HEADSTART IN HISTORY

D1098211

REFORMATION AND
REBELLION 1485-1750

SERIES EDITOR: ROSEMARY REES

STEVE ARMAN

SIMON BIRD

MALCOLM WILKINSON

Heinemann is an imprint of Pearson Education Limited,
a company incorporated in England and Wales, having its registered office at Edinburgh
Gate, Harlow, Essex, CM20 2JE. Registered company number: 872828
Heinemann is the registered trademark of
Pearson Education Limited

© Steve Arman, Simon Bird, Malcolm Wilkinson 2002

First published 2002

ISBN 978 0 435 32303 5

08

10 9 8

Produced by Gecko Ltd, Bicester, Oxon

Illustrated by Gecko Ltd, Roger Penwill and Geoff Ward

Original illustrations © Heinemann Educational Publishers 2002

Cover design by Hicksdesign

Picture research by Jenny Silkstone

Printed and bound in China (CTPS/08)

Photographic acknowledgements
The authors and publisher would like to thank the following for permission to reproduce photographs:
AKG London: 27A, 41D, 78A, 159A, 161A, 203B; AKG/Erich Lessing: 22.1, 23.3, 68B, 169J; AKG/Musee du
Louvre: 23.4; AKG/Rabatti-Domingie: 170L; Archivi Alinari: 169K; Blair Castle Collection: 33A; Bridgeman
Art Library: 82C, 95A, 150H, 176B, 198G, 202A, 235A, 240B; BAL/British Library: 100F; BAL/Burghley
House Collection: 19A; BAL/Chateau de Versailles: 20C; BAL/Christies Images: 193B, 213A; BAL/Crown
Estate: 123A; BAL/Fitzwilliam Museum, University of Cambridge: 206E; BAL/Hermitage, St Petersburg:
205D; BAL/Houses of Parliament, Westminster: 101G; BAL/Ipswich Borough Council Museums and Galleries:
46A; BAL/John Bethell: 47B; BAL/Johnny van Haeften Gallery, London: 250A; BAL/Lambeth Palace Library:
62A, 83D, 121G; BAL/Loseley Park: 65A; BAL/National Portrait Gallery: 23.6, 53A, 87A; BAL/Phillips: 10C;
BAL/Pinacoteca di Brera, Milan: 168I; BAL/Royal Holloway and Bedford New College: 10B; BAL/Scottish
National Portrait Gallery: 29C; BAL/Simon Gillespie Studio: 10A; BAL/Trustees of Weston Park: 97C;
Calderdale Museums and Arts: 220A; Corbis: 22.2, 23.5, 49C, 53B, 58G, 67A, 183D, 190C, 192A, 193A;
Fotomas Index: 73A, 109A, 112G, 134C; Giraudon: 172N; Historical Archive: 43E, 55C, 92D, 107C, 171M,
173A, 179F, 182A, 194C, 228F; Hulton: 18E, 31C, 36D, 116B, 144C, 154F, 177C, 224A; Mary Evans Picture
Library: 35B, 40A, 113A, 162B, 199A, 236B; National Army Museum: 137F; National Portrait Gallery: 230A;
National Trust Photographic Library/Andreas von Einsiedel: 90B; National Trust Photographic Library/
Michael Caldwell: 209H; Pepys Library, Magdalene College, Cambridge: 244A; Public Record Office: 29D;
Royal Collection: 149G; Shakespeare Centre Library: 165A; University of Utrecht: 166C

Cover photograph: © AKG Photo/Lausanne, Musee Cantonal des Beaux-Arts. Picture is *Huguenot Wars:
St Bartholemew's day Massacre, 23–24 August 1572*, by Francois de Valois.

Written acknowledgements
The authors and publishers
gratefully acknowledge the
following publications from
which written sources in the
book are drawn. In some
sources the wording or
sentence structure has been
simplified.

H.A. Clement, *The Story of Britain 1485–1714* (Harrap, 1941): 21G
C.S.L. Davies, *Peace, Print and Protestantism* (Paladin, 1977): 86D
Desiree Edwards-Rees, *Ireland Story* (London, 1967): 134E
Margaret Elliot, *Britain under the Tudors and Stuarts* (CUP, 1958): 97E
John Guy, *The Public Career of Sir Thomas More* (Yale, 1980): 21F
Christopher Haigh, *English Reformations* (Oxford, 1993): 86B
Angus McInnes, *The English Town* (Historical Association, 1980): 228G
R. Tittler, *The Reign of Mary I* (Longman, 1983): 86E
Neville Williams, *Henry VIII* (Weidenfeld and Nicholson, 1973): 18F
P. Williams, *The Tudor Regime* (Clarendon, 1979): 86C

Conversion chart for general reference		
£1 = 20 shillings (20s)	1kg = 2.2 pounds (lbs)	1 litre = 1.76 pints
1s = 12 old pence (12d)	1lb = 16 ounces (16 oz)	1 pint = 20 fluid ounces (20 fl.oz)

Tel: 01865 888058 www.heinemann.co.uk

Contents

1 Kings, Queens and Parliament 5

2 The Early Reformation, 1510–47 38

3 The end of Catholic England 65

4 The Stuart Crisis: Civil War to Glorious Revolution 95

5 The Making of the UK: Stability and Unity 129

6 The Renaissance and the Scientific Revolution 156

7 A Changing Society 1485–1750 188

8 The 'World We Have Lost' 215

Index 251

1 Kings, Queens and Parliament

King marries six times and beheads two wives along the way!

The King is executed!

Headlines like these would shock today's newspaper readers let alone those of a few hundred years ago! But this is what actually happened in this period with Henry VIII and Charles I. Why? The answer lies in two key words: power and control. Of the Tudor and Stuart monarchs, one king (Henry VII) became monarch through battle and most of the other kings and queens rose to power as a result of desperate political struggle and fiendish intrigue. The succession was rarely certain. Once crowned, all monarchs needed power and influence to hold on to their position and to control their lands and people. These were difficult and dangerous times to be a monarch.

In this book we are going to look at the ideas of power and control amongst Tudor and Stuart kings and queens. For instance, how did these monarchs come to the throne? How did they overcome rebellions and maintain their control over nobles, lords and the Church? Our investigations will lead us to look at Henry VII's rise to power in 1485 through to James II's move to exile in France in November 1688 and then to William and Mary sharing power with Parliament.

In early modern England, kings and queens played a very significant role which had a great impact on every level of society. The flow diagram on page 7 shows the workings of power in 1485 at the beginning of the Tudor dynasty.

Gaining and maintaining power and control

In this period, kings and queens had to use many different methods and means to gain and maintain their control. These included:

- **Battles** – e.g. the Battle of Bosworth in 1485 (see page 12); this is a good example of a potential king overcoming enemies or traitors in order to seize power.

- **Rebellions** – this is armed resistance to the established government; the monarchy had to put down and overcome any attempts by potential claimants to the throne to send a clear message to any potential trouble-makers; see the cases of Simnel and Warbeck on pages 17–8.

- **Revenues/taxation** – revenue is income raised by the monarch through taxes on the people. To remain in a strong position, a monarch had to be financially well off. A key way of increasing revenue was by raising taxes. This was also supported by leading nobles, who operated an efficient legal system that raised revenue through fines.

- **Images of power** – royalty had to show off their wealth and power to strengthen their position. They did this by royal progresses (visiting) and tournaments (jousting events) in the early Tudor period. Late Tudor and Stuart monarchs impressed through banquets, visitations, and great castles and palaces. The monarchy also needed to maintain good international relations (foreign policy); this was achieved through foreign visits (e.g. by ambassadors) and by the arrangement of royal marriages between nations.

- **Relations with the Church** – As the Church played a key role in people's lives, it was important for the monarch to keep on good terms with it, e.g. by using churchmen like Thomas Cranmer (see page 53) and Thomas Wolsey (see pages 46–7) as chief advisers.

- **Relations with nobles and Parliament** – see the flow diagram which explains the balance of power at this time.

KING and QUEEN (monarch)

Marriage within powerful families could increase a monarch's power and status.

Sources of money: customs/rent from royal lands and loans from wealthy merchants. Taxes were only for emergencies.

Military support: monarchs had to rely on the nobles when an army was needed.

THE COUNCIL

The monarch's close advisers:

The Lord Chancellor was the most important person who held the Great Seal, used on all key documentation.

Other key nobles, churchmen and country gentlemen advised the monarch and carried out important decisions.

PARLIAMENT

Parliament met where and when the monarch decided, e.g. Westminster.

It was only called when the monarch commanded.

It was made up of the Lords and the Commons.

The Lords: nobles, bishops, abbots and judges. The Lord Chancellor was in charge and sat on a special seat called the 'woolsack'.

The Commons: gentlemen who were elected from the counties and some important towns.

Not everyone was eligible to vote in the elections. To vote you had to rent land to the value of 40 shillings or more from the local landowner.

The Speaker was in charge and decided what was to be discussed, who would speak and for how long.

He informed the monarch about the discussions and carried out the monarch's instructions.

The Lords and Commons (together with the monarch) were the ruling classes. The tasks they performed were to:

a) make Acts of Parliament, i.e. the laws which everyone had to obey. Commons, Lords and monarch all had to agree

b) raise taxes when the monarch needed them – this was a source of conflict!

c) advise the monarch.

RULING CLASSES IN THEIR COUNTIES

Members of the Lords and the Commons were the ruling classes in their counties. They used Justices of the Peace (JPs) and the local gentry to:

a) collect taxes; they decided how much everyone should pay and how much everyone collected

b) raise troops when necessary for the monarch

c) maintain law and order; a significant number were JPs which meant deciding the fate of the poor and the unemployed, fixing wages and apprenticeships, licensing ale houses and repairing roads and bridges.

THE REST OF THE POPULATION

They had to obey all of the above!

Establishing the Tudor monarchy

In these ways, monarchs gained and maintained power and position. In 1485 Henry VII became the first monarch of the Tudor dynasty. He had to work really hard to hold on to the throne, especially in the crucial early years of his reign. England was just coming out of a very unsettled period and he faced a number of problems:

- He needed money.

- He had to have peace with other countries like France.

- The nobles were trying to gain more power.

- The families of York and Lancaster were still fighting each other, as they had throughout the Wars of the Roses (1455–85).

Henry VII's son became King Henry VIII in 1509. He is a good example of a Tudor monarch who was successful at maintaining and displaying his power. He was also very determined to become a more powerful and respected king. In 1520 Henry VIII met his great rival Francis I, king of France, just outside Calais in France. This meeting is known as the Field of the Cloth of Gold and demonstrated the power and wealth of Henry because he was dressed in silver and gold cloth (see Source C on page 20). This was a typical example of the style of the 'new monarchy'.

Before the coronation of Henry VII there had been some 30 years of war between the House of Lancaster and the House of York. Known as the Wars of the Roses, they lasted from 1455–85. When Edward IV died in 1483 there was a question of who exactly would become king. Prince Edward became Edward V but, because he was too young to rule, his uncle Richard acted as regent. This is a person appointed to administer or rule the country in place of a monarch who is too young to do so himself. That same year, Richard crowned himself Richard III. The story goes that, in spring 1483, he took the princes Edward and Richard to the Tower of London in order to keep control over them. During the months that followed the princes disappeared and were never seen again. It is not clear what happened but it would appear that they were murdered – this remains one of the great unanswered questions of history! However, in 1502, Sir James Tyrell, a supporter of Richard III, confessed to suffocating the two princes in the Tower in 1483 on Richard's orders. But why did he wait so long to make his confession? And in 1674 (nearly 200 years later) the bones of two children aged between ten and twelve were discovered under some stairs in the Tower. Were they the bones of the two young princes?

THE FAMILIES OF LANCASTER AND YORK

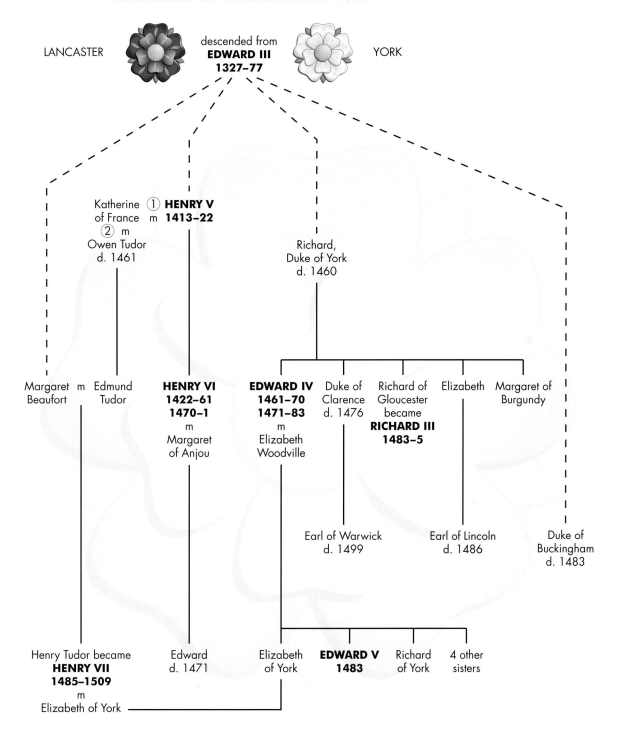

LANCASTER   descended from
               EDWARD III   YORK
               1327–77

Katherine ① **HENRY V**
of France m **1413–22**
② m
Owen Tudor
d. 1461

Richard,
Duke of York
d. 1460

Margaret m Edmund   **HENRY VI**   **EDWARD IV** Duke of   Richard of   Elizabeth Margaret of
Beaufort   Tudor   **1422–61**   **1461–70**   Clarence   Gloucester   Burgundy
                         1470–1   **1471–83**   d. 1476   became
                         m   m   **RICHARD III**
                         Margaret   Elizabeth   **1483–5**
                         of Anjou   Woodville

                                           Earl of Warwick   Earl of Lincoln   Duke of
                                           d. 1499   d. 1486   Buckingham
                                                                                          d. 1483

Henry Tudor became   Edward   Elizabeth   **EDWARD V** Richard   4 other
HENRY VII   d. 1471   of York   **1483**   of York   sisters
1485–1509
m
Elizabeth of York ———

REIGNING SOVEREIGNS ARE IN CAPITAL LETTERS

Dotted lines indicate that previous generations have been left out.

*The English royal family
tree from Edward III to
Henry VII.*

Digging deeper

Murder in the Tower?

This episode in history is a good example of a struggle for power and control. The key players are:

Richard III, painted after his death, from a portrait by an artist who had seen Richard.

Richard III: uncle to the sons of Edward IV, he ruled as regent instead of the eldest prince, Edward. Because Richard wanted to have complete control he 'looked after' the princes and locked them in the Tower of London.

Prince Edward and Prince Richard painted by Millais.

The Boy Princes: the eldest became Edward V aged twelve, and therefore was too young to rule on his own so Richard ruled for him. The other prince in the Tower was Edward's brother, Richard, Duke of York, aged only ten.

Henry VII, painted by Michael Sittow in 1505. The king wears a collar of the Golden Fleece.

Henry VII: known as Henry Tudor, he became the first Tudor king when he defeated Richard III at the Battle of Bosworth in 1485. Was he responsible for murdering the princes?

Your task is to work out 'Whodunnit?'.

Carefully read the background information and then consider who the main suspects are with a reason to get rid of the two princes. Copy out the table, allowing yourself plenty of room to write.

Then, using the information and your own knowledge, complete the table by listing all the possible suspects. Be sure to note down motives and the reasons behind your decision.

Suspect	Motive	Reasons for choosing this person (give detailed explanation)

Background information

Spring 1483
Richard and one of his supporters, Buckingham, took Edward V from Lord Rivers, in whose charge the princes had been left. Rivers was executed soon afterwards. Edward was taken to the Tower to get ready for his coronation. The princes' mother, Elizabeth Woodville, allowed her younger son to join his brother.

Unanswered question:
Elizabeth Woodville was scared of Richard and his desire for power. She realised how much of a threat her children could be to him, because they had a direct claim on the throne. Why were the princes allowed to be put in the Tower if their mother was scared of Richard III?

June 1483
The two princes were declared illegitimate, which weakened their claim to the throne, and their uncle, Richard of Gloucester, was crowned King Richard III. By doing this he was also declaring that their siblings (brothers and sisters) were illegitimate as well, so they would not have a strong claim to the throne either. This included their sister, Elizabeth of York, whom Henry VII was to marry in 1486. If the princes were alive when Henry took over the Tower, it wasn't in Henry's best interests to keep them alive and legitimate because their claim to the throne was better than his. However, he needed their sister to be legitimate so that he could marry her and unite the houses of Lancaster and York.

Unanswered question:
Did Richard want to help the princes or was he taking the crown for ambitious reasons and to protect the country?

August 1483
Rumours quickly spread that the two princes had been murdered in the Tower. Richard III did not take any action and ignored the rumours. Buckingham was constable of the Tower at that time so he could control everything that happened there.

Unanswered question:
When rumours began about the princes in the Tower, why didn't Richard produce the boys?

October 1483
Buckingham made contact with Henry Tudor, who was in exile in France, and rebelled against Richard. He was captured and executed. Henry tried to land from France but quickly retreated to the safety of Brittany.

Unanswered question:
Why did Buckingham rebel? Had he found out about the princes, or was he claiming the throne?

7 August 1485
Henry landed with a small army at Milford Haven in Wales where he gained a great deal of support.

22 August 1485
Henry defeated Richard and his army at the Battle of Bosworth and Richard III was killed (see page 12). Henry VII became king – the first Tudor. In 1486 he married Edward IV's daughter, Elizabeth of York, which united the families of Lancaster and York.

Unanswered questions:
Did Henry VII murder the princes because they were a threat to his power? Were they still alive even in 1485?

Why didn't Henry VII accuse Richard of murdering the princes, particularly as he had already accused him of other evil deeds?

Remember to use all the information available when completing your table.

Henry VII gains power

The Battle of Bosworth, 22 August 1485

Wearing his crown, King Richard III charged forward into battle with his army to defeat finally Henry Tudor's men. In the heat of battle, Richard was killed and his Yorkist army fled. Henry's soldiers found Richard's crown stuck in a bush. Henry wanted to prove to everyone that Richard had been killed, so he ordered that Richard's naked body be slung over a mule and taken to Leicester. There it was paraded before the people, so declaring Henry's ascension to the throne. Later, with great ceremony, Henry was crowned king. When Parliament was summoned, the date of his reign was backdated to 21 August, one day before the Battle of Bosworth. Therefore anybody who had fought against the new king on 22 August could be tried for treason – that is, an attempt to get rid of, or depose, the sovereign king.

What actually happened at Bosworth?

The battle took place at Ambien Hill, Bosworth, Leicestershire between the armies of the Yorkist king, Richard III, and the self-pronounced Lancastrian king, Henry Tudor, who had returned from exile in France. There was also a third army present, that of Sir William Stanley and his brother, Thomas, Lord Stanley, which was held back. The question was – for whom would they fight? Henry's army was out-numbered by the Yorkist army. Henry was hoping for the support of the Stanleys, but as yet had not received it.

A plan of the Battle of Bosworth at its start.

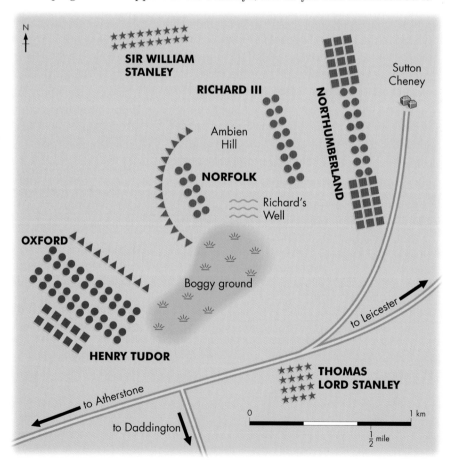

Key

YORKISTS
▲ Archers

● Men-at-arms (on foot)

■ Men-at-arms (mounted)

STANLEY
★ Men-at-arms and Archers

TUDOR
▲ Archers

● Men-at-arms (on foot)

■ Men-at-arms (mounted)

Each symbol represents 100 men

King Richard ... arranged his footmen and cavalry. In front he placed his archers under the command of John, Duke of Norfolk. Behind this leading body followed the king himself, with a hand-picked body of soldiers.

Account of the battle by the historian, Polydore Vergil, written before 1512. It is based on accounts of men who were at the battle.

There was a third section of the army fighting for the king, led by Northumberland. It brought up the rear. Henry's armies were positioned close to the marshland, which acted like a fortification for them. As Henry's men marched forward past the marsh, Richard III ordered his soldiers to charge them. First archers sent their arrows into Henry's advancing army, then foot soldiers moved in starting hand-to-hand combat. The Earl of Oxford's troops with his men grouped closely together countered this attack and in a triangular shape charged the enemy.

The battle was now in the balance. Who would win?

Richard drew near to Henry, and burning with anger, he spurred on his horse. Henry saw King Richard approaching ... King Richard killed several in his first charge, threw down Henry's standard and its bearer, William Brandon. Then he fought John Cheney, a much stronger man than most. He stood against the king, who with great strength smashed him to the ground. Henry held out against the charge much longer than his men thought possible. They began to give up hope ... Then surprisingly William Stanley came to the rescue with his 3000 men. Straight away King Richard's men fled, leaving Richard alone, fighting manfully in the thickest press of his enemies.

Again historian Polydore Vergil gives an account of the battle.

With the help of Stanley's men now fighting with Henry, Richard was killed. His crown was found in a bush and placed triumphantly on Henry's head.

Activity time

1   Using the map on page 12 and the information above, as well as your own research, draw and label a diagram of what took place on 22 August 1485. Indicate the positions of the armies and their movements and shape.

2   Fighting with the king!
    How might a foot soldier fighting closely alongside Richard III have reported what happened at Bosworth? In diary format write up details of what happened including the outcome of the battle, the surprise of the Stanleys fighting against the king and what a foot soldier would have thought of the whole event. Remember when looking at these sources that Polydore Vergil was a supporter of the Tudors, so his views may be biased in their favour.

Maintaining power and overcoming problems

Henry VII had secured a great victory at Bosworth and, with it, the 30 years of war between the Yorkists and Lancastrians had come to an end. But the Wars of the Roses had left England in disorder and Henry now faced many problems. For example, the nobles were unsettled, law and order had crumbled and Henry needed money to provide a strong financial base upon which to rule the country. Previous wars like the Hundred Years' War with France (1347–1453) had left the royal coffers empty. Henry knew that he had to secure his position to hold on to power and he had to act fast to solve the problems crown and country faced, as well as restoring authority. Perhaps his most important challenge was to try to win over his people. He was not a generous man by nature but was sharp and cunning. He knew full well that money formed a solid foundation for his power, therefore he wanted to acquire as much as possible and spend as little as he could.

SOURCE A

That of the three affections which naturally tie the hearts of the subjects to his Sovereign, love, fear and reverence, he had the last in height, the second in good measure and so little of the first as he was beholden to the other two ... He was a prince sad, serious and full of thoughts.

Sir Francis Bacon writing about Henry VII in 1585.

Henry had to tackle the following issues during his reign:

- money
- gaining support and making policies
- foreign policy and alliances, including marriage alliances
- overcoming rebellions – see pages 17–18 on Simnel and Warbeck.

Money

Henry needed to secure a significant fortune, which he could use to rule the country. So he set about fining his enemies in the Court of Star Chamber – a special court to deal with cases that were unsuitable for the ordinary law courts (see page 15). He also confiscated land and when he made a treaty with a foreign power he often demanded payment to him.

Henry employed Sir Richard Empson and Sir Edmund Dudley to raise money. They revived old laws and fined people for having broken them, which made them the two most unpopular men in England at the time. One of their favourite ways of raising money was by using forced loans or benevolences (giving of gifts to the king). In 1492, when he was preparing to go to war with France, he raised large sums of money in this way. London alone contributed £9000 to Henry's war funds – and in the end there wasn't a war! At the end of his reign Henry left a fortune of £4,500,000 to his son, the future Henry VIII.

Gaining support and making policies

Henry was helped to strengthen his power by two things:

- The country needed law and order following the Wars of the Roses, which had been a long period of upheaval.

- By 1485 the number of barons was reduced and their status weakened because some had died in the wars and others had lost land.

Henry started by taking back all land which the crown had lost or given away since 1455, and he attacked the practice of livery and maintenance. This was when barons employed large numbers of armed retainers who wore the livery and badge of their lord and supported him on every necessary occasion. If any of them got into trouble and were brought before a court, the lord would fill the court with other armed men and bully the jury into pronouncing a favourable verdict. This was known as maintenance. Henry passed a law against livery and maintenance at the start of his reign, and enforced it fully.

Also in 1487 Henry passed the Act which reorganised the Court of Star Chamber at Westminster. Henry strengthened the power of this court and used it for cases of rebellion and lawlessness. It was not bound by detailed rules of procedure and acted quickly and efficiently even using torture to obtain evidence! In its early years the Court of Star Chamber was very popular with people who wanted good order and prompt justice – as Sir Francis Bacon said later, 'Justice was administered in his time.'

Henry also made it his policy to strengthen the middle classes. He gave them more power and say in the running of the country, which was to help him establish law and order. They were employed as royal servants and officials and were business-like and dependent on the king. Members of the middle classes were also appointed as Justices of the Peace and had many duties to carry out (see flow diagram on page 7). This increased involvement in official duties made them more important and raised their standing in society at the same time as giving Henry more support.

Foreign policy and alliances

In 1492 Henry VII and the king of France, Charles VIII, signed the Treaty of Etaples whereby Henry was paid a large sum of money to avoid war with France. This was due to the fact that Charles VIII's marriage proposals had effectively annexed (joined) Brittany to France, which upset Henry.

Other treaties which gave Henry VII further power and control were:

- Poynings Law (1494) – through this Henry secured control over Ireland. All the laws passed by the Irish Parliament had to have the agreement of the English government and all laws passed by the English Parliament were to automatically apply to Ireland.

- A commercial treaty with Flanders (1496); he also encouraged Cabot's voyage across the Atlantic (see page 185).

There were also a number of key diplomatic marriages which secured good relations with both Scotland and Spain. These led eventually to the union of England and Scotland in 1707, when James VI of Scotland became James I of England in 1603 (see page 33) and Henry VIII's marriage schemes led up to the English Reformation:

- In 1501 Henry's eldest son Arthur married a Spanish princess, Catherine of Aragon, thus securing an alliance with Spain.

- In 1503 Henry's daughter Margaret married James IV of Scotland which created an alliance with Scotland.

- Henry's youngest child Mary married Louis XII of France, thus forming an alliance, and later married Charles, Duke of Suffolk.

These marriages established good links between important and influential families.

Key features of Henry VII's reign

- defeat of rebellious opposition

- increased control over nobles, particularly by the statute of livery and maintenance and the Court of Star Chamber

- increased wealth, mainly through fining and benevolences

- successful foreign policy and marriage alliances

- expansion of foreign trade and exploration

Question time

1 Describe six separate ways in which Henry VII strengthened his power. Explain the reasons behind them and try to provide evidence to support your ideas.

2 Explain the importance of the following factors during the reign of Henry VII:
   a livery and maintenance and the Court of Star Chamber
   b diplomatic alliances and marriages
   c Poynings Law (1494)

   Which do you think was the most important and why? Consider the social, political and economic issues in your answer.

Digging deeper

Pretenders to the throne: the rebellions of Simnel and Warbeck

This box gives you a lot of information about two rebellions which Henry had to deal with early in his reign. The information in black is factual; the information in colour panels is source material. When using sources such as Polydore Vergil, remember to be aware of bias.

Historians always need to ask who the person supported or why the source was written, because this will indicate if the views in the source can be trusted.

Lambert Simnel

Lambert Simnel, son of an Oxford tradesman, claimed in 1487 to be the young Earl of Warwick. He was trained by Yorkist supporters and a priest, Richard Simons, for the part.

This Yorkist plot to overthrow the House of Tudor was supported by Margaret, Duchess of Burgundy. She provided men and money, as well as paying for Simnel to travel to Ireland, a traditionally strong Yorkist area, to gain further support.

Henry VII paraded the real Earl of Warwick (who had been held captive in the Tower) through the streets of London.

In Dublin, Simnel was crowned king. He then crossed to England to seize the throne.

Henry sent an army to defeat Simnel's forces at Stoke in 1487.

SOURCE B

He first taught the boy courtly manners ... He changed the boy's name and called him Edward. Later he went with him to Ireland. There he secretly called a meeting with a large number of Irish nobles, whom he understood by common rumours to be opposed to Henry VII.

Polydore Vergil on Simnel's training to be Earl of Warwick.

SOURCE C

The front line of the king's army charged the enemy with such strength that it at once crushed the remaining leaders of the enemy. Thereupon the remaining enemy troops turned and fled.

Polydore Vergil writes about the Battle of Stoke, 1487.

SOURCE D

The false boy king was indeed captured with his backer Richard [Simons], but each was granted his life – the innocent lad because he was too young to carry out any crime and the teacher because he was a priest.

Polydore Vergil on Simnel's capture and punishment.

Perkin Warbeck

Perkin Warbeck claimed to be Richard, the younger of the (supposedly) murdered princes in the Tower.

Margaret of Burgundy also supported his claim. He also gained support from Ireland, Flanders and Scotland.

Henry VII was on the look-out!

In 1496 James IV, King of Scotland, invaded England on Warbeck's behalf. This led to a rebellion in Cornwall by Yorkist supporters. They were defeated in 1497 at Blackheath in Kent.

In a desperate attempt, Warbeck landed in Cornwall to try to revive the rebellion but failed and was captured in 1497.

Warbeck confessed and was imprisoned in the Tower.

In 1499 Perkin Warbeck and the Earl of Warwick were executed. This removed all of Henry's rivals, finally bringing to an end the Wars of the Roses.

SOURCE E

Perkin Warbeck, a portrait drawn in about 1540, perhaps copying an original. Warbeck came across as a striking individual to whom people could easily be attracted.

SOURCE F

Henry was not to be rid of the impostor for six years ... but when other sovereigns claimed to be convinced of Perkin's royal birth, saying that they were satisfied with his identity from birthmarks, even the King of England began to have doubts, for the bodies of the princes in the Tower had never been found.

Modern historian, Neville Williams, writing in 1973.

SOURCE G

And the Friday next following was made within the palace at Westminster a scaffold of pipes and of hogsheads [barrels]. And there in a pair of stocks he was set a good part of the morning ...

The Great Chronicle of London in November 1491.

SOURCE H

[Perkin and a man called Edwards] were drawn from the Tower unto Tyburn and there hanged until dead, whose bodies were after buried at the Friar Augustines within London.

The Great Chronicle of London, 23 November 1491.

Now answer the following questions:

1   How likely was it that Simnel and Warbeck were who they claimed to be?

2   Why did Henry treat Simnel and Warbeck so differently?

3   Are you surprised at the ways in which Henry dealt with his problems? Could he have done any differently and better?

What sort of king was Henry VIII?

Henry VIII became king in 1509 following the death of his father, Henry VII. How did Henry VIII rule and what was his style as a ruler? How did he display his power and control the country?

Henry VIII is a very famous person in English history. This is mainly because of three things:

- He married six times – two of his wives were beheaded!

- He made himself head of the Church in England.

- He made himself very wealthy from the dissolution of the monasteries (see pages 56–7). By closing the monasteries he also weakened the power of the Catholic Church in England.

When Henry became king at the young age of seventeen, he was in a very fortunate position. His father, Henry VII, had left him a peaceful kingdom, plenty of money in the royal coffers, and there was no obvious or real threat of war from neighbouring countries such as France or Spain.

The young Henry VIII, c. 1510, by a contemporary artist, Joos van Cleve.

SOURCE B

Could you but see how nobly he is bearing himself, how wise he is, his love for all that is good and right, and specially his love of learning, you would need no wings to fly into the light of this new risen ... star ... how proud our people are of their new sovereign ...

These words of a courtier, Lord Mountjoy, in 1509 show that it appeared to be a time of great hope and promise for England.

What does this view of Henry coming to power suggest to you? Why would Lord Mountjoy have this view of Henry?

Machiavellian prince or true Renaissance man?

The Renaissance was a period of massive change across Europe (from approximately 1450 to 1675), which saw a renaissance (rebirth) of interest and learning in the arts (see Chapter 6). The term 'a Renaissance man' was popularised by Castiglione in 1516 in his book called the *Book of the Courtier*. A Renaissance man was seen to be someone who was accomplished in many different areas, who was brave, witty and courteous, and civilised and learned.

Niccolo Machiavelli was an Italian writer (see also page 159). He wrote a famous book called *The Prince* in 1513, when Henry was 21. It offered advice to keep monarchs and rulers in power by using various means such as deception, opportunism and manipulation. From this name comes the term we use today: 'Machiavellian' – making the best of chances available, controlling and influencing situations using trickery and deception.

Read through the following evidence about Henry VIII to help you draw your own conclusions about him: was he a Machiavellian prince, or a true Renaissance man?

- Empson and Dudley were lawyers for Henry VII. They were unpopular because they imposed fines on the people (see page 14). At the start of Henry VIII's reign, in 1510, Henry executed them both. This made him popular and gave him prestige amongst the people.

SOURCE C

The Field of the Cloth of Gold, 1520, illustrated by an unknown contemporary artist.

- Henry VIII employed the German artist, Hans Holbein, and the composer, Thomas Tallis. Holbein painted portraits of Henry and his family. Henry even chose his fourth wife (Anne of Cleves) from one of his paintings (see page 23)! However, soon after their marriage, Henry divorced her saying she looked like a Flanders mare – a horse!

- At the Field of the Cloth of Gold in 1520, Henry had a meeting with Francis I of France in order to impress him (see Source C). It lasted for nearly two weeks and in this time the kings and their courtiers feasted, danced, jousted and even a special palace was built near Calais.

- In 1513 Henry VIII executed the Earl of Suffolk. He was the leading Yorkist claimant to the throne and was accused of treason. In 1521 the Duke of Buckingham was executed because he was also accused of treason. He was England's most powerful nobleman and had a claim to the throne if Henry died.

SOURCE D

His majesty is ... extremely handsome ... very accomplished, a good musician, composes well, is a most capital horseman, a fine jouster, speaks French, Latin and Spanish, is very religious ... he is extremely fond of tennis, at which game it is the prettiest thing in the world to see him play.

Report from the Venetian ambassador in London, 1515.

SOURCE F

Henry preferred hunting, dancing, dallying, and playing the lute. In his more civilised moments, Henry studied theology and astronomy; he would wake up Sir Thomas More in the middle of the night in order that they might gaze at the stars from the palace roof.

A modern historian, John Guy, writing in 1984.

SOURCE E

I believe he [Henry VIII] favours me more than any other subject in England ... however ... have no cause to be proud, for if my head could win him a castle in France it should not fail to go.

Sir Thomas More, one of Henry VIII's chief advisers, speaking in 1525.

SOURCE G

It was the young king's character and accomplishments that appealed most to the nation, especially after the cold reign of Henry VII. The new king was in many ways a child of the Renaissance. Among his accomplishments were theology, music, and languages. In person he was handsome and strong.

The historian H.A. Clement writing in 1941.

Activity time

1 Using all the information above, decide which pieces of evidence support the two different points of view that Henry is:

   a A true Renaissance man

   b A Machiavellian prince

2 Write two structured paragraphs, using the opening sentences below. In your writing use supporting evidence from the sources as well as your own knowledge.

   Paragraph A: Henry is a good example of a true Renaissance man, because he loved astronomy ...

   Paragraph B: By executing the Duke of Suffolk and the Duke of Buckingham, Henry displayed Machiavellian characteristics ...

Divorced, beheaded, died, divorced, beheaded, survived!

Henry VIII is very famous for having six wives. Why did he keep remarrying and what were the results of his marriages? How did Henry make decisions and who advised him?

Think about the theme of power and control here. One of the main reasons why Henry had so many wives was because he wanted to produce a male heir to be the next king. This would make sure that he and his family kept control of the country (see Chapter 2 for more details).

FACTFILE

Wife number 1: Catherine of Aragon, a Spanish princess

Born: 1485   **Died:** 1536

Married: First to Arthur Tudor, son of Henry VII, thereby forming a Spanish alliance with England. When Arthur died in 1502 Catherine was allowed to marry his younger brother, the future Henry VIII, with the Pope's special permission.

Children: Mary, born 1516, was brought up as a Catholic and later became queen.

Why marriage ended: Catherine was divorced from Henry in 1533 and ended up living in seclusion with her daughter in England. She had not been able to provide Henry with a male heir and had suffered many miscarriages and pregnancies that resulted in still-births. Also, Henry had become attracted to lady-in-waiting Anne Boleyn (see below) as Henry felt that Catherine had become too old and unattractive (see pages 51–2).

FACTFILE

Wife number 2: Anne Boleyn

Born: 1507   **Died:** 1536 (beheaded)

Married: In secret, January 1533. Henry's first marriage was annulled (cancelled) in May 1533 and Anne was crowned queen in June.

Children: Elizabeth, born September 1533 and brought up as a Protestant. She later became Queen Elizabeth I.

Why marriage ended: Beheaded at the Tower of London in May 1536 after being tried on charges of adultery (affairs with different men). Anne was probably beheaded for not producing a son and heir to the throne, but historians have argued that the most likely reason may have been her affairs. She also considered herself to be more important than she actually was and tried to advise Henry.

Wife number 3: Jane Seymour

Born: 1509   **Died:** 1537

Married: 1536

Children: Edward, born 1537, the future king Edward VI.

Why marriage ended: Jane died twelve days after giving birth to Edward. Henry had been genuinely fond of her and mourned her death.

FACTFILE

Wife number 4: Anne of Cleves, a German princess

Born: 1515   **Died:** 1557

Married: January 1540, forming a diplomatic alliance with the German Protestants. She was chosen for Henry by Thomas Cromwell from a painting by Holbein (seen on left). Henry is said to have likened her to a horse when he eventually met her!

Children: None.

Why marriage ended: Henry divorced Anne in June 1540. Anne remained unmarried and lived in England on a generous pension for the rest of her life.

FACTFILE

Wife number 5: Catherine Howard

Born: 1521   **Died:** 1542 (beheaded)

Married: In 1540 as the result of the ambitious Catholic Duke of Norfolk (a Howard).

Children: None.

Why marriage ended: Protestant enemies of the Howards accused Catherine of adultery and so she was beheaded.

FACTFILE

Wife number 6: Catherine Parr

Born: 1512   **Died:** 1548

Married: When Catherine married Henry in 1543 she had already been widowed twice.

Children: None to Henry.

Why marriage ended: Catherine was the only wife to outlive Henry. She skilfully managed Henry in his decline and looked after Henry's children and brought the family back together. She remarried after Henry's death but died in childbirth.

Question time

Using the factfiles on pages 22–3, and through your own research, answer the following questions in essay format:

1   Why did Henry VIII have six wives?

2   Which do you think was the most important wife? Explain your answer. You can add extra information from your own independent research.

Hanging on to the throne

A case study

Henry VIII had three children all of whom were to become monarchs of England. They all had their own specific problems to deal with. In Chapter 3 we shall look at the reigns of Edward (1547–53) and Mary (1553–8). We are also going to investigate the reign of Elizabeth (1558–1603) in that chapter. Here, however, we shall look at certain aspects of Elizabeth's reign to see how important it was for a monarch to remain in power by using certain skills, such as the ability to compromise and use advisers wisely.

Problems facing Elizabeth

When Elizabeth came to the throne in 1558, there were five key areas that she had to manage carefully in order to maintain her rule and keep England prosperous, peaceful and under control. These were:

- religion

- marriage

- foreign relations, for example with Spain

- poor people and beggars

- threats to the throne – such as from Mary, Queen of Scots.

How did she deal with them? What did she do? Some of these issues are covered in more depth in Chapter 3. Here we are going to describe her problems and ask what an adviser at that time might have suggested she should do to make sure that she held on to the throne.

Activity time

Copy the table below. Allow enough room to write. Complete it once you have read about the options Elizabeth had for dealing with her problems. Be sure to give a full explanation for the solutions you choose.

Problem	Solutions	Explanation
Religion		
Marriage		
Foreign relations		
Poor people and beggars		
Threats to the throne		

Issue 1: Religion

Mary I has just died (1558) and left the throne to Elizabeth, her half-sister. She asked Elizabeth to allow Catholics to worship freely and to maintain Catholicism as the state religion. What should Elizabeth do?

Options

a   Continue with Mary's Church, keeping England Catholic.

b   Go back to the Protestant Church. Maybe let Catholics worship privately?

c   Go back to the Protestant Church. Be strong and burn as heretics anyone who objects.

Considerations

● What kind of Church is wanted?

● How does Elizabeth want to be viewed by her people?

Issue 2: Marriage

The advisers, particularly William Cecil, suggested to Elizabeth that she should get married to secure England an heir to the throne.

Options

a   Stay single and be in control.

b   Marry a Protestant Englishman and then hope for a Protestant heir to the throne.

c   Marry the Catholic king, Philip II of Spain, her dead half-sister Mary's husband, thereby ensuring a good alliance with Spain, and no wars.

Considerations

● Who would be in control in England, Elizabeth or her husband king?

● Who would succeed after her death?

Issue 3: Foreign relations

Catholic Spain and France continued to watch Protestant Elizabeth's actions and offered suitable important men for her to marry. Scotland was concerned about how Elizabeth's actions would affect it. Elizabeth didn't want to go to war, which was expensive, but how should she keep these countries happy and at peace with England?

Options

a   Be willing to let Catholics worship freely and maintain relations with the Pope.

b   Be strong and pass Acts that make her head of the Church of England and also introduce a new prayer book. Establish control over the clergy and reduce the control of the Pope over the Church of England.

c   Avoid persecuting the Catholics, like Edward VI had done (see Chapter 3). This will keep the Catholic countries happy.

Considerations

- War is easily started yet Elizabeth doesn't want to be controlled from abroad.
- What will Protestants and Catholics think of her?

Issue 4: Poor people and beggars

During Elizabeth's reign, as a result of changes in agriculture (the enclosure movement) many people began to starve and die. They turned to begging or stealing food just to live. Elizabeth's advisers instructed her to be firm with the poor and beggars. What should she do?

Options

a   Pay no attention to this problem because it is not a new thing to happen – there are always people starving.

b   Be kind, give them more food and help them in their crisis. This will make her popular with the poor and they will remain loyal and not rebel.

c   Take strong action. Pass laws to stop people from begging and clear them off the streets.

Considerations

- Elizabeth doesn't want riots or rebellions to break out.
- If Elizabeth is too kind, poor people might come to always expect help?
- Can she afford to give more to the poor?

Issue 5: Threats to the throne – Mary, Queen of Scots

Elizabeth's Scottish cousin, Mary, Queen of Scots, was a Catholic. Mary had a strong claim to the English throne, in which she was supported by other Catholic countries. After her husband was murdered, Mary fled from Scotland and lost her Scottish throne. With her Catholic cousin imprisoned in England, what should Elizabeth do?

Options

a   Keep Mary imprisoned in England, out of harm's way.

b   Hand Mary back to the Scots, who will probably execute her.

c   Try to help Mary get back her Scottish throne.

Considerations

- Helping Mary would look good (especially with Catholic countries).
- Mary is a threat to Elizabeth's throne.
- Mary is Elizabeth's cousin.

Digging deeper

What to do about Mary, Queen of Scots?

As we have just seen, Elizabeth I had many difficult decisions to make and issues to sort out during her reign. One of her main concerns was the number of Catholic plots to overthrow her rule. In this section we shall look at these plots more closely and the problem Elizabeth had of: 'What to do about Mary, Queen of Scots?'

Mary's background

Mary Stuart became Queen of Scotland in 1542 when she was less than one week old. Her father, James Stuart (or James V) had just died and her mother, Mary of Guise, ruled in her place as regent. Mary Stuart was taken to France in order to be brought up as a Catholic and a lady of the French court. She married a French prince, Francis, at the age of fifteen. After one year of their marriage, Francis became King Francis I of France, thus making Mary Queen of both Scotland and France.

Francis died in 1560 and Mary returned to Scotland a year later, to rule as queen. But on her return she found that Protestantism, a main division of Christianity following the Reformation and the break from the Roman Catholic Church, had taken hold in Scotland. This meant that the Scottish people did not want a Catholic queen, though they accepted Mary's rule because she tolerated Protestantism.

In 1565 Mary married Lord Darnley, who was her cousin, giving birth to a son, James, the following year. However, Mary's marriage to Lord Darnley was unhappy and they soon drifted apart. Then, in February 1567, Darnley died in suspicious circumstances following a mysterious explosion. Mary's supporter and lover, Lord Bothwell, was accused of plotting Darnley's murder, though there was no firm evidence against him. The situation worsened

Mary, Queen of Scots, in her teens. Contemporary portrait.

in May 1567 when Mary married for a third time – Lord Bothwell! Mary was now seen to have played a part in Darnley's murder, and there was a rebellion against her in Scotland. After formally resigning her throne, Mary escaped to England and her infant son, James, was crowned king of Scotland.

Mary arrived in Cumbria in 1568 and almost at once was seen to be at the centre of attempts to overthrow Elizabeth. English Catholics, supported by France and Spain, wanted Mary to become queen. Elizabeth soon realised that Mary was a major threat to her position and power.

Plots

At this time there were a number of important plots aimed at overthrowing Elizabeth. One of these plots was in effect promoted by the Pope when, in 1570, he issued a Bull (statement) which declared that Elizabeth had been excommunicated (thrown out of the Catholic Church and declared a heretic).

> ### SOURCE B
>
> I take away Elizabeth's false claim to the throne … and English nobles and subjects are let off all promises, loyalty or obedience to her. I forbid nobles and subjects to obey her orders and laws …
>
> *An extract from the Papal Bull of 1570.*

Because of this declaration the Pope appeared to be encouraging plots against Elizabeth. Hence one year later …

The Ridolfi Plot, 1571

Roberto di Ridolfi, a wealthy banker from Florence, hoped to rescue the Duke of Norfolk and Mary (who were both imprisoned in the Tower at this time) in order to depose Elizabeth. Ridolfi was backed by Spanish forces. However, Sir Francis Walsingham, one of Elizabeth's supporters, who built up and became head of a large spy network in Europe, soon discovered the plot and in 1572 the Duke of Norfolk was executed. The situation at this time seemed to be getting very dangerous for Elizabeth, but she had made a very powerful ally in Sir Francis Walsingham who she subsequently employed as her 'spy-master'.

In 1583 Walsingham uncovered the Throckmorton Plot, a failed attempt to take over England with Spanish help. Also, in 1585, Walsingham unearthed the Parry Plot – a plan by an MP to murder Elizabeth. But Walsingham could not prove Mary's involvement until the following year, when he found out about the Babington Plot.

The Babington Plot, 1586

In 1585 Walsingham began to employ a double agent, a priest in touch with Mary, who gave him a copy of all letters she received and sent. A local brewer, also in Walsingham's pay, smuggled the letters in the false bottom of a beer barrel, in and out of Chartley Manor where Mary was imprisoned.

A group of Catholic gentlemen led by Anthony Babington plotted to kill Elizabeth and wrote to Mary to plan her escape. Walsingham had tricked Mary into thinking that her way of sending and receiving coded messages was completely secret. This idea was actually Walsingham's, so as soon as Mary used the system, he was ready to decode and copy all the messages. The letters provided the evidence to hang the plotters and prove that Mary was involved too. When it reached him, Walsingham's secretary in London drew a gallows on the outside of Mary's letter, telling of the plan for her escape.

Mary is beheaded

At 8 o'clock on a cold February morning in 1587, Mary Stuart was beheaded for her part in the plot to overthrow Elizabeth. She was carrying a crucifix and wearing a white veil on her auburn hair. She was very dignified, saying her Latin prayers loudly and firmly. It was revealed she was wearing crimson petticoats – the colour of martyrdom. The executioner held up her severed head but dropped it, showing that she wore a wig and had short grey hair. As she was beheaded, her little dog ran out from beneath her skirts.

 Activity time

1   The real Babington code is shown in Source D. Using the code try to work out what the following message means. (You will find the answer at the end of this chapter on page 37.)

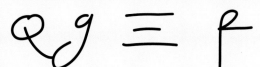

Now write out the following message in Babington code: *Elizabeth must die. Long live Mary.*

Capital letters are found in the second column; lower case are found in the third column.

2   Write a letter that Elizabeth might have written to her cousin, Mary, who was being imprisoned. Include in your letter an explanation of the following points:

a   the background to the forthcoming execution

b   the evidence from the various plots

c   the predicament that Elizabeth was in

d   how Elizabeth arrived at her decision.

SOURCE C

The execution of Mary, Queen of Scots, in 1587 – a drawing made by a Dutch artist soon after the event.

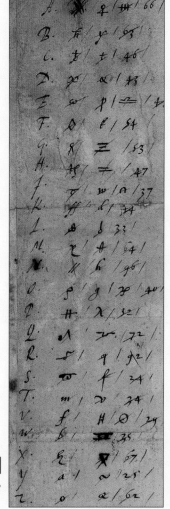

SOURCE D

Key to the Babington code.

Gaining wealth and power

Court life

As well as using their power to establish control, monarchs used their wealth to demonstrate their status, to impress visitors and their own subjects. Henry VIII did this at the Field of the Cloth of Gold in 1520. Elizabeth and later monarchs continued this tradition.

SOURCE A

We were admitted into the Presence Chamber hung with rich tapestry, at the door stood a gentleman in velvet with a gold chain whose office was to introduce to the queen any person of distinction who came to wait on her ... Next came the queen very majestic upon her head she had a small crown and she had on a necklace of exceeding fine jewels. Her air was stately and she was dressed in white silk bordered with pearls of the size of beans. She spoke very graciously to one and another in English, French and Italian. She was guarded on each side with 50 gentlemen with guilt battle axes.

This report was given by a German politician called Hentzner who visited Queen Elizabeth in 1598.

For monarchs and other wealthy people, dinners were extravagant occasions. A dinner for five or six people might include a round of brawn, two geese, six woodcocks, 18 pigeons, a sirloin of beef, six hens, four partridges, four snipe, four joints of veal, six rabbits, one pheasant, 36 larks, butter, eggs, spices, fruit, bread, ale, white and red wine and rosewater.

Peasants and common people did not have such grand lifestyles, but how do you think the list of food and drink above compares with the kind of food a common person would eat at a meal?

The queen's progresses

Queen Elizabeth went on tour around the country each year – this was called a 'progress'. These progresses were like her summer holiday and gave a good opportunity for many of her subjects, other than just Londoners, to view and admire her. Elizabeth would often ride in a carriage and, along the road, country people would come flocking to see her.

When Elizabeth visited towns, the people there made special preparations for her. They would decorate the main street, write poems like the one in Source B, hang up verses outside their houses, put garlands of flowers in the streets and offer gifts to her of gold and silver cups, plates or money. They would also put on entertainment, such as in 1578 when Elizabeth visited Norwich and a citizen called Thomas Churchyard arranged a show which included water nymphs ready to sing and dance for her as well as an actor dressed up as the Greek god, Mercury.

These visits and shows were very important because they gave a clear indication of the power and position of the monarch. Public appearances increased the loyalty and devotion of English people to their monarch, which were reinforced through gifts and allegiance. They also provided the town and countryfolk with a clear image of their monarch as quite often people at that time would never leave their county or even their town.

SOURCE B

No sooner was pronounced the name,
But babes in street 'gan [began] leap;
The youth, the age, the rich, the poor,
Came running all on heap,
And, clapping hands, cried mainly out,
'O blessed be the hour!
Our Queen is coming to the town,
With princely train and power.'

An unidentified contemporary writer describes a progress in verse.

Finally, what about the cost of these progresses? The monarch would not have to pay a penny towards them! That was down to local business people and show organisers who would sometimes lose a great deal of money just to impress the monarch. The nobles at whose houses she stayed had to put up the royal entourage at their own expense. In fact the queen would actually increase her wealth in a big way with all the gifts she received!

Elizabeth and Parliament

Look carefully at the picture of Elizabeth at the House of Lords (Source C). Members of the House of Commons are also present. She is listening to a speech from the Speaker of the House of Commons, who is standing in the middle of the members. In his speech he asks the queen to give the members of the House of Commons two key rights or privileges: freedom of speech and freedom from arrest. Thus they could say what they liked in the House of Commons and would not be arrested for anything they said.

SOURCE C

Queen Elizabeth attending Parliament. A contemporary engraving.

Elizabeth's Parliament helped her to rule the country. There, Acts of Parliament were passed to raise taxes and deal with major issues, such as the country's religion and how the poor should be looked after (see the table below). In Elizabeth's 44-year reign, Parliament held 13 sessions and met for a total of 140 weeks.

Throughout her reign, Parliament and Elizabeth worked together quite effectively; although it was always Elizabeth who had the final say, using the nobles, gentry and other key figures like Sir Francis Drake as advisers on important issues.

Date	Parliament	Acts passed/debates
January to May 1559	First Parliament	Act of Supremacy, Act of Religious Uniformity, Treason Act
January 1563	Second Parliament	Act for Relief of the Poor
April to May 1571	Third Parliament	Act against the Pope and Roman Catholics
February to April 1593	Eighth Parliament	Act against Catholics living in England, great debate on the government's attempt to raise extra taxes
October to December 1601	Tenth Parliament	Debate on government monopolies, Act for Relief of the Poor

Question time

1 What impression do you get from the tone of the report in Source A on page 30?

2 In what ways is Elizabeth's power displayed in Source A?

3 What image of Queen Elizabeth and her power do you get from Source B?

4 Why are freedom of speech and freedom from arrest important privileges for members of the House of Commons?

James I – transferring power

Elizabeth I died on 24 March 1603. She had had no children, so left no heir, and the English throne therefore passed to her cousin, James VI of Scotland, the son of Mary, Queen of Scots. He now became James I of England, which meant that he united the crowns of England and Scotland.

James I of England with his mother, Mary, Queen of Scots, painted in 1583.

James was faced with two main problems throughout his reign – Parliament and religion – both of which served as threats to his power.

Parliamentary problems

- Towards the end of her reign, Elizabeth had many problems with Parliament, because members hated paying heavy taxes to fund the wars with Ireland and Spain.

- England had become a trading nation, and there was a growth of wealthy merchants and industrialists who became members of the House of Commons. They wanted more say in how the country was run and more power for the Commons.

- There was the question of how often Parliament should be called. Also, how much of a role should ministers have in running parliamentary affairs to ensure that James got all the money he needed for his reign? The scene was set for a direct clash between king and Parliament.

Religious problems

- James had been raised as a Protestant in Scotland, where the extreme Protestants, the Puritans, had been very powerful.

- He hoped to give Catholics the opportunity to worship freely in their own church.

- His chief adviser and secretary, Robert Cecil, warned him that this would leave Catholics free to plot to kill him and so seize the throne.

- James had to decide whether he should carry on Elizabeth's plan of attacking all Catholics, or declare as king that Catholics should be able to worship freely, with parliamentary support.

Activity time

1 a List the problems facing James I, using key words.

   b Put these problems into the order in which you think James should deal with them.

   c Give reasons why you have chosen this particular order.

    Lay out your ideas in a table like this:

Problems (in order)	Reasons for choosing this order

2 Write a paragraph explaining the actions James should take and why he should take them.

Digging deeper

The Gunpowder Plot, 1605

A contemporary engraving of the Gunpowder conspirators.

The story of the Gunpowder Plot is full of intrigue, mystery and unanswered questions. It is a story which illustrates how religious discontent can lead to rebellion and even assassination attempts. It was a real threat to James I and his reign and a major event in British history. We still remember the Fifth of November today, celebrating Bonfire Night with fireworks and the burning of a Guy as a reminder of Guy Fawkes.

SOURCE C

The plan was the idea of Robert Catesby, a Catholic. He and other Catholic gentlemen would blow up the Houses of Parliament when King James I went there to make a speech.

In spring 1605, Thomas Percy rented a cellar nearby. It led under the House of Lords. Barrels of gunpowder were brought in and covered with wood and coal. The group had appointed Guy Fawkes, a Yorkshire gentleman and ex-soldier, to set off the powder. Meanwhile, the rest went to their country homes and waited. James was due to open Parliament on 5 November.

At 7 o'clock on 26 October, Lord Monteagle was about to have dinner when one of his servants brought him a letter. It had been given to him by a stranger in the street. The letter was written by Francis Tresham, one of the plotters and Lord Monteagle's cousin. The letter warned him not to attend Parliament. 'They shall receive', it said, 'a terrible blow'. Monteagle did not really know what to make of it. Even so he took it to Cecil, the king's chief minister. Cecil took the letter to the king.

On 4 November the cellar was searched. A heap of coal and wood was found. There was also a man who said he was called John Johnson. That evening the cellar was searched again. This time the gunpowder was discovered. John Johnson was arrested. In the Tower of London he was tortured and admitted he was Guy Fawkes. He confessed about the plot on 8 November.

The other plotters were tracked down to the Midlands. A number, including Catesby and Percy, were shot dead. One called Rokewood was taken prisoner. The survivors, including Guy Fawkes, were found guilty of high treason. In January 1606 they were dragged to the place of execution. There they were hanged, drawn and quartered. Their hearts were cut out and their insides burned in public.

An account of the Gunpowder Plot from Robert Cecil, the king's chief minister.

Source C gives one interpretation of the Gunpowder Plot – the government's version. But there are other things to remember about 5 November which may shed a different light on things:

- Cecil's spies were constantly watching leading Catholics.

- James' speech to Parliament was originally planned for 7 February, then planned for 3 October and finally it was to be on 5 November.

- The rented cellar was owned by a government official who died suddenly on 5 November.

- Why was Percy (a Catholic well known to Cecil's spies) allowed to rent a cellar under the Houses of Parliament in the first place?

- All gunpowder was stored in the Tower of London and you had to have a license to buy it. Cecil did not allow any investigations into the Tower stores from early 1604 onwards.

- Cecil knew of the plot in October, so why did he wait until 4 November to search Parliament's cellars?

- Monteagle's name was removed from the plotters' accounts and he was given a large pension.

- Some handwriting experts believe the letter given to Monteagle was a forgery.

- Tresham was arrested later and died mysteriously in the Tower of London.

- Cecil gave three different accounts of Guy Fawkes' arrest.

- Guy Fawkes' confession is different from the government version.

- Were Catesby and Percy shot to prevent them from talking?

- Why did the man who shot them receive a pension of 2 shillings a day for life?

- The plotters were unarmed.

- Look at the picture of Guy Fawkes' signature (Source D). Why was it so different prior to his torture?

Guy Fawkes' signature before and after torture.

So there was a threat to the king in 1605, or so it appeared! There are different interpretations of events – some historians would argue that Robert Cecil devised the whole plot to attack Catholics and make them appear a serious threat to the king. Some would argue that Cecil actually knew about the plot and used it to his advantage for propaganda purposes. Others would point out that Cecil's account is actually accurate and correct.

 ## Question time

What you need to do now is to use all the evidence here, as well as your own research, to create a well supported and clearly argued answer to the essay question:

'To what extent was the Gunpowder Plot a real threat to James I?'

Remember to divide your essay into three sections:

- An introduction should set out the key points you are going to make in your essay.

- In the main part of the essay you should use your own knowledge to analyse the events of 5 November. Use the sources to back up your main arguments.

- In your conclusion, draw together the main strands of your essay.

Trouble brewing between king and Parliament

Religion was not the only problem facing James I. Many MPs increasingly demanded a greater share in policy making, to keep taxes down and to help the cause of Protestantism abroad. The disagreements between James I and Parliament grew steadily worse as time went on. They were further compounded by James's belief that monarchs had the divine right to rule – in other words that they were appointed by God. This set the scene for a great rift between the king and Parliament which was to result, eventually, in the Civil War during the reign of James I's son, Charles I. He became king in 1625 and also believed in the divine right of kings (see Chapter 4).

Assessment section

1 Choose either Henry VIII or Elizabeth I and answer the following question in an essay style.

'Was Henry VIII or Elizabeth I a good or a bad monarch?'

Support your opinions with detailed evidence.

2 Answer the following essay question.

'How important to monarchs were the issues of power and control during the Tudor and Stuart period?'

Give examples of, and reasons for, how the monarchs maintained their power and control.

3 'To what extent were there major threats to the monarchy during this period?'

In your answer make reference to key people and events, such as Mary, Queen of Scots and the Gunpowder Plot.

4 Write a speech which can be used during a class debate about the events leading up to the 'Murders in the Tower'. You must put forward a clear line of argument that explains what happened. Remember, you will be debating this in class, so make sure your answers can be backed up with theory and/or evidence.

Further reading

Jeremy Black, *History of England* (Dolphin Publications, 1993)

Plantagenent Somerset Fry, *The Kings and Queens of England and Scotland* (Dealerfield Books, 1990)

British History: Tudors and Stuarts 1485–1714 (Kingfisher Books, 1997)

Answer to coded message on page 29: dogs

The Early Reformation, 1510–47

In 1513, Henry VIII and his queen, Catherine of Aragon, went on a pilgrimage to the Abbey of Hailes, in Gloucestershire. They lit candles, knelt before statues of the saints and the Virgin Mary, and kissed the monastery's most treasured possession, a holy relic (see page 39). This particular relic was a phial (or bottle) which was said to contain the blood of Christ. Henry hoped that God would reward him for this devotion by giving him a son.

At the start of his reign Henry VIII, like all Christians in western Europe, belonged to the Roman Catholic Church of which the Pope was the head. The English king was a particularly loyal and devoted Catholic, quite prepared to persecute, or treat cruelly, those who criticised the Church or its priests.

A few years after his pilgrimage, Henry published a book in which he attacked the views of a German monk called Martin Luther (see pages 39–41). Luther had rejected the Pope's right to be the head of the Christian Church. The Pope was so pleased with Henry that he gave the king a new title – Defender of the Faith. In Latin, this is *fidei defensor*: FD for short. If you look at the coins in your pocket, you will see that these letters are still there, above the queen's head.

Sweeping religious changes

Henry began his reign as a good Catholic, but within 20 years everything had changed. He had divorced Catherine of Aragon, the Abbey of Hailes was closed down and the monks were thrown out. By then, every other monastery in England had been shut down and their relics and treasures had been destroyed or confiscated by the king. The law was also changed, so that it was illegal to venerate statues or relics; and pilgrimages were condemned. Henry had also turned against the Roman Catholic Church and the Pope. Those who dared to defend the Pope as head of the Church were executed – killed for repeating what the king himself had written in 1521. Instead the ideas of the Protestant reformer, Martin Luther, were now introduced. And most importantly, the king declared himself the head of the Church in England.

It seemed to some English men and women that the world was turned upside down during Henry's reign, and perhaps they were right. The changes begun by Henry VIII are called the Reformation. This resulted in England and Scotland becoming Protestant countries, no longer part of the Roman Catholic Church. This split meant that, for centuries, Protestants and Catholics were enemies.

Even today in the United Kingdom there are still many reminders of the Reformation and divisions exist between Catholics and Protestants. Did you know that in the last 30 years over 3000 people have been killed in violence in Northern Ireland? One cause of the troubles there has been mistrust and hatred between Catholics and Protestants. This continues to be a major problem for British prime ministers. Also, it remains against the law for either Prince Charles, or his son, Prince William, to marry a Roman Catholic. Even football is affected by the events of the Reformation: Glasgow's two teams, Celtic and Rangers, represent the separate Catholic and Protestant communities of the city.

What was the Reformation and why did it happen?

To answer this question you will need to study events in Germany and Italy, as well as in England. Most historians are agreed that the Reformation began in Germany, so we shall start there.

Martin Luther and Rome

In the winter of 1510, when Henry and Catherine of Aragon had only been married a year, a young German monk called Martin Luther went on a pilgrimage to Rome. This was the home of the Pope and the headquarters of the Catholic Church, and to a pilgrim it was a holy city. Rome was also the city of St Peter and St Paul, and many of the early Christian martyrs. Just by visiting Rome, Luther was performing a holy action which would help him enter heaven after his death. Luther walked about 800 miles to reach Rome, and on his first sight of the city he lay flat on the ground and called out, 'Hail, Holy Rome!'

Like most pilgrims visiting Rome, Luther went to the sacred shrines of the city, fasting, praying, and touching the holy relics.

Digging deeper

Relics

Relics were sacred objects preserved in many churches throughout Europe. They might be the bones of a dead bishop or saint, or the possessions or clothes which once belonged to them. The more holy the person, the more valuable were the relics. The most precious of all were relics of Christ himself (such as the phial of Christ's blood at Hailes Abbey), his disciples, or the Virgin Mary. Some churches claimed to have pieces of the cross on which Christ was crucified, a strand of hair from his beard, thorns from his crown, straw from the manger where Jesus was born, or even bottles containing the Virgin Mary's milk.

The Church taught that a Christian could obtain indulgences by viewing these relics. This meant that God's punishment for sin would be lessened. It was believed that, when a person died his or her soul did not go straight to heaven or hell, but to purgatory, where people were punished for their sins. This was a place of suffering, but the time a soul spent in purgatory could be reduced by obtaining indulgences.

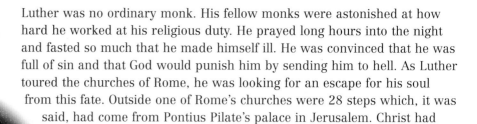

Luther was no ordinary monk. His fellow monks were astonished at how hard he worked at his religious duty. He prayed long hours into the night and fasted so much that he made himself ill. He was convinced that he was full of sin and that God would punish him by sending him to hell. As Luther toured the churches of Rome, he was looking for an escape for his soul from this fate. Outside one of Rome's churches were 28 steps which, it was said, had come from Pontius Pilate's palace in Jerusalem. Christ had climbed them, so the Church taught that if a Christian climbed them on his hands and knees repeating prayers as he went, then he could release a soul from purgatory. Luther regretted that his parents were still alive because he would have liked to release them. He chose to release his grandfather but, as he wearily reached the top, he was filled with doubt about the teachings of the Church regarding purgatory. Could it really be so simple?

Luther also noticed other things about Rome which disturbed him. The Pope and the cardinals, the most important members of the Church, lived in luxurious palaces. Luther had grown up believing that Christians were meant to follow Christ's example and live simply. This was why he had become a monk. Now he heard stories of the extravagance of the Popes, how they broke their vow of celibacy by keeping women, how they dressed in the finest silks and held huge banquets. Pope Julius was not actually in Rome when Luther came; he was leading an army besieging a castle. Dressed in armour and riding a huge warhorse, he had charged at the head of his army, yelling threats against his enemies. This was not quite how Luther expected the Pope to behave!

Elsewhere in the city Luther met Italian priests who rushed through the words of the Mass, the Roman Catholic service of Holy Communion. One priest said seven Masses in the time it took Luther to say one: the priests received a payment for each Mass. He also noticed how much money the Church was making from charging people to view relics.

The storm breaks in Germany

Martin Luther returned to Germany a troubled man. He wanted to save his soul from damnation (going to hell) but he was not sure how because his faith in the Catholic Church had been shaken. He became professor of theology at the University of Wittenberg, and his lectures on the Bible were very popular because he was an excellent speaker. One day in 1517 some of his students told him about a Dominican preacher, John Tetzel, who was travelling through Germany selling indulgences. Tetzel had been instructed by the Pope to grant indulgences to the faithful who would pay according to their wealth. The money would help the Pope's grand scheme to rebuild the Basilica of St Peter's in Rome. Tetzel entered each market place at the head of a solemn procession. He would set up his cross and then speak to the crowd. Luther heard that he was making wonderful claims (see Source B). The listeners were then encouraged to put their coins into a large coffer (or box) that Tetzel's priests carried everywhere. At the end of his speeches, Tetzel reminded his audience: 'When the coin in the coffer rings, the soul from purgatory springs.'

SOURCE B

Listen to the voices of your dear dead relatives and friends, saying, 'Pity us, pity us. We gave birth to you, we brought you up, we left you our fortunes. Now you ignore us for the sake of a few coins. Will you let us lie here in flames?' Remember that you are able to release them.

Tetzel speaking about the benefits of buying indulgences.

SOURCE C

Why doesn't the Pope build the Basilica of St Peter's with his own money?

Before long all the churches, palaces, walls, and bridges of Rome will be built out of our money. We Germans cannot attend St Peter's.

From Martin Luther's Ninety-Five Theses *of 1517.*

Hearing Tetzel's speech proved the final straw for Luther. He could not believe that God's forgiveness could be purchased so easily. He decided to protest and wrote down all the reasons why he thought it was wrong for the Church to sell indulgences – 95 in all! As a university lecturer he hoped to start a debate, so he pinned his arguments, or *Ninety-five Theses*, to the door of the main church in Wittenberg.

Martin Luther's action succeeded in starting a heated debate. The Church was furious: indulgences were a major source of money and Luther seemed to be threatening that. The sellers of indulgences, especially the monks of the Dominican order, turned on Luther, but he also had friends and supporters who defended him. Much to his surprise, Luther became famous overnight. Copies of his *Theses* were printed and distributed throughout Germany. Luther had written them in Latin, the language of the Church, but now they were translated into German so that ordinary people could read them. Luther had based his arguments against indulgences on his careful reading of the Bible, but to many ordinary Germans he soon became a hero who was defending them against greedy priests and foreign popes.

SOURCE D

The Dominican preacher, Tetzel, selling indulgences. A nineteenth-century German print.

Calls for reform of the Church

Anti-clericals

For many years some Germans had been complaining about the Church and the corruption (or misbehaviour) of the clergy or ministers of the Church, such as priests, bishops, cardinals and the Pope, as well as monks and nuns. These people are known as anti-clericals, which means being 'against the clergy'. They made public their disapproval of the way the clergy behaved. Some of the German bishops lived in palaces and ruled as princes, collecting taxes and commanding armies; they were also often noblemen. Some of them were the bishops of more than one diocese or area, as well as being the abbot of two or more monasteries and the priest for several village churches. Obviously the bishops could only be in one place at a time, even though they collected income for each of the different posts they held, so people complained that they were not looking after their congregations properly. On the other hand, many ordinary priests were very poor and uneducated – they could not even read Latin. Anti-clericals also argued that uneducated priests could not look after the needs of ordinary people and teach them religion.

Humanists

Another group of people who criticised the clergy were the humanists. These were university scholars, who were horrified by the ignorance of some of the clergy. A famous humanist was Erasmus, who made fun of priests and monks, who 'brayed like donkeys in church, repeating the words of psalms they don't understand'. Above all, Erasmus said the Church had twisted the meaning of the Bible. Jesus had been a poor man who encouraged spirituality and humility, but his followers – the bishops, the cardinals and the Pope – were rich. Erasmus said that the clerics cheated ordinary people: they frightened them with pictures of hell and then encouraged them to escape the pains of purgatory by paying the Church, i.e. to view relics of dead saints. Erasmus used his scholarly learning to show that many of the items people claimed to be relics were in fact fakes. For example, there were enough fragments of Christ's cross preserved in monasteries to make several trees, and, although it had only taken four nails to crucify Christ, hundreds could be seen as precious relics. Also, the arm of St Andrew looked suspiciously like a pig's bone!

Humanists and anti-clericals both complained that some of the priests were misbehaving:

- They were expected to imitate Christ and set an example to their people by leading simple lives in purity and honesty, but many could be found in the inns, drinking and gambling.

- Some lived with women despite their vow of celibacy, which prevented them from marrying.

- Often they were greedy, forcing poor farmers to pay tithes – one tenth of the harvest – even when the harvest had failed.

- Some daring humanists went further and criticised how the congregation in church only received bread, not wine, at Mass or Communion. They said that the service was based on Christ's Last Supper, when Jesus had given his disciples both bread and wine as his body and blood. In the Roman Catholic Church only the priests received the wine.

Anti-clericals and humanists had often called for the reform of the Church. They wanted to improve the Church and end the corruption and ignorance of the clergy. This is where the word 'Reformation' comes from.

German woodcut of c.1520 making fun of the Pope. He is seen here as an ass playing the bagpipes!

Luther attacks the Pope

Erasmus wrote his criticisms of the Church in Latin; scholars read them, but ordinary people could not read Latin. Most Germans were illiterate – they could not read or write. However, humanists and anti-clericals made sure that when Luther attacked the sale of indulgences he found many supporters. Pictures and cartoons in the form of woodcuts quickly spread Luther's message to illiterate Germans. The pictures showed greedy monks, and the Pope growing fat by feeding on Germany. The Pope was made fun of, pictured as a donkey, playing the bagpipes (see Source E), or even as the devil.

Luther was ordered by the Church to withdraw his criticisms, but he stood his ground. He said he would only back down if he were shown the passage in the Bible that allowed the sale of indulgences. Very quickly his ideas moved on. Like all Christians, to Martin Luther the Bible was the Word of God. Now he said the Pope had no power to order Christians to believe anything that was not in the Bible. He said the New Testament contained nothing about relics, or purgatory, or even popes! These were dangerous words. All Christians were expected to follow the Pope without question and Luther was now challenging the Pope's authority to rule the Church. This was heresy, a crime punished by being burnt at the stake.

Luther's complaints against the Church

- Indulgences were a fraud.
- Popes claimed powers to which they had no right.
- The Church ignored what the Bible said.
- Christians were not being taught true religion by the Church.
- The Church was greedy and was not concerned with spiritual things.

The Diet of Worms

Pope Leo X was furious with Luther and wanted to punish him. He persuaded the 20-year-old ruler of Germany, Charles V, to bring Luther to trial. Charles was also the King of Spain and Holy Roman Emperor, but despite these titles his power in Germany was limited. Also, Luther thought he could count on the protection of the prince who ruled in Wittenberg, Frederick the Wise, who was proud of the famous scholar his university had produced. Despite the efforts of his friends who tried to persuade him not to go, in 1521 Martin Luther agreed to attend the meeting of the German Parliament, or Diet, in the town of Worms, to answer the charge of heresy. (Luther spoke little English, so he wouldn't have got the joke about the Diet of Worms!)

At the meeting, Luther refused to give way when he was told that what he was saying was heresy. He defended himself by asking his accusers to prove him wrong by quoting the Bible, but all they could do was tell him that the Pope, bishops and councils of the Church did not agree with him. Luther was defiant, saying 'Here I stand! So help me God', but he left Worms quickly because his life was now in danger. Charles V banned him as an outlaw, and the Pope condemned him as a heretic. On the road back to Wittenberg, Luther's coach was attacked by horsemen, and he was captured. Luther's disappearance started rumours that he had been murdered, but he had been kidnapped by his friend, Prince Frederick the Wise, and taken to one of his castles to protect him from enemies.

Luther stayed in hiding for a year but eventually returned to Wittenberg. There he was welcomed as a hero and led the reform of the Church. Within a few years great changes took place:

- The Pope's authority was ended, services were held in German (not Latin), priests were allowed to marry and monasteries were closed down.

- There were no more relics, pilgrimages or statues of saints.

- Congregations now began to receive both bread and wine at Communion.

- Before long, Luther's followers were called Protestants – they had, after all, begun the protest against the Roman Catholic Church.

This was the start of the Reformation in Europe and it soon spread from Wittenberg.

Activity time

1 Using the summary of Luther's complaints explain why he attacked the Roman Catholic Church.

2 Find evidence in this section to explain why many Germans saw Luther as a hero.

The Church in England

In England Henry VIII was horrified by Luther's attack on the Church and wrote a book attacking the German monk (see page 38). However, Luther's ideas spread quickly to England, where the man responsible for defending the country against heresy was Cardinal Thomas Wolsey. In 1521, soon after the Diet of Worms, Wolsey organised a public bonfire outside St Paul's Cathedral to burn Lutheran books confiscated in England. The bishops were ordered to track down anyone who was spreading Luther's ideas, either by preaching or in print.

Discontent with the Church in England

There seemed to be many reasons why English men and women were attracted to Luther's teachings. The English Church certainly had problems:

- It was led by greedy men, like Wolsey, who did not set an example of Christian holiness (see page 46). Some of the bishops were the holders of many church posts and the incomes from them made them very rich.

- Parish priests were often uneducated and seemed to be more interested in getting money from their congregations than giving them spiritual help. Priests collected fees for baptisms and burials, and many other services. They also received tithes, a payment by farmers of a tenth of their harvest.

Some people resented paying tithes, and sometimes this resentment led to violence. For example, at Hayes in 1530 a large group of villagers refused to pay their tithes, so the priest, Henry Gold, and his brother tried to seize the villagers' cattle. The villagers fought back and, led by the local innkeeper, they allowed their cattle to trample the priest's corn. The villagers also stole his vestments (the robes he wore to perform Mass). Matters came to a head with a riot during Mass and threats to the priest; eventually the archbishop had to settle the affair.

The case of Richard Hunne

Also at this time, Londoners remained uneasy about what had happened to Richard Hunne, a wealthy London merchant. In 1511 Hunne's baby son had died. The usual practice when someone died was for the priest to demand a mortuary (a payment for performing the burial service). Instead of money the priest would be given the baby's christening robe, no doubt a beautiful and expensive piece of clothing. Hunne, however, refused to pay, and as a result he was excommunicated, banned and cursed by the Church. Hunne brought his case to the king's court, because he said the Church had damaged his business, but the bishop of London accused Hunne of heresy and had him arrested. Hunne was imprisoned in the bishop's cell, where he was found hanged in 1514. The bishop said that Hunne had committed suicide out of shame because he was a heretic, but a month later a jury inquiring into Hunne's death declared that he had been murdered. There had been signs of a struggle in his cell, and also evidence that Hunne had been strangled before his neck was broken.

Hunne had been a respected merchant, and many Londoners now believed that he had been killed on the bishop's orders because he was a troublemaker.

People called for his murderers to be put on trial, but, because the people responsible for Hunne's death were members of the Church, they had benefit of clergy. This meant they had the privilege of not being tried for crimes in the king's courts: they could only be brought before the Church's own courts, and the bishop refused to start a trial. Anti-clericals said that it was wicked that the Church could ignore the law like this, in order to cover up a murder. They attacked the Church, saying that what had happened to Hunne showed that the Church was corrupt, and had too much power.

Digging deeper

Cardinal Wolsey

Although Thomas Wolsey's life began in humble circumstances, he rose to become the most powerful person in the land after the king. After training in law at Oxford University, he entered the service of the Archbishop of Canterbury and quickly showed that he was highly talented and intelligent. He was also hard working and ambitious, and the young King Henry was looking for men like Wolsey to serve him.

Under Henry VIII, Wolsey became the Lord Chancellor, responsible for governing England. Wolsey also held many posts in the Church, each of which provided him with an income. Although not a monk, he became the Abbot of St Alban's Abbey; he was made Archbishop of York, a city he only visited just before his death. Wolsey was also made a cardinal by the Pope. Cardinals were the most important priests in the Roman Catholic Church, and when a pope died they chose the new one. He also became the papal legate – the pope's special representative in a country – for England.

In this way, Wolsey became both powerful and rich. He was a proud man, who dressed in the finest silks, velvets and furs. His appetite was huge, and he grew very fat (see Source A). His palace at Hampton Court was grander than the king's – here Wolsey kept over 500 servants and entertained his guests to magnificent banquets, surrounded by fine furniture, tapestries, and a dazzling collection of silver and gold plate. Nobles seeking favours would present Wolsey with gifts in the hope that he would help them.

SOURCE A

Cardinal Wolsey. A contemporary portrait after Hans Holbein the Younger.

Hampton Court Palace.

Wolsey's procession to court through the streets of London was a colourful spectacle. A nobleman would go ahead of him, carrying his cardinal's hat on a velvet cushion, other gentlemen carried two large decorative pieces of silver, shaped like columns, to be placed either side of his throne in court. There were also horsemen and servants dressed in Wolsey's household livery (uniform). Wolsey himself sometimes rode a donkey, as Christ had done when entering Jerusalem, and might also be seen sniffing at a hollow orange soaked with herbs and vinegar, to protect him either from the smell or the diseases of the crowds that filled the streets.

Wolsey's pride and power made him many enemies. Several of the great nobles despised him because of his low birth. He was also unpopular with anti-clericals (see page 42), who were horrified that the Church in England should be led by a man who seemed greedy for wealth and had little spiritual virtue. They mocked his pride and dismissed him as a 'fat maggot'. Nevertheless they had to respect his power.

 ## Activity time

Find out more about Wolsey's palace of Hampton Court.

Luther's ideas spread to England

Against this background of corruption in the Church in England, Luther's ideas began to gain ground. In Wittenberg in 1525, Englishman William Tyndale, an associate of Martin Luther, had translated the New Testament into English with a commentary to show how much the Roman Catholic Church had moved away from the true Word of God. Another Lutheran, Thomas Bilney, gave sermons attacking relics and images, and the veneration (or worship) of saints. Bilney told people that such practices were not necessary to enter heaven, and that purgatory was an invention of the Catholic Church simply to make people pay money for indulgences. He called the veneration of images idolatry.

Stories were soon being told of the tricks performed by some priests. At Leominster the congregation was filled with wonder when a 'Holy Maid' appeared in the rood loft. (The rood loft was the space above the arch leading to the altar in which there hung a cross, or 'rood', with the figure of Christ on it.) A young woman was seen kneeling at the foot of the cross and was said to be living on nothing but 'angels' food'. During Mass the congregation were amazed to see the Communion wafer (bread) miraculously rise from the plate held by the priest and travel to the Holy Maid's mouth. Thousands came to witness this miracle and gave donations to the priest. However, the bishop decided to investigate this 'miracle' and the Holy Maid was shown to be a fraud. It was discovered that the Communion trick had been carried out with fine hairs and, when questioned, the Holy Maid confessed to sleeping with the priest, who had planned the whole deceit.

Other attacks were made about the corruption of the clergy. Simon Fish wrote a petition to the king accusing the clergy of idleness, drunkenness and sinfulness. He said that many priests and friars took advantage of their position to seduce the virtuous housewives of their parish, so that husbands did not know whether their children were really their own. Fish wrote that people should 'tie these holy idle thieves to a cart and whip them naked through the streets'.

Wolsey's response to increased attacks on the Church was another public bonfire of Lutheran books. Suspected heretics were made to parade through London in shame with bundles of sticks tied round their necks. These sticks represented the kindling wood that would be used to start the fire when heretics were burned at the stake. They were intended to warn people away from Lutheran ideas – but how long before people would really be burnt at the stake?

Were the complaints about the Church widespread?

Anti-clericals and humanists found plenty to complain about in the English Church. They were highly educated people who often had contempt for the ignorance and superstition of both priests and ordinary people. But many historians now think that their evidence gives us a false impression of the Catholic Church, and have found other evidence to suggest that most people were content with the Church. People in general continued to go on pilgrimages and processions, venerate holy relics and give money for shrines and images. Indeed, the amount of money that people were spending on the decoration of their churches was actually increasing at the start of the Reformation. New statues of Jesus, Mary and the saints were being carved, sculpted, and painted up and down the country, and the money for these was raised by the people themselves, not priests or bishops. In some places steeples and towers were rebuilt in the latest style.

Increasingly in England at this time donations were made to priests for Masses for the souls of people's dead relatives. Money was also being left in wills to pay for the upkeep of statues and other images. The number of young men becoming priests was growing and, despite the spread of Lutheran writings, booksellers were selling even more books of Catholic prayers and meditations. None of this evidence suggests that the Catholic Church was an organisation that was in decay and unpopular with the English people. Apart from the anti-clericals and humanists, who were few in number, it could therefore be argued that there was no great demand for a Reformation in England.

Activity time

1   Draw a table with two columns headed:

A corrupt Church	A popular Church

In each column write down the evidence in the section you have just read to show either that the Church was corrupt or that it was popular with the people.

2   Read the following statements about the Church:

- It was corrupt and unpopular with English men and women.
- It was popular and well run.
- It was corrupt, but popular.

Which of these statements seems to you to be best supported by the evidence?

The King's Great Matter

To understand why the English Reformation occurred, we must return to Henry VIII himself and the problems of his marriage with Catherine of Aragon. Catherine was the daughter of the King and Queen of Spain. Catherine's nephew, Charles, became Charles V, the Holy Roman Emperor and King of Spain in 1519. He banned Luther at the Diet of Worms (see page 44).

Henry married Catherine when he became king in 1509, at the age of eighteen, and to begin with they were very happy together. However, they seemed to have no luck producing children. A baby boy was born in 1510, but he soon died. Other pregnancies followed, but ended in miscarriage. At last, in 1516, a healthy baby girl was born, named Mary. However, Henry urgently wanted a son to succeed him as King of England. In 1518 Catherine became pregnant again and Henry was busy making plans for the expected arrival of his heir. Sadly, tragedy again struck when the baby, a girl, was born dead. Catherine was now in her late thirties and it seemed increasingly unlikely that she would conceive again. Henry was worried for the future of his Tudor dynasty if he could not have a son. Also, he believed the problem lay not with him but with Catherine, since he had fathered a son by one of the ladies at court, Bessie Blount. With little thought for Catherine's feelings, Henry had proudly christened the boy Henry Fitzroy, a surname that means 'king's bastard'. (Bastard is a word used for someone who is born illegitimately, or outside marriage.) However, he knew that he needed a legitimate heir to succeed him as king, that is, a son born to his wife.

Doubts about his marriage

After many years of trying for a son with Catherine, Henry began to doubt whether their marriage was proper in the eyes of God. Catherine had actually been married before, to Henry's older brother, Arthur, when she and Arthur were both fifteen. However, Arthur had died after only four months of married life. To preserve the friendship between England and Spain, Catherine had been quickly betrothed to the young Henry. Now Henry was starting to believe that this marriage was forbidden by the Bible. In the Book of Leviticus it was written, 'If a man shall take his brother's wife it is an unclean thing. They shall be childless'. Henry began to convince himself that he had sinned by marrying Catherine, and so had been cursed by God who would not allow him a son. When the marriage between Henry and Catherine had been arranged, the Pope had granted his permission for the marriage to take place. Henry now began to claim that the Pope did not have the right to set aside the law of God.

In 1527 Henry publicly declared his doubts about his marriage to Catherine of Aragon, and asked the Church to examine whether his marriage to Catherine was wrong. It sounded a simple case, but Henry did not mention one particular fact about his private life, which was being whispered about throughout the Court – he had also fallen passionately in love with one of the ladies who attended Queen Catherine. While Catherine was by now an ageing woman of 42, Anne Boleyn was only 26. She had dark hair and beautiful eyes, and a flirtatious manner that bewitched Henry.

Henry was six years younger than his wife, Catherine, and still fit and vigorous. Catherine had stopped dancing long ago, but now Henry enjoyed dancing with Anne. Anne teased Henry: she said she was a virtuous girl who would not make love with him unless she was his wife. A marriage to Anne was very appealing to Henry: it would resolve Henry's difficulties over the succession, and give him 'the one who I value the most of all women'.

Wolsey's problems

In Henry's time, divorce, as we know it today, was forbidden by the Church. Only God could end a marriage – by death. However marriages could be annulled – the Church could declare that the man and woman had never been properly married. To get a marriage annulled it was necessary to prove that there was something wrong with the original marriage; that, for example, it broke the law of God. It was usually necessary to bribe the leaders of the Church to make an annulment, and this should not have been a problem for Henry and Wolsey.

Catherine's stubbornness

Henry VIII now ordered Cardinal Wolsey to persuade the Pope to annul his marriage to Catherine of Aragon, on the grounds that it was against the law of God. However, several difficulties lay in the path of the king and his chancellor. First, Catherine would not allow herself to be so rudely pushed aside. She was the daughter of the King and Queen of Spain and the aunt of the present King of Spain and Holy Roman Emperor, while Anne was just a maid of honour. Also, Catherine believed firmly in the justice of her marriage to Henry. She now embarrassed Henry by publicly kneeling before him and calling out, 'I have been to you a true, humble and obedient wife. Take of me some pity and compassion'.

Lack of support from the Church

A second problem was the attitude of the Church. Another passage in the Bible seemed to contradict Leviticus, and many scholars believed that the Pope did indeed have the right to permit a marriage such as Henry's to Catherine. One of the most respected bishops in England, John Fisher, strongly defended the queen, for whom many people felt sympathy. Also, as Wolsey soon discovered, the Pope himself was unwilling to admit that his predecessor could have made an error. Such an admission would suggest that popes were not chosen by God to rule his Church, but were merely humans who made mistakes.

Pope held captive by Charles V

However, the most serious difficulty, and one which could not be overcome, was that in 1529, when Wolsey was trying to change the Pope's mind, the Pope was actually the prisoner of Catherine's nephew, the Emperor Charles V, whose soldiers had captured Rome! Charles was certainly not going to allow the King of England to humiliate his aunt.

The break with Rome

As the king's Great Matter dragged on, Henry became more and more frustrated and angry, infatuated with Anne Boleyn, and desperate for a son. The first to suffer was Wolsey. In Henry's eyes he had failed him, so was dismissed by the king in shame. This was too much for the great cardinal, who died just soon enough to avoid a trial and, possibly, execution for treason.

Henry VIII now began to listen to some of the anti-clericals who were saying that the Church had too much power. Anne Boleyn lent him a copy of a book by William Tyndale (see page 48) who had written that the king, not the Pope, was really the head of the English Church. Tyndale claimed that popes and bishops had taken the power that really belonged to monarchs.

Cranmer and Cromwell

Henry now appointed two men to his Council who shared some of those views which opposed the Roman Catholic Church. The first was Thomas Cranmer, who now became the Archbishop of Canterbury. Cranmer had been to Luther's Germany and had secretly married – it was still against the law in England for priests to marry. The second man was Thomas Cromwell, a skilful lawyer whom the king trusted the way he had once trusted Wolsey. Cromwell may also have promised to make Henry 'the richest prince in Christendom'. He was to replace the Pope with the king as the head of the Church in England. Henry would then have full control over all the property of the Church in England. In Germany, Lutheran princes had closed down the monasteries and confiscated their property.

SOURCE A

Archbishop Cranmer by Gerlack Flicke, 1546.

SOURCE B

Thomas Cromwell. A contemporary portrait after Hans Holbein.

Matters became urgent late in 1532, when Anne at last gave in to Henry and began to sleep with him. She soon became pregnant. Henry was anxious to make sure that the child was legitimate and could succeed to the throne, so he married Anne in secret, in February 1533. Two months later Archbishop Cranmer held a court, which declared that the marriage of Henry and Catherine had been unlawful in the sight of God, so should be regarded as never having happened. Catherine of Aragon was now informed that she had never been Henry's wife, but had merely been living with him in a sinful relationship, and her daughter Mary was declared a bastard. She also had to endure Anne, six months pregnant, being crowned Queen of England, in June 1533.

When the baby was born it must have been a disappointment for Henry – it was a girl, Elizabeth. He even cancelled a tournament he was planning in celebration. Anne must have been disappointed too – she had been so confident that the child would be a boy that she had written his birth announcement in advance. God was thanked for assisting her 'in the deliverance and bringing forth of a prince'. The document shows that the letter 's' was added in different handwriting at the end of the word 'prince' (to mean 'princess').

Now it was Thomas Cromwell's turn to help Henry. Using all his skills as a lawyer, he persuaded Parliament to change the laws of England, declaring an end to the authority of the Pope over England's Church. In the future, the king would be the Supreme Head of the Church of England. The clergy would pay taxes to him, and all people had to accept that Henry had the right to marry Anne Boleyn. By the Act of Succession of 1534 nobles, monks and priests had to swear an oath that they agreed to this – to deny the right of Anne to be queen or of her heirs to inherit the throne was now treason, punishable by death. This seemed to be enough to frighten most people into obedience, but some Carthusian monks refused to take the oath. They were dragged through the streets of London and hanged, drawn and quartered at Tyburn. Bishop Fisher (see page 52) who had supported Catherine was now beheaded, and a month later so was Sir Thomas More. Sir Thomas More had once been Henry's friend, a man of great learning who was admired throughout Europe. These executions horrified people in many countries.

Digging deeper

Executions

SOURCE C

Executioners hanging, drawing and quartering their victims. This contemporary illustration shows the execution of the Gunpowder Plotters in January 1606.

The punishment for treason was always death, but how traitors died depended on their position in society. Noblemen and women were usually beheaded with an axe, as happened to Sir Thomas More and Bishop Fisher, but commoners would be hanged, drawn and quartered (see Source C). This process began with the traitor being dragged through the streets of the town tied to a sled, nearly naked. Next the traitor was hanged, but would be cut down after hanging and revived, so that he or she were alive whilst being disembowelled. For disembowelment, the executioner used a sharp knife to cut open the stomach and remove the person's guts, meanwhile keeping the victim alive and conscious for as long as possible. The victim's arms and legs were then cut off and, finally, the traitor was beheaded. In the case of the Carthusian monks and their abbot who refused to accept Henry VIII as head of the Church of England it is said that their hearts were ripped out and rubbed 'hot and steaming' over their mouths. The Carthusian abbot's arm was brought back to his abbey and nailed to its door, whilst the monks' heads were displayed on spikes above London Bridge.

Compared to this, the beheading of noblemen and women seems merciful! It also allowed them an opportunity to die with dignity. Sir Thomas More was even able to joke on the way to his death. Time spent in prison had left his legs stiff, so he asked the executioner to help him up the steps to the scaffold; he said he would manage by himself on his way down. As More placed his head on the block he carefully moved his beard out of the way, saying that his beard had not committed treason.

Henry attacks the monasteries

Now that Catherine had been publicly shamed by her marriage being declared sinful, there was the risk that Charles V (see page 52) would invade England in support of his aunt. Henry had lived an extravagant life which meant there was little money to defend the country. This problem was solved by Cromwell. He ordered an inspection of the monasteries, the results of which were carefully sifted through to show that the monks were guilty of breaking their vows. Parliament was then persuaded to order the closing of all the smaller monasteries in 1536. Later, Henry and Cromwell closed all of the monasteries in England, so that, by 1540, all monks, nuns and friars had been thrown out of their communities. Many of the abandoned monasteries were ancient and beautiful buildings; now the king's commissioners took their treasures to London – even the lead from their roofs. In some cases precious manuscripts, which had taken months to write, were thrown out and burned; in London, a butcher bought an abbey's library in order to use the paper to wrap his meat! The monasteries had owned a quarter of all the land in England and Wales. All of this now became the property of the king, an event called the dissolution of the monasteries.

Digging deeper

The dissolution of the monasteries

Henry gave Cromwell a new job in 1535: he became the Vicar General. This meant that Cromwell was responsible for supervising the Church, since the king was too busy to do it himself. So Cromwell ordered an inspection of the monasteries and nunneries in England in Wales. The inspection was quite a remarkable operation, since there were over 800 monasteries to visit. Cromwell picked a team of lawyers to travel the country and visit each one, inspecting the behaviour of the monks and nuns. The team completed the inspection in six months, and Cromwell was able to prepare a report of their findings to present to Parliament.

The report presented to Parliament painted a very unholy picture of the monasteries, with little dedication to religion and devotion to God – the purposes for which they had been established. Monks were also shown to neglect good works, such as teaching and healing, or copying books. MPs were deeply shocked to learn that the monks and nuns were regularly breaking their vows of poverty and celibacy (see

Source D). Evidence was produced of monks living with several 'wives', often nuns from a nearby convent, but sometimes the daughters of farmers. Nuns were found with six or more children, while some abbots lived in luxury through selling off the abbey's silver. Monks were found to be drunken, or more fond of fishing than praying.

SOURCE D

The abbot delighted much in playing at dice and cards, and therein spent much money. There was here much frequence of women coming to this monastery.

The report on Bury St Edmunds abbey *from the comperta, the collection of inspectors' reports made by Thomas Cromwell. Bury St Edmunds in Suffolk housed one of England's greatest monasteries, but even there the inspectors found corruption.*

When their enormities [sins] were first read in the Parliament house, they were so great and abominable that there was nothing said but 'down with them'.

Protestant preacher, Hugh Latimer, recalls the impact of hearing Cromwell's report read out in Parliament. From Edward Hall's Chronicle 1555.

The inspectors of the monasteries were carefully chosen by Cromwell, and were lawyers who shared the views of the humanists and anti-clericals. These inspectors scoffed at the religious treasures stored in the monasteries, regarding relics as 'vanity and superstition' and as tricks to separate the simple folk from their money. The inspectors mockingly reported to Cromwell when they found 'the coals with which St Lawrence was toasted, St Edmund's toenails, St Thomas Becket's penknife'. They also found that monks kept girdles which had supposedly been worn, round the waist, by holy women in the past. For a small fee, local women could borrow these girdles during pregnancy, to protect them from the pains of childbirth. Various skulls were also kept as cures for headaches. In several places jars of 'saint's blood' and 'Virgin's milk' were also found, and some were sent to London to amuse Cromwell and the king, who were scornful of such superstitions.

This damning report on the monasteries of England and Wales was exactly what Cromwell needed. A horrified Parliament was easily persuaded to order the closing in 1536 of all the smaller monasteries. Parliament was told that this would help the spiritual reform of the larger monasteries, but this was probably untrue. Henry and Cromwell may already have been thinking of closing down all monasteries.

These smaller monasteries were as thorns, but the great abbots were putrefied old oaks, and they must needs follow.

An MP writing about the closing of the smaller monasteries in 1536. From Edward Hall's Chronicle 1555.

Cromwell planned the dissolution of the monasteries very well. His inspectors' reports might have contained some truth, but historians agree that they had deliberately exaggerated the corruption of the monasteries. There is plenty of other evidence from the time showing well-behaved and religious monks and nuns, but little was said about this to Parliament. The anti-clerical lawyers who visited the monasteries seemed only to be looking for evidence of misbehaviour. Sometimes the monks were bullied to give the answers the visitors wanted. The inspectors also questioned the servants of the monks, who sometimes had personal grudges against the abbots and were keen to speak against them.

The evidence presented to Parliament provided the excuse for closing the monasteries, but the real reason for them being stripped of their treasures was clearly Henry's urgent need for money. In addition, perhaps it was the third of their vows which made Henry want to get rid of monks and nuns – their vow of obedience to the Pope!

The ruins of Fountains Abbey, Yorkshire.

Question time

Historians have worked hard to explain why the English Reformation happened. Unfortunately they do not all agree! Here are two of their explanations:

a The English Reformation began because the priests, monks and nuns were corrupt. They misbehaved and were very unpopular.

b The English Reformation happened because Henry VIII quarrelled with the Pope over his divorce.

These are very different explanations. Historians interpret the past, and they often have different points of view. By now you should be able to find evidence to support each of these points of view.

1 Write a paragraph for each point of view, presenting evidence to support it.

2 Write your own conclusion after studying the evidence. For this you should say which point of view (or explanation) you think is correct. Remember your conclusion has to fit the facts.

The Pilgrimage of Grace

How would English men and women react to the closing of the monasteries? Henry and Cromwell did not have to wait long before they found out. Although much of England stayed quiet, in the north there was a major rebellion in the autumn of 1536. This was known as the Pilgrimage of Grace.

Discontent began in Lincolnshire, but soon spread to Yorkshire. Before long, a huge army of some 40,000 rebels had gathered and was heading south. Their leader was a one-eyed lawyer, Robert Aske, who had links with some of the courtiers who had supported Queen Catherine and were hostile to all that had happened under Cromwell and Cranmer.

Not rebels, but pilgrims

Aske declared that his followers were not rebels, but pilgrims. This was a clever move, since as rebels they would be traitors and punishable with death. As pilgrims, however, they wished to petition Henry for Grace for the Commonwealth. By this Aske meant that Henry should be freed from the evil and wicked advice of heretics like Cromwell and Cranmer, the monasteries should be reopened, and Princess Mary, Catherine of Aragon's daughter, should have her right to the throne restored. The 'pilgrims' included many of the gentry from Yorkshire, Lancashire, Durham and Cumbria, as well as their tenant farmers. Monks and priests headed the procession as they advanced south, carrying a banner of Christ on the cross. The pilgrims sang hymns and wore a badge of the Five Wounds of Christ, showing how Christ's Church was bleeding because of all the changes taking place.

This popular uprising alarmed Henry VIII – he had never faced a rebellion on this scale. After 27 years on the throne, Henry was used to the obedience of his people. He saw rebels not just as traitors against the crown, but as the enemies of God, since he believed himself to be God's chosen ruler of England. Also, rebellion would probably have reminded him of the dark days of the Wars of the Roses before his father, Henry VII, had gained the throne. But what could he do? Aske and his followers had a huge force, while his own army, under the Duke of Norfolk, was small and badly paid.

The Duke of Norfolk rushed north to try to halt the pilgrims' progress towards London. He reached Doncaster, where he was able to prevent the rebels using the bridge crossing. Here, he was helped by several things:

- It was a wet autumn and the river meadows were flooded, making it difficult for the pilgrims to advance.

- Although the ordinary folk who made up the pilgrim army were angry, many were reluctant to move further south so late in the year. How long would they be away from their families? What would happen to those they left behind? Campaigning was never comfortable, even for trained soldiers in the sixteenth century, so the thought of being outdoors in the winter in unfamiliar country would have been frightening for Aske's band of untrained pilgrims.

- Many of the gentry who were the leaders of the rebellion were torn between their loyalty to the king and their support for the rebellion. They knew that, if they took part in battle against the king's army, they could never expect to be pardoned.

Promise of a pardon and a hearing

Aske was aware of the difficulties the pilgrimage faced, so he decided to accept the Duke of Norfolk's offer to meet for talks at Doncaster. Norfolk had little choice: his army was too small to attack the rebels directly. However, Norfolk now used all his cunning to turn the situation in the king's favour. He played for time, hoping that the pilgrims would grow tired and go home, or that the gentry leaders would abandon the pilgrimage. Norfolk wrote to the king, 'I beseech you to take in good part whatsoever promise I make to the rebels, for surely I shall observe no part thereof.'

Upon meeting with Norfolk, Aske was taken in by the promises of a general pardon for all the rebels, and that Parliament would meet to discuss the pilgrims' complaints. Two of the rebel leaders were also invited to London to present their petition to the king – they returned with reports of the king's kindness and understanding. By the beginning of December the patience of the rebels was exhausted, and Aske was now able to persuade them to return to their homes and to trust in the king's honour. In a dramatic gesture of loyalty, Aske tore off his pilgrim's badge of the Five Wounds of Christ and declared, 'We will all wear no badge nor sign except the badge of our sovereign lord the king.' But Robert Aske had been deceived – Henry had no intention of keeping his word. The promise of a pardon had not been written down and, in any case, Henry believed that promises made to rebels need not be kept.

Henry punishes the traitors

In January 1537 there was a riot in Hull, which reflected the pilgrims' impatience at there being no news of the promised Parliament to discuss their complaints. The riot provided Henry with the excuse he needed to punish the rebels. He ordered Norfolk that 'dreadful execution be done upon a good number, by hanging them up in trees, and by quartering them'. Henry's intention was that punishment should be widespread through the villages of Yorkshire and Lancashire; in all, nearly 200 northerners were killed in revenge for the pilgrimage. The prior at Cartmel in Lancashire, who had taken part in the pilgrimage, was ordered to be hanged from the steeple of the priory church. Other rotting bodies were left dangling from the trees, to serve as a warning of what would happen to people if they disobeyed their monarch.

Robert Aske, who had tried so hard to keep the rebellion peaceful, was arrested and examined. He defended his actions (see Source A). Aske may have been trying to save his own life, but his words also serve as a final tribute to the disappearing monasteries (see Source B). Aske was eventually taken to York where he was tried and sentenced to be hanged in chains. This involved him being placed alive inside a hooped cage, which was then suspended from the top of the castle walls for all the inhabitants of the city to see. Aske was left to die a slow death, at the mercy of the crows and ravens, which would pluck at his weakening body.

The abbeys of the north parts gave great alms [charity] to poor men and laudably served God. By occasion of their suppression [closing] the divine service of Almighty God is much diminished, great number of Masses unsaid, to the distress of the faith. The temple of God is ruined and pulled down, the ornaments and relics of the Church unreverently used.

Robert Aske defends his actions in leading the Pilgrimage of Grace when he is questioned in 1537.

No hospitality is now kept in those places. Many of the abbeys were in the mountains and empty places, where the people be rude of condition and not well taught the law of God, but when the abbeys stood the people not only had worldly refreshing in their bodies but also spiritual information and preaching. The abbeys were one of the great beauties of this realm to all men.

In 1537 Robert Aske pays tribute to the worth of the monasteries in northern England.

Ultimately, the Pilgrimage of Grace failed. With the deaths of many of its supporters, abbots were more quickly bullied into surrendering their abbeys to the crown, in return for not being accused of supporting the rebellion. The abbots of Glastonbury and Reading refused to hand over their monasteries, but they too were hanged.

Activity time

Work together in small groups to answer these questions about the dissolution of the monasteries and the Pilgrimage of Grace.

1 Were the monasteries as corrupt as Henry and Cromwell said they were? Study the evidence about the behaviour of the monks and compare it with what Aske said about them. What is the difference?

2 Is the evidence of the written sources reliable? To help you decide you must think about what makes any evidence reliable. Ask yourself questions about who has written it. Does the author have a reason to twist the truth, or exaggerate something? You need to know the author's opinion about the subject. Is he or she biased?

3 Discuss the ways 'the truth' can be altered according to who is telling it. You can do this in groups by telling each other about things that have happened to you, where your view of what happened is not the same as other people's. Try to work out why this is so.

4 Why did the Pilgrimage of Grace fail? Does this mean that Henry had the support of the people for the changes he was making?

The coming of reform

During the reign of Henry VIII, Thomas Cromwell and Archbishop Cranmer were the two men in England with the most power to bring about religious reform. Encouraged by the failure of the Pilgrimage of Grace, they decided to continue to attack Catholicism. This was because they disliked some of the rituals (or religious practices) of the Roman Catholic Church.

Banning of statues and relics

In 1538 Cromwell issued orders banning pilgrimages and the celebration of many of the saints' days. Relics could no longer be displayed for worship, and orders were given for some to be smashed or burned. The great tomb of St Thomas Becket, the Archbishop of Canterbury murdered in 1170, was demolished, but not before the rubies and the gold which adorned the tomb had been sent to the king. Cromwell also sought out for destruction the most famous statues, which were believed to perform miracles. The shrine at Walsingham, to which Henry himself had gone with Catherine of Aragon, in the hope that God would send him a son, was also destroyed: its famous statue of the Virgin Mary, said to perform miracles, was brought to London and publicly burnt with other relics. One statue of a Welsh saint was destroyed in the same fire as that which consumed a Franciscan friar who denied that the king was head of the Church. Cromwell also ordered all priests to preach against superstition and the worship of relics.

SOURCE A

Frontispiece of the Great Bible of 1539, showing Henry VIII handing out the word of God to Cromwell and Archbishop Cranmer.

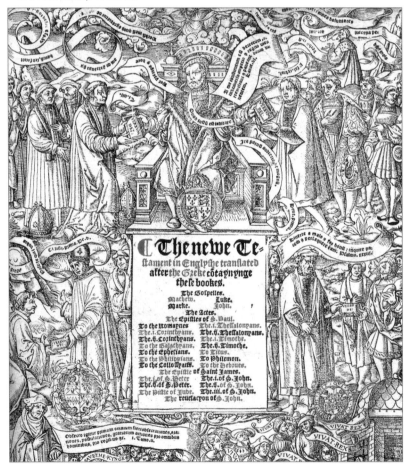

Bible translated into English

Until this time, the Bible was still only available in Latin, a language which few English people could read. Cromwell arranged for an English translation to be made, which all churches were ordered to purchase so that everyone could read 'the word of God'. He also held talks with the Lutheran princes from Germany where Protestantism was now well established. However, Cromwell's intentions were not only religious – he also hoped that the German Lutherans would make useful allies against Catherine of Aragon's nephew, Charles V. By the late 1530s, it looked as though England would soon become Europe's next Protestant country.

Rejection of Protestantism

However, Cromwell had made a serious error in leading the English Church towards Protestantism. While Henry VIII believed himself to be the Supreme Head of the Church and had become less superstitious, he was still far from being a Protestant. He could not accept the Protestant idea that priests should marry, nor their wish to abolish the Catholic Mass, the service where the bread and wine changed into the body and blood of Christ.

At court, Cromwell had made many enemies who disliked the recent changes he had made. They accepted the end of the Pope's power in England, and they had also bought or been given land that had once belonged to the monasteries but – like Henry – they detested Protestant ideas. These men included the Duke of Norfolk, who had crushed the Pilgrimage of Grace (see pages 59–61). Whilst Cromwell investigated Lutheranism, his enemies gained influence with the king, who had already drawn back at the idea of an alliance with the Lutherans.

The Act of Six Articles, 1539

Thus, in 1539, Parliament made a new law, the Act of Six Articles, which firmly outlawed Protestant beliefs. To refuse to believe in the Catholic Mass was now a crime punishable by burning at the stake. Priests who had married were ordered to separate from their wives. The congregation continued to have only bread at Communion, not wine. Henry showed how seriously he viewed this when, in 1540, three Protestants were burnt at the stake, alongside three Catholics who declared that the Pope was head of the Church in England. German Lutherans were disappointed with Henry, about whom they wrote, 'The rich treasures, the rich incomes of the Church, these are the Gospel according to Harry.'

Cromwell is beheaded

Cromwell had been so closely associated with religious reform that it was not long before his enemies were able to persuade the king that his powerful minister was also guilty of heresy. They had a new way of doing this since the king was now hopelessly in love with Catherine Howard, the eighteen-year-old niece of the Duke of Norfolk, who was Cromwell's enemy. In 1540 Thomas Cromwell was arrested in the council chamber. Norfolk and the other nobles tore from him his badges of rank. They despised him because, like Wolsey, he was of low birth. Cromwell, who had done so much for Henry, was now abandoned by him and beheaded. Later, the king was to express regret for this execution and blame it on Cromwell's enemies.

In the 1540s it seemed as though England's Reformation was over, and disappointed Protestants left the country. Even Cromwell and Cranmer's great work in producing an English Bible seemed threatened when Henry ordered that it should not be read by women or the lower classes. When Henry died in 1547, his funeral service was strictly Catholic, with priests chanting in Latin, candles and incense burning, and prayers said for his soul on its journey through purgatory. However, within a few years of Henry VIII's funeral, England had become Europe's most important Protestant country.

Assessment section

1 Thomas Cromwell is one of the most important figures in Tudor history. See what else you can find out about him. His downfall in 1540 is closely linked to Henry's marriage to Anne of Cleves. Try to find out why. You can use your school library or the Internet to find out as much as you can.

2 In this chapter you have studied England's Reformation under Henry VIII. Now write an extended answer to the following question:

'What changed in the Church in England during Henry VIII's reign?'

Remember that writing about change means comparing how things were done at the beginning of the reign with how they were done at the end of the reign. Use the outline below to help you.

- How was the Church run?

- What did Christians believe?

- How did they worship God?

- What happened to those people who disagreed with the way the Church was run?

In your answer you should refer to:

● the Pope	● the Supreme Head
● monasteries	● shrines
● relics	● purgatory
● saints	● Protestants
● Catholics	● indulgences

Further reading

Eric Ives, *Anne Boleyn* (Oxford, 1986)

J.J. Scarisbrick, *Henry VIII* (Methuen, 1968)

R. M. Warnicke, *The Rise and Fall of Anne Boleyn* (Cambridge, 1989)

The end of Catholic England

After Henry VIII's death in 1547, Protestants were able to reform the Church in England under his son, Edward VI. Edward's death in 1553, however, brought the Catholic Queen Mary to the throne. Roman Catholicism was restored, and Protestants were persecuted, but only for five years. Mary died in 1558 and the reign of her half-sister Elizabeth I (1558–1603) saw Protestantism firmly established in England.

A boy king

In Chapter 1 you read how Henry married six times in an effort to produce a male heir. With his son Edward's birth in 1537, Henry appeared to have solved the problem of his succession. However, the risks to the life of a young child were great in the sixteenth century and Henry was therefore eager to produce a second son. Also, Edward's mother, Jane Seymour, died of a fever only twelve days after Edward's birth. Death after giving birth was sadly all too common in the sixteenth century. There were no antiseptics, and little understanding of the importance of hygiene. Jane probably developed puerperal fever, also called childbed fever, as a result of a blood infection after the tearing of skin during childbirth. Some historians have even suggested that Henry's doctors were so anxious that his son should be born, that the baby was effectively ripped out of Jane's body, with fatal consequences for her!

Despite three further marriages, Henry had no more children. When he died in 1547, he was succeeded by his only son, Edward, who was just nine years old.

SOURCE A

A contemporary portrait of Edward VI.

The Church in England, 1547

Edward's health was good and, like all the Tudors, he was exceptionally intelligent. Henry had greatly valued education, so had employed the best available tutors for his son. He had wanted Edward to be trained by the most fashionable methods of the time so the men chosen had been leading humanists. Humanists were scholars who valued the importance of reading the Bible (see page 42). Many of them were critical of traditional Catholic teachings, which often contradicted the 'Word of God' as found in the Scriptures. Edward VI was therefore brought up to study the Bible in the Protestant manner, even while his father was burning Protestants at the stake (see page 63). Edward's half-sister, Elizabeth, who was now fourteen, was brought up in a similar way. But Mary, the eldest of Henry's children, remained a Roman Catholic. King Henry VIII's children were therefore divided over what religion England should have.

Somerset and the royal council

Edward's reign lasted only six years, but during that time the English Church was completely changed from how it had been on Henry's death. Edward was probably too young to make much difference himself, and during his reign he was led by noblemen. Henry had known that the nobles were divided into factions, and had worried that this might lead to civil war while his son was a child king. In his will Henry had therefore tried to ensure that the nobles worked together on a council which would rule England. But now Edward's uncle, the Duke of Somerset, made himself the Lord Protector of the Realm. Somerset was the brother of Jane Seymour, Edward's mother, and he had cleverly used this to his advantage as Henry had grown old and weak. Like the new king, Somerset was a Protestant. He made sure that Catholics were removed from the royal council; the leading Catholic noble, the Duke of Norfolk, was kept in the Tower of London.

Somerset began to make changes to the Church but he acted cautiously. He knew there were dangers if too much changed too quickly. Enthusiastic Protestants wanted to abolish the Mass and replace it with a Protestant service in English. They wanted bishops to be abolished, priests to be able to marry, and the Church to be stripped of much of its land. They also wanted churches to be plain and simple, with no statues, ornaments and images. Somerset feared that these changes would anger the ordinary people who were still attached to their traditional religion. There could be another rebellion like the Pilgrimage of Grace in 1536 (see pages 59–61). Somerset was also advised by the Archbishop of Canterbury, Thomas Cranmer, to move slowly. The Act of Six Articles of 1539, which had outlawed Protestant beliefs, was abolished. Protestants would no longer be burned at the stake for refusing to accept Catholic doctrine.

For Protestants, Edward VI's reign had positive effects. The censorship of books and sermons was relaxed, so Protestants now found they could say and write opinions which, a few years before, would have been considered heresy – a crime punishable by death. Some Protestants had fled from England during Henry's last years on the throne. Now they returned, and were joined by European Protestants who were themselves fleeing persecution in Catholic countries.

Calvin and the Puritans

In Chapter 2 we saw how Martin Luther had begun the Reformation in Germany. By 1547 many Protestants had begun to follow the teachings of John Calvin, a French Protestant who had fled for safety to the Swiss city of Geneva. Under Calvin's leadership, Geneva was fast becoming the leading Protestant city in Europe. Calvin was far less patient with Catholics than Luther had been. From Geneva he encouraged Protestants elsewhere to set up new churches which would defy the law in Catholic countries. Individual communities were encouraged to run their own churches according to the plan laid down for them by Calvin in Geneva.

Calvinists, as John Calvin's followers were known, had to be prepared for martyrdom. This meant that they were not afraid of persecution, because they believed that it would be glorious to die for their faith. Calvin strongly believed in predestination. This is the idea that God has already decided whether people would go to heaven or hell before they were even born. Men and women were thus divided into two groups: the Elect and the Reprobate. The Elect were chosen by God for eternal life in heaven, while the Reprobate were damned and would endure forever the punishments of hell. This might seem a very shocking idea today, but for Calvin's followers there was a comforting aspect to it: everything that happened had been planned by God, so everything had a purpose. In this respect, it did not matter what might happen to you in life because it was all part of God's plan. Calvinists did not need to ask why tragedy might strike them, for example, when a child died. Calvinists believed that God knew the reason for it, and that was enough. They believed that they were playing a part as witnesses in the unfolding of God's purpose for humanity.

The Calvinists' beliefs made them stubborn and dangerous enemies of Catholicism, which they identified with the devil. They did not fear torture, imprisonment, or death by burning, because they believed that God had a purpose for their martyrdom. It would be difficult for Catholic rulers to stamp out this new form of Protestantism by force.

A contemporary portrait of the Protestant reformer, John Calvin.

A strict moral code

There was another remarkable aspect to Calvin's teaching. Luther had expected Christians to live virtuously and to obey the laws, but he did not interfere in people's private lives or tell them how to behave. Calvin was quite different: he drew up a strict moral code which all citizens of Geneva must obey. Calvin believed that Christian life should be based upon the Bible, and that rules for behaviour could be found in the Old and New Testaments.

The moral code was intended to enforce godly behaviour, and included rules on how citizens should dress and behave:

- Only simple plain clothes were permitted; fashionable styles, jewellery and make-up could not be worn.

- Ribbons in women's hair were seen as idle and vain, and temptations of the devil.

- Men and women had to cut their hair short and avoid fancy styles.

- Sex outside marriage was also strictly forbidden, and those caught in adultery (a sexual relationship with someone other than your husband or wife) might even be put to death.

- Music and games were discouraged, because they were not thought appropriate for godly people.

- Dancing around the maypole was ended.

- Drunkenness and gambling were punished severely.

- Theatres were closed down and replaced by Bible readings and sermons.

- Every Sunday at midday, the children of Geneva had to recite the catechism, the statement of the beliefs of the Church.

- Church buildings (see Source B) and services were to be very plain, with the congregation joining together for prayers and singing psalms without music.

- Committees of elders ensured that the rules were obeyed and gave out punishments for those who broke the rules. This would usually involve public shaming, where the wrong-doer would be humiliated in front of their fellow citizens.

We might think today that this moral code must have been very unpopular, but this doesn't appear to have been the case. Of course some people never accepted it, and were forced to leave Geneva, but for many people following the moral code was worthwhile and offered hope of getting to heaven.

Digging deeper

The Calvinist road to heaven

Although Calvin said that only God knew who was saved and who was damned, he also taught that the Elect could be recognised by their good behaviour. He often quoted the line in the Bible: 'A good tree cannot bring forth evil fruit.' On the other hand, Calvin said that the Damned could not prevent themselves from doing evil, because evil was in their nature. By this Calvin was saying that people do not behave well or badly out of choice, but because of their nature. In other words – people do not have free will. God has predestined (already decided) whether they are good or sinful. If a Christian could avoid evil by following the moral code strictly, Calvin said that they could take this as a sign that they had been chosen by God. This might mean that they were one of the Elect. They would enjoy salvation, that is they would go to heaven and join the company of the saints when they died.

The Elect.

What you have just read is quite difficult. Try it like this:

You are a godly citizen of Geneva.

- You dress soberly, avoid all sin and wickedness.

- You pray aloud with your family several times a day.

- You listen intently as passages are read from the Bible.

- You avoid frivolous and foolish behaviour, such as singing, dancing and drinking in taverns, because such behaviour is ungodly.

▼

Can you be sure of salvation?
NO! Only God knows his plan for humanity.

▼

Is there any hope for you?
YES! You may have been chosen by God for salvation!

- Your behaviour is obviously good.

- People do not behave well just because they want to – people behave well because it is in their nature to be good.

- God's people, the Elect, are good.

- If your behaviour is good then it is a sign of election.

Should you jump up and down for joy?
Certainly not! You should show no false pride or vain optimism.

The Reprobate (Damned).

Calvinism spread quickly through Europe, with small groups springing up in many countries. Calvin's followers were usually educated people, or at least they were able to read the Bible. In England, Calvinists were more common in the towns and in the south-east, because it is nearest to Europe. In England they were often called Puritans, because of their wish to lead pure lives. For the next hundred years, Puritans were to play a major part in English history, as you will read in Chapter 4.

Question time

1 Identify each of the following terms and write a sentence of explanation:

a predestination   b Elect

c Reprobate   d the moral code

e free will.

2 In small groups, discuss Calvinist ideas. You should consider the following questions. When you have finished, discuss your ideas with the class.

- What do you think of the idea of predestination?

- If you believed that God had already decided your future, would it affect how you behaved?

- What is meant by having no free will?

- Do you believe people are born good or evil?

- How would your life be affected today if your family adopted Calvin's strict moral code?

- What sort of people in the sixteenth century would have welcomed Calvin's ideas?

- Do you know of any societies in the world today which have similar ideas to those of Calvin?

3 'Calvin's ideas spread rapidly because many people found them worthwhile and believed that they offered hope of getting to heaven.' How do you explain this opinion? Find out more about Calvinism to help you write your answer.

The Edwardian Reformation, 1547–53

By Henry VIII's death, little had changed in the way English people worshipped despite the efforts of Archbishop Cranmer and Thomas Cromwell (see page 53). A few shrines had been dismantled, for example Becket's at Canterbury, but this was for political rather than religious reasons. The burning of candles before statues and images had been stopped since 1538, but in most other ways religion at the start of Edward VI's reign continued as it had at the start of Henry VIII's reign.

An end to Catholic ceremonies

Although Edward's uncle, the Duke of Somerset, and Archbishop Cranmer acted cautiously, the religious changes they set in motion were eventually to have huge effects in England. As Protestants they first set out to stop idolatry – the worship of statues and images. Roman Catholic ceremonies had been full of rituals involving statues of saints, and now orders went out to churches to remove their statues. Traditional ceremonies were also banned.

Banning of the St George's Day ceremony

Across the country, churchwardens began the task of hiring men to remove the statues of St George and the Dragon that were used in traditional processions on St George's Day, 23 April. Usually the statues of St George, the patron saint of England, and his horse were dressed in elaborate costumes so that they could ride through the streets. But now, even the costumes were sold. In the larger towns, like York and Norwich, the St George's Day ceremony was an important holiday in the life of the community and guilds (groups of craftsmen in the same trade) had been formed to organise the occasion. These guilds were now abolished and their property confiscated. This must have shocked many ordinary English people, but to Protestants the ceremony was nothing but superstition.

Banning of the Corpus Christi processions

Another very popular procession took place on the public holiday of Corpus Christi, which means the 'body of Christ'. Catholics believed that the bread at Communion becomes the body of Christ when blessed, or consecrated, by a priest. On the feast day of Corpus Christi a procession passed through the streets carrying a shrine, protected by a canopy, under which could be seen the consecrated host. This was a wafer of bread which had been blessed by a priest and so, Catholics believed, had become Christ's body. The priests would carry the shrine with councillors and members of the Corpus Christi guild marching behind them, singing hymns and carrying banners, crosses or torches. As the host passed by, people would kneel down in the streets bareheaded in adoration of Christ's body. Often the shrine was of silver or gold and the canopy made of fine velvets and damask embroidered with gold thread. In York, the fronts of houses were decorated with tapestries and flowers.

The Corpus Christi procession took place in June, and in many towns the climax of the procession was the performance of a play. This was always in the open air, usually on top of a wagon, and told biblical stories. In large towns like York, a whole series of different plays was performed as the wagon was wheeled through the streets. The actors were sometimes professionals, but often were members of the guild. Always the plays were colourful occasions, with bright costumes, music and special effects to represent dramatic events like Noah's flood or Jonah in the whale.

Protestants hated the sight of Christians worshipping what to them was just a piece of bread, and so this ceremony and the guilds which organised it were banned.

Banning of the Easter rituals

Easter was the most important time in the Catholic year, so there were many special rituals around this time. Many of these ceremonies were now banned, for example, the ceremony of 'creeping to the Cross' on Good Friday, which marked the remembrance of Christ's death on the cross (crucifixion). It was the custom for priests to crawl on their hands and knees along the floor of the church and kiss a crucifix (a cross with the figure of Christ on it) lying before the altar.

The crucifix would then be carried down the church for the congregation to kneel before and kiss. Henry VIII and Catherine of Aragon had themselves performed this ritual.

Also banned was the Easter sepulchre. This was a miniature tomb, sometimes carved in stone, but often made of wood and canvas. On Good Friday a statue of Christ would be laid in this tomb, and would then be 'watched' until Easter by local volunteers, as a remembrance of how Christ's tomb was guarded by soldiers. A candle or lamp would be kept burning above the sepulchre until after dark on Saturday when everyone would gather as the priests put out every candle in the church. This part of the ceremony marked the ending of Christ's physical life. Then, in complete darkness, a priest would strike flints to start a new fire, which would be used to light the largest candle in the church, from which all the other candles in the church were re-lit. This part of the ceremony marked Christ's resurrection to new life in heaven.

The loss of 'merry England'

Corpus Christi, creeping to the Cross, St George's Day, Easter sepulchres – these are just a few of the ceremonies and rituals that filled the Christian year. Catholic religion in England had been full of colour and drama, of excitement and entertainment. Ceremonies and processions were popular and involved ordinary people in their daily lives. However, with the Duke of Somerset and Cranmer coming under the influence of Calvinist Protestants, there would be no place for idolatry and superstition. Some of the bishops even tried to stop celebrations at Christmas. John Hooper, bishop of Gloucester, banned the playing of games on Sunday. For peasants, Sunday was their only day off during the week; to Puritans, Sunday was the Lord's Day and should be spent in prayer and quiet meditation. In 1552 Dr John Caius referred to the celebrations of the ritual year when he regretted the loss of 'the old world, when this country was called merry England'.

More religious changes were to follow:

- In 1547 chantries were abolished. These were special chapels that were founded by money from a person's will. In the chantries, priests prayed for the founding person's soul in purgatory. However, the belief in purgatory was now condemned and all chantry property confiscated by the crown.

- In 1549 Archbishop Cranmer wrote a new Prayer Book with services in English, so that English people could now worship God in their own language.

Protestants were delighted with the progress that was being made in reforming the Church in England.

SOURCE A

Edward sits on the throne with Somerset beside him. His father lies on his deathbed, passing on his authority to Edward. Beneath Edward lies the Pope and in the corner can be seen two monks. A painting by an unknown artist in c.1570.

Look carefully at Source A and answer the following questions:

1 What is happening to the Pope and the monks?
2 What is happening in the painting on the wall?
3 Try to explain why this painting (Source A) was made.

Revolt again!

The Duke of Somerset and Thomas Cranmer had at first tried to make England's Protestant Reformation a slow and steady process, because they knew that many of the nobles and bishops were not in favour of change. However, by the summer of 1549 they were feeling more confident. The most important Catholics had been removed from the council and were in the Tower. Bishops who opposed the changes had been sacked and replaced by enthusiastic Protestants. Now, Somerset was becoming rather arrogant and was not listening to the advice of others. Instead of holding full meetings of the council, he was simply meeting with his close supporters in his own house. This was a huge new palace which was being built along the banks of the Thames using money confiscated from the chantries and guilds. Somerset seemed to think that nothing could prevent him and Edward from doing 'God's work'. However, to his opponents it seemed that for Somerset 'God's work' meant lining his own pockets with treasure stolen from the Church! Somerset's over-confidence and arrogance led to a summer of revolt in 1549 and, ultimately, his own downfall.

The Prayer Book Rebellion, 1549

The new Prayer Book was introduced in the early summer of 1549. Priests who refused to use it were punished severely. In London the new Prayer Book seems to have been accepted by many people. However, for people elsewhere in England, its introduction was one change too many. Over the course of the previous two years, village people had experienced the Protestant attack on their traditional ceremonies and customs, and the abolition of their statues. So, with the introduction of the new Prayer Book in 1549, when priests began to say the Mass in English, there were riots in many English villages.

In Devon and Cornwall, opposition to the new Prayer Book turned into full scale rebellion. People set about replacing all the statues and images which had recently been removed from their churches. One of the complaints of the rebels was that the new church service was 'like a Christmas game', by which they meant it seemed silly. The Cornish language was probably still spoken in some villages, and the rebels said, 'We Cornish men (whereof certain of us understand no English) utterly refuse this new English'. Archbishop Cranmer replied to this complaint by asking how many of them understood Latin! The rebels also demanded punishment of heretics as had been carried out in Henry VIII's time. This meant that they wanted to see Archbishop Cranmer, whom they thought was a heretic, burned at the stake.

Eventually the rebels from towns and villages across Devon and Cornwall, led by their priests, began to march towards London. The rebels had the support of many of the local gentry, but they lacked a clear leader. Only when the rebels reached Exeter were they halted, because the city was held by Protestants who were loyal to the government. The rebels then began to lay siege to Exeter.

The Prayer Book Rebellion of 1549 placed the Duke of Somerset and Edward VI in difficulty for a number of reasons:

- England was at war with France and Scotland, so there were no soldiers to send to Exeter to quash the rebellion.

- Religious discontent was made worse by the hardship from which many English people were suffering. The harvest had failed the year before, so there was a serious shortage of food and food prices had become very high.

- People were angry with their landlords who made them pay rent while they were starving.

- In Norfolk another revolt was begun by peasants who were angry that landlords were enclosing the fields where they grazed their animals. A huge rebel army, led by Robert Kett, captured Norwich in Norfolk (see pages 216–7).

- At this time there were also outbreaks of trouble in Yorkshire.

This was as dangerous a moment for the Tudors as during the Pilgrimage of Grace in 1536. For six weeks it looked as though the rebel armies might advance on London. Eventually, however, the king was saved by soldiers returning from France and Scotland, so at last the royal armies were strong enough to march to Devon and Norfolk.

The rebels had no cannon or cavalry and were massacred. Lord Russell, who led the king's forces, was ordered to make examples of traitors. One such example was Robert Welsh, the vicar of the church of St Thomas in Exeter. He was hanged from a gallows built out over the top of his church tower. He was dressed in his vestments, with a holy water bucket and sprinkler, a bell, rosary beads and 'such other like popish trash hanged about him'.

Edward survived the Prayer Book Rebellion of 1549, but not the Duke of Somerset. After the rebellion the nobles on the council lost their trust in Somerset, and overthrew him in October 1549. He was sent to the Tower and eventually beheaded.

The Duke of Northumberland

The man who replaced the Duke of Somerset as regent was the Duke of Northumberland. He had led the army which had crushed the rebels in Norfolk and was an able and clever leader. Also, it seems that he was more interested in power and governing England well, than in religious change.

The Reformation gathers pace

Despite the rebellions of 1549, there was no halt to the Reformation:

- Priests had begun to marry and have families.

- The congregation now received both the bread and the wine at Communion, instead of just the bread.

- The Communion bread and wine were served in cheap wooden or pewter cups and plates, not the beautiful gold plate that had been used before.

- The Catholic belief in transubstantiation was condemned: a Christian was no longer allowed to believe that the Communion bread and wine changed into Christ's actual body and blood. Instead the service simply commemorated the Last Supper that Jesus had with his disciples before his arrest.

- Archbishop Cranmer wrote a second Prayer Book which did away with the Mass completely. Mass was now replaced by a service called the Lord's Supper.

- The stone altars, which had been richly decorated with fine fabric, crosses and candles, were taken out of churches and replaced by plain wooden tables.

- Paintings on church walls were whitewashed over.

- Priests were renamed ministers and now wore simple black clothes, rather than the colourful robes, or vestments.

- The government sent commissioners round to all churches to confiscate their gold and silver plate. Protestants were pleased to see an end to what they called idolatry, but many ordinary people were shocked that the crown was greedily stealing possessions from their villages.

There was little resistance to the Protestant Reformation now. Those who didn't like the changes were too frightened to rebel.

The death of Edward VI

A complete turnabout in the Protestant Reformation in England came in 1553 when King Edward, still only fifteen, fell ill with tuberculosis. There was no hope of his recovery and it was known that, when he died, Princess Mary would become the queen according to Henry VIII's will. This put the Duke of Northumberland in a panic. Mary had stuck stubbornly to her Catholic religion during Edward's reign, refusing to obey her brother's orders to stop attending Mass in her private chapel. Northumberland knew that, as a Protestant, he would be unlikely to survive if Mary became queen. In a desperate bid to prevent Mary coming to the throne, Northumberland revived the claim to the throne of Lady Jane Grey, a girl of only seventeen who was a descendant of Henry VII. To preserve his own power Northumberland then married her to his son, Guildford Dudley. When Edward finally died on 6 July 1553, he proclaimed Lady Jane Grey the Queen of England.

Nearly all the court and politicians accepted Lady Jane Grey as queen. Indeed, her claim was a good one since the claims to the throne from Henry's two daughters depended on marriages which had been annulled. Nevertheless, once Mary Tudor began to assert her claim to the throne, support for Northumberland and Lady Jane Grey quickly disappeared. The fact that Mary was Henry VIII's daughter was greatly to her advantage. Elizabeth, Mary's Protestant half-sister, also refused to have anything to do with Northumberland's scheme to stop Mary ascending the throne.

Mary Tudor had successfully avoided capture by Northumberland and had raised support for her claim to the throne. Her supporters soon took London, capturing the unfortunate Lady Jane Grey and her husband after a reign of only thirteen days! When Mary herself entered the city on 3 August 1553, the bells in every church rang all day and the people celebrated with street parties. Northumberland, disguised in rags as a beggar, was captured in the market place in Cambridge. He was brought back to London and beheaded as a traitor. Few people mourned him.

The Tudor family tree.

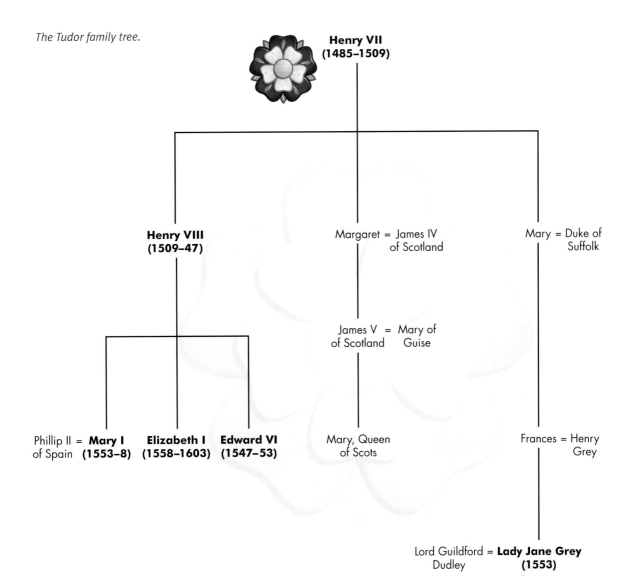

Henry VII
(1485–1509)

Henry VIII
(1509–47)

Margaret = James IV
of Scotland

Mary = Duke of
Suffolk

James V = Mary of
of Scotland   Guise

Phillip II = **Mary I**
of Spain   **(1553–8)**

Elizabeth I
(1558–1603)

Edward VI
(1547–53)

Mary, Queen
of Scots

Frances = Henry
Grey

Lord Guildford = **Lady Jane Grey**
Dudley   **(1553)**

Activity time

1   Describe the changes made to the inside of a church during Edward VI's reign.

2   On page 75 you have read how Robert Welsh, the vicar of the Church of St Thomas in Exeter, was hanged after the Prayer Book Rebellion. How might one of Robert's congregation, who survived the rebellion, describe the changes to St Thomas' Church, and the events which took place before, during and after the revolt?

You could write this as a diary between the end of Henry's reign and 1552. Remember your diary entries will need to express a point of view about the religious changes.

Mary Tudor triumphs

When Mary Tudor gained the throne she became England's first female sovereign for 400 years. Henry VIII had left instructions in his will that, if Edward died without producing an heir, then his elder half-sister, Mary, would become queen.

When her father had died, Mary Tudor was already 21. She had endured a lifetime of bitterness and rejection. Her mother had been removed from the throne and banned from court, and had been left to die alone, separated from her only child. Mary had felt these events deeply. She had also been declared illegitimate (born outside marriage), and she had seen the overthrow of the religion she had been brought up in. Loyal to her mother, Mary remained a Roman Catholic. She still believed that only the Pope could be the head of the Church in England.

SOURCE A

A contemporary portrait of Mary Tudor by Antonio Moro.

As queen, Mary had the opportunity not just to put an end to the religious changes, but to reverse everything that had happened to the Church since the time when her father had divorced her mother in 1532 (see page 54). Mary was determined to return England to the Roman Catholic Church. She was helped by the enthusiasm of many English people as, across the country, townspeople and villagers began to repair and restore the damage done to their churches by the Protestant reforms. Statues of saints and stone altars were now restored (sometimes villagers had hidden them in the churchyard). Ceremonies and processions were revived, and the Mass was permitted once again. Even in London, where there had been more support for Protestantism, there was enthusiasm for the return of Catholicism.

Marriage to Philip II of Spain

Mary Tudor was 37 years old when she became queen. The heir to her throne was her 20-year-old half-sister, Elizabeth, a Protestant woman. If she was to have any chance of giving birth to a son to keep England Catholic after her death, Mary needed to marry quickly. So, in 1554, Mary married her cousin, Philip II of Spain.

Philip was the son of Charles V, the ruler of the Holy Roman Empire, and Charles had been the nephew of Mary's mother, Catherine of Aragon. Philip had also been looking for a chance to revive his family's influence in England, as well as an ally against his enemy, France. Mary felt herself to be close to the Spanish, not only because they were her mother's people, but because Spain had remained fiercely loyal to the Catholic Church. Although she had never met Philip, she felt sure that he would now help her in her great task to restore Roman Catholicism in England.

However, there was opposition to Mary's marriage to Philip. Many of Mary's subjects disliked foreigners, and didn't take well to the 9000 Spaniards that came to London for Philip's wedding. Many also feared that England would end up being ruled by Spain, because a female queen was bound to be ruled by her husband.

Wyatt's Rebellion

Sir Thomas Wyatt, a knight from Kent, decided he would try to prevent Mary's marriage to Philip by leading a revolt to replace Mary with Elizabeth. In January 1554 Wyatt gathered an army and marched to London, scattering the small royal army, whose soldiers threw away their weapons and livery (uniform) and fled back to London. However, Wyatt gained no support from elsewhere in England, and Elizabeth wisely refused to support him. Even so, Wyatt's army successfully entered London and marched through the outskirts, actually passing beneath the windows of the Palace of Whitehall to the west of the city, from where Mary could look down on the rebel horsemen. The gates to the palace were closed only just in time.

When Wyatt finally reached the gates of the city of London he found that they too had been closed, by citizens loyal to Mary. Mary had refused to flee London and had spoken directly to Londoners, asking for their support. Now they turned out in large numbers to fight for her. Wyatt's men were outnumbered, and there was bloodshed in the narrow streets of the city. Wyatt himself was captured, and tried for treason – for plotting to overthrow the monarch.

Mary decided that she had to punish the rebels severely and 120 were hanged, their bodies left to rot slowly on gallows both in London and in the villages from where they had come, as a terrible warning to others. Wyatt himself was hanged, then disembowelled. His head was cut off and left to rot on a spike over the gateway to London. Lady Jane Grey, who had been in the Tower of London throughout, was now brought out and beheaded along with her husband.

Now Mary had to decide what to do about her half-sister, Elizabeth. She was a Protestant and would take the throne if Mary died. This situation might encourage Protestants to attempt to kill Mary. Evidence suggested that Elizabeth had been sympathetic to Wyatt. For a while Elizabeth's life hung in the balance as Mary kept her in the Tower; after all Elizabeth was none other than the daughter of Anne Boleyn, who had taken Mary's mother's place on the throne! Eventually Elizabeth was removed to Woodstock where she remained a prisoner at her sister's mercy.

Catholicism restored

After overcoming Wyatt's Rebellion in 1554, Mary was at last able to restore the Pope as head of the English Church. Religious rituals, including the Mass, were brought back; services were once again in Latin; and priests who had married were ordered to separate from their wives. Leading Protestant bishops and priests, including the Archbishop of Canterbury, Thomas Cranmer, were arrested on charges of heresy. It was not possible to reopen the monasteries, however. Although the abbey buildings might have been repaired, their land had been acquired by the nobles and gentry during the dissolution of the monasteries (see pages 56–7). Without land the monks had no income and Mary could not afford to buy it back. And if she chose to confiscate the land she would be faced with rebellion by Catholics as well as Protestants.

Mary made it illegal to use the Protestant Prayer Book written by Archbishop Cranmer, and, at the end of 1554, Parliament restored the old law which said that heretics must be burnt at the stake. Mary was a deeply religious woman – a priest heard her confession daily (when she asked forgiveness of God for wrong-doings), and she attended Mass several times each day. She believed it was her duty to God to restore Catholicism as the true faith of all English men and women. She would have failed in her duty if she had allowed Protestants to continue to worship, since in her view they were heretics (followers of the devil rather than of Christ).

Bloody Mary

With the old law about the burning of heretics restored, so began the burning of the Protestant heretics. Mary believed that only by burning their 'wicked' bodies could their 'evil' be destroyed and their souls released at God's mercy. This has become one of the most famous points in England's history – in just three years about 300 Protestants were burned at the stake, an average of nearly two every week. Most of these burnings took place in south-east England, in and around London, where Protestantism had won most support. Very few took place in the north, with only one in Yorkshire, for example. The regions furthest from London and the south-east had been least affected by Protestantism, perhaps because they are further from Europe.

The scale of this persecution was unusual in Tudor England. Burnings of heretics had occurred before – 81 during Henry VIII's 38-year reign – but now they were in far greater numbers and more frequent. The victims were sometimes famous and important people, and included Archbishop Cranmer and other bishops. But often those burnt at the stake were ordinary villagers and townspeople, whose only crime was to hold the 'wrong' beliefs. Such people often died bravely, praying loudly, and showing few signs of fear, clinging to their faith to the end. It was difficult for the onlookers to see these people as wicked friends of the devil. Many people admired the victims, seeing them as martyrs who were willing to die for their faith. As a result of these public burnings of heretics, Mary came to be known as 'Bloody Mary'.

Digging deeper

Burning at the stake

Mary's burnings of heretics can still arouse shock today, so let's examine what happened to the victims. Most of our evidence comes from John Foxe, a Protestant who carefully gathered the stories of the burnings by speaking to eye witnesses. He wrote the *Book of Martyrs* which was not published until 1563, after Mary's death. It quickly became a bestseller and helped to turn people against Mary. Although Foxe appears to have got the basic facts right, his purpose was clear. The stories are told from the point of view of the victim. For hundreds of years, English readers would feel sympathy for these 'innocent' men and women, and shudder with horror at the cruelty of Bloody Mary and the Catholic Church.

SOURCE A

... and so Rogers was brought to Smithfield, saying the psalm 'Miserere' by the way, all the people wonderfully rejoicing at the constancy, with great praises and thanks to God for the same. And there in the presence of a wonderful number of people, the fire was put unto him. When it had taken hold both upon his legs and shoulders, he, as one feeling no pain, washed his hands in the flame, as though it had been in cold water. Most mildly this happy martyr yielded up his spirit into the hands of his heavenly Father.

Foxe's description of the burning of the first victim, John Rogers, in 1555.

SOURCE B

Some of the onlookers wept, others prayed God to give them strength, perseverance and patience, to bear the pain and not to recant [abandon Protestantism]. Others gathered the ashes and bones and wrapped them up in paper to preserve them. Others threatened the bishops.

The Spanish ambassador reports the burning of John Rogers in a letter to Philip II of Spain on 5 February 1555.

At the first burning of heretics in 1555, the Spanish ambassador feared that there might be a revolt. The government hired soldiers to guard the victims, to prevent attempts to release them. In order to persuade the public that the punishment was deserved, Mary ordered sermons to be delivered before the fire. However, whilst there was sympathy for the victims from the crowd, others may have come along just to see the spectacle. Also, more enterprising people did a roaring trade selling cherries!

The burning of Bishops Latimer and Ridley

When the Protestant bishops, Latimer and Ridley, were burned at the stake, their friends tied bags of gunpowder around their necks, hoping that they would explode and bring them a quick death. According to Foxe's *Book of Martyrs*, Latimer called out bravely to Ridley, 'Be of good cheer, Dr Ridley. We shall this day light such a candle as I trust shall never be put out.'

Unfortunately, it was a wet day so the wood only smouldered. Latimer managed to twist himself towards a flame and the gunpowder exploded killing him instantly. However, the crowd watched in horror as the fire burned the lower part of Ridley's body, causing him agony, until some friends lifted a burning faggot up to his neck 'and he was seen to stir no more. The dreadful sight filled almost every eye with tears.'

SOURCE C

The burning of Latimer and Ridley from Foxe's Book of Martyrs. *Heretics would be chained to a stake with bundles of wood piled around them. Note here the soldiers and the priest in the pulpit delivering a sermon in Latin.*

Sometimes sympathisers of those being burnt would deliberately use green wood – this made lots of smoke which could choke the victims to death, so that they didn't suffer the agony of being burned alive. More often the victims' flesh would burn while they remained conscious. Eyewitnesses talk of sometimes seeing the blood and fluids in the victims' bodies boil and burst out of their flesh as scalding steam.

The burning of Bishop John Hooper

Hooper had been one of the most enthusiastic Protestant reformers during Edward VI's reign. With Mary on the throne, he was tried and condemned for heresy, but then given several chances to recant – to admit publicly that he no longer held Protestant beliefs. Hooper refused. His burning in 1555 was one of the most horrible. When he was brought to Smithfield to be burnt, he first forgave the man whose job was to make the fire, and then Hooper actually helped him pile up the wood. But, as often happened with winter burnings, the wood was damp and the fire wouldn't burn well. At first, a strong wind blew the flames away, singeing Hooper's hair and blackening his skin. The bishop prayed loudly throughout. Then the fire got going again and burnt his legs, before it went out again. Now Hooper cried out, 'For God's love, good people, let me have more fire.' When the fire was started again, it flared up and reached the bags of gunpowder that had been tied to his knees, but the wind took the explosions out into the air away from him. He then had to endure a slow and agonising death lasting nearly three quarters of an hour, as the fire slowly crept up his body. All the while, he continued to pray.

SOURCE D

The burning of Archbishop Cranmer from Foxe's Book of Martyrs.

The burning of Archbishop Cranmer

The most famous victim of Bloody Mary's reign was Thomas Cranmer, the Archbishop of Canterbury, who had granted Henry VIII's divorce from Catherine of Aragon, Mary Tudor's mother. Cranmer had been imprisoned for several years and had been forced to watch the burning of his friends, Latimer and Ridley. Eventually Cranmer recanted and, in a signed confession, promised to give up his Protestant beliefs and return to Catholicism. However, despite recanting, he learned that he would not be spared. At his burning, Cranmer was expected to repeat his confession, but instead he denied it boldly and confirmed his Protestant beliefs.

SOURCE E

Fire being now put to him, he stretched out his right hand and thrust it into the flame, and held it there a good space, before the fire came to any other part of his body, crying out with a loud voice, 'This hand hath offended.' As soon as the fire was got up he was very soon dead, never stirring or crying. Surely his death much grieved every man. His friends sorrowed for love, his enemies for pity, strangers for a common kind of humanity whereby we are bound one to another.

A Catholic eyewitness describes the burning of Archbishop Cranmer.

Question time

1   Study each of the burnings mentioned above in Sources A–E. Copy out examples of words or phrases which tell you that the writer had sympathy for the victim.

2   Most of the evidence above comes from John Foxe, who was a Protestant. He suggests that people sympathised with the heretics. Two passages above are written by Catholics (Sources B and E). Do they contradict what Foxe has written?

3   Does the evidence of the two Catholic writers make Foxe's evidence more, or less, believable? Explain your answer. You should consider whether bias always makes evidence unreliable.

4   Why do you think that Cranmer held out his right hand into the fire (Source E)?

5   Look at Source E. Can you explain what the Catholic eyewitness at Cranmer's burning meant by the phrase 'a common kind of humanity'?

Facts and figures about the burning of heretics

Number of men	222
Number of women	51

Number of men and women burnt as heretics during Mary Tudor's reign, according to John Foxe's records. As many as 60 of the martyrs – 20 per cent – were under 21 years old; only 25 per cent were over 35.

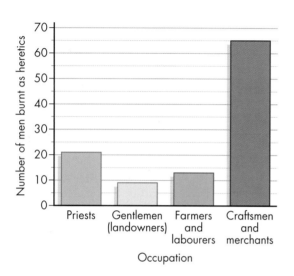

Occupations of 108 of the men burnt as heretics during Mary Tudor's reign. Craftsmen include weavers and other cloth workers, tanners, brewers, painters, smiths, butchers, bricklayers, tallow makers, shoemakers, tailors and other creative trades.

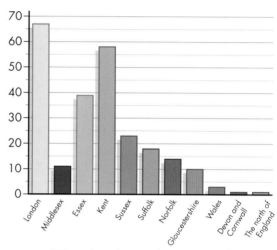

Numbers of martyrs from different areas, where known.

Activity time

Study carefully the facts and figures about the victims of burnings.

1 What can you work out about the type of people who were Protestants from the occupation figures?

2 Find an atlas and a copy of a map of England that includes the counties in the graph where the victims came from. Draw fires in areas where burnings took place. Use the following scheme:

NUMBER OF BURNINGS	NUMBER OF FIRES
below 10	one
10–19	two
20–49	three
50+	four

Study your results on the map. What does it show about the concentration of the burnings? Can you find reasons why Protestants were concentrated in this area?

Mary's death in 1558

The burnings made Mary unpopular with many people in and around London, but she had other problems too. War had broken out with France in 1557, and French armies had captured the northern town of Calais, that had belonged to the English for over 200 years. This was a humiliating defeat for Mary, and the war also gave rise to higher taxes. Also at this time, there was a famine because of a bad harvest, food prices were high, and there was an epidemic of flu. These events increased her unpopularity with the English people.

In 1558, Mary still had no heir. She had had little opportunity to get pregnant, since her husband, Philip II of Spain, spent hardly any time in England. Also, Philip's main interest in England was to have an ally in his war against France, and he showed no affection towards his wife. Philip's absence depressed Mary. Twice she thought she was pregnant and celebrations were ordered, but no baby was born. Rumours circulated that Mary had miscarried (lost the baby during pregnancy). Some people ridiculed Mary for imagining she was pregnant even though she was now 42 years old. Some thought that Mary's lack of children was God's punishment of her for burning heretics.

Despite these difficulties, by 1558 it looked as though Mary's effort to restore Roman Catholicism had been successful. Most people accepted the traditional religion they had grown up with, and the persecution of Protestants frightened others into obeying the law. While there had been sympathy for the heretics that were burnt at the stake, there were no rebellions in protest at what was happening.

However, one event was about to put an end to Roman Catholicism in England – Mary became ill in 1558 and by the autumn her condition worsened. Lonely and depressed, with no children and an absent husband, Mary I died on 17 November. Apart from the brief reign of James II in the seventeenth century, this was to be the last time an openly practising Catholic would sit on the throne of England.

When Mary's half-sister, Elizabeth, heard of the queen's death, she fell to her knees. Elizabeth had come close to execution at the start of Mary's reign (see page 80), but now she had succeeded her Catholic half-sister to the throne. Placing the ring that had been taken from Mary onto her own hand, she quoted a verse from the Psalms, 'This is the Lord's doing and it is marvellous in our eyes'.

Activity time

Investigation

SOURCE A

As the bloody rage of this persecution spread neither man, woman nor child, wife nor maid, lame, blind nor cripple was spared. Whoever he were that believed not as they did on the Pope, whether he were wise or simple, all went to the Fire.

John Foxe, writing in 1563, gives his verdict on the religious persecution during Mary's reign.

SOURCE B

Mary's reconstruction of Catholicism was a success. The evidence from the parishes is of considerable and continuing support for traditional services and celebrations.

A modern historian, Christopher Haigh, writing in 1993.

SOURCE C

Persecution did not eliminate heresy; and scattered congregations of Protestants met in many places. But the Protestant clergy, the leaders of their Church, were either executed or exiled.

A modern historian, P. Williams, writing in 1979.

SOURCE D

One of the more unpleasant lessons of history is that persecution often works.

A modern historian, C.S.L. Davies, writing in 1977.

SOURCE E

John Foxe's detailed account of nearly all the executions still evokes images and heightened emotions. It cannot be insignificant that the work enjoyed at least five editions in its first quarter century, and that it came to be one of the most frequently printed works in the English language.

A modern historian, R. Tittler, writing in 1983.

Read Sources A–E. Now produce an extended piece of writing in which you judge Mary's attempt to restore Roman Catholicism. The following two views may help you organise your ideas:

- Mary failed because she did not have the support of the English people.

- Mary achieved the restoration of the Catholic religion but her early death and her failure to have a son destroyed her efforts.

Be sure to use, and explain, the following words: persecution, heretic, martyr.

Protestant triumph

Elizabeth was 25 when she became queen in 1558. Since her mother's execution in 1536, when she was a baby, her life had been extraordinary. More than once she herself had come close to being put to death. Elizabeth was now a striking and confident young woman, who made a great impression on all who met her. She enjoyed the attention of her male courtiers, but would resist their wishes that she should marry. Clearly she had inherited qualities from both her mother and father. She was witty and intelligent, well educated and could speak several languages. Elizabeth was also deeply committed to the new religion of Protestantism.

A contemporary portrait of Elizabeth I on her accession to the throne in 1558.

At Elizabeth's coronation, an English Bible was presented to her and, according to a contemporary report, 'she did take it with both hands, kiss it and lay it upon her breast'. This was a clear message of her intentions and, certainly, the burnings of Protestants stopped immediately. Parliament was then called to change the laws, and in 1559 passed a new Act of Supremacy and an Act of Uniformity. The monarch once again became the head of the Church in England.

Puritans – followers of a new, stricter form of Protestantism (see pages 67–70) – were unsure about whether a woman could really be the head of the Church. The Protestant translator of the Bible, William Tyndale, had described women as 'the weaker vessel', while the Scottish Calvinist, John Knox, had written a book attacking women rulers as 'the monstrous regiment of women'. Puritans also had strong ideas about how the Church should be cleared of all things Roman Catholic. They wanted to complete the Reformation that had been halted by Edward VI's death in 1553.

The Elizabethan Religious Settlement

Elizabeth, however, had her own ideas about the Church, and was not going to allow herself to be told what to do. Elizabeth was also keen to avoid her half-sister's mistakes. She knew that too much change would upset the English people, who liked their traditional religion. She believed that, although services should be in English, the ministers could wear the robes previously worn by Catholic priests. Crucifixes (crosses with the figure of Christ on them) would be permitted. If Catholics wished to believe that the priest turned the bread and wine into the body and blood of Christ (transubstantiation), then Elizabeth maintained that that was still possible. Most importantly, Elizabeth insisted that the Church would be ruled by bishops. Puritans wanted to abolish the bishops and set up a Calvinist-style church.

By 1563 Elizabeth's Parliament had passed several laws to make sure that everyone accepted her as the head of the Church in England. These laws are known as her Religious Settlement.

Avoiding extremes

Elizabeth's intention was for her Church to avoid the extremes of Roman Catholicism and strict Protestantism. Her hope was that this would please most English people, so she could avoid rebellion and civil war. She said she 'would not make windows into men's souls', meaning that she was prepared to let people follow their own beliefs provided they obeyed her laws and attended church. However, for those devout Catholics who could not accept a service of worship that was not the Mass, there was no persecution if they refused to attend church, merely a fine. These Catholics became known as 'recusants' and included many nobles and gentry.

It looked as though England had at last found a peaceful solution to its religious disputes, based on the tolerance, or acceptance, of people's individual beliefs. However, this situation did not last, for several reasons:

- There were many courtiers and members of Parliament who had little intention of tolerating the ideas of those who disagreed with them.

- Roman Catholics believed that Protestants were heretics and devil-worshippers.

- Protestants did not just want a Protestant Church, they also wanted to destroy the Pope and his Church.

- In Rome, the Pope refused to accept Elizabeth's right to the throne because she was a bastard (illegitimate) and the daughter of the 'sorceress', Anne Boleyn, who had bewitched Henry VIII. In 1570 the Pope excommunicated Elizabeth and declared that anyone who killed her would be serving God. During Elizabeth's reign, this made life difficult for Catholic recusants in England who were loyal to their queen, because the government could no longer trust them.

The Northern Rebellion, 1569

As you read earlier (pages 26–9), another problem arose for Elizabeth when Mary, Queen of Scots, arrived in England in 1568 and was imprisoned by Elizabeth. Mary was a Catholic and was the granddaughter of Henry VIII's sister, Margaret (see family tree on page 77). Elizabeth was worried that Catholics might support Mary's claim to the throne rather than that of 'the bastard' Protestant, Elizabeth.

In 1569 a revolt broke out in the north of England in support of Mary, Queen of Scots. The Mass was restored in Durham Cathedral, and the new bibles and English Prayer Books were torn up. The revolt was led by the northern Earls of Northumberland and Westmoreland and supported by the Duke of Norfolk, whom they hoped to marry to Mary. However, Elizabeth could count on the loyalty of many of the nobility; the army that marched north found little resistance as the rebels fled. Northumberland was captured and beheaded in August 1572, and Elizabeth ordered the hanging of at least one man from each village that had taken part. The Duke of Norfolk was placed in the Tower and beheaded in 1572, after the Ridolfi Plot of 1571 (see page 28).

A clampdown on Catholics

After the Northern Rebellion, there was little room for religious tolerance. Elizabeth came under pressure from her supporters to kill her prisoner, Mary, Queen of Scots. Elizabeth's secretary, Sir Francis Walsingham, operated a network of spies and double agents to keep an eye on Catholic families (see page 28). New laws made it treason for Catholic priests to enter the country, and for English men or women to shelter them. Also, the fines imposed on Catholic recusants increased. Many Catholic recusants found that they were now unable to pay the fines for absence from church. Some now grudgingly obeyed the law, but others simply stopped paying and either lost their land or were imprisoned. In this way, prisons began to fill with Catholics suspected of treason.

Walsingham was determined to protect the queen from Catholic traitors. His soldiers were sent out to search the houses of Catholic nobles for priests who might be hiding behind panelling – in 'priest holes' (see Source B on page 90) – or up the chimney. In the dungeons, Walsingham's torturers got to work. They used all sorts of means to get information about the movement of priests, their contacts, whom they had met, or where they had been hidden. The information was then used to find Catholics guilty of treason, and this was followed by the inevitable, cruel traitor's death. To Catholics, however, Elizabeth's victims were seen as martyrs, killed just as cruelly as those Protestants burned by Mary Tudor (see pages 80–4).

Digging deeper

Traitors or martyrs?

Sir Francis Walsingham was able to make life very uncomfortable for Roman Catholic priests. He had agents spying on them and soldiers searching for them. It must have been very difficult for them to know whom they could trust. Walsingham's searchers kept watch at the ports: they searched bags, and opened letters and packets. They were looking for any evidence that might put them on the trail of Catholic plotters. Walsingham also employed double agents: these were men who pretended to be Catholics, but who were really spies for Elizabeth. The spies would get themselves into the jails where Catholics were imprisoned, and start up a conversation with them, encouraging the prisoners to confide in them. Any information – the names of priests in England and the houses where they were staying – would then be fed back to Walsingham who would send out his searchers.

Fortunately for priests, there were plenty of places to hide in Elizabethan manor houses. Priest holes (small, secret hiding places) were cleverly concealed either behind the wooden panelling of rooms, beneath a staircase, under a hearth or behind a chimney. Sometimes, in an emergency, a priest might hide up a chimney. However, the searchers quickly found out about this, so even in summer they would order fires to be lit in all the hearths. In some of the better-built priest holes, a man could lie hidden for several days, having to stay completely silent as the soldiers camped out in the house waiting for the slightest hint of movement. The searchers would use the handles of their swords to sound the panelling, searching for hollow places. Sometimes they would thrust their swords right through.

SOURCE B

The priest's hole in Moseley Old Hall, Staffordshire.

With Walsingham's spies, soldiers and torturers in action, it was a terrifying time for Catholic priests during Elizabeth's reign, and for any Catholic family in whose house a priest was found, since the punishments were severe. Catholics were risking their lives by sheltering priests, but they were convinced that they had a duty to God to keep their faith alive. The priests themselves were prepared to risk death because they believed that they were doing God's work. If they were caught they would face a long interrogation, which would usually take place in a prison cell, about their movements and their contacts.

Edmund Campion

One of the most famous priests at this time was Edmund Campion, who travelled around England in secret, saying the Mass in the homes of recusant gentry. He would disguise himself as a merchant or even a labourer, taking care to hide his rosary beads and the plate and cup used for Mass. If searchers came to the place where he was staying, he would have to be hidden. Edward Campion was eventually caught after hiding in a house for two days. It took 60 soldiers to discover his hiding place.

After being captured, Campion was interrogated by Walsingham's soldiers. Campion refused to answer any questions, so he was chained to a wall in a filthy cell, with no toilet and no food, and kept in darkness with nothing but rats for company. Eventually torture was used to try to break down his resistance but, even when iron spikes were driven under his finger and toenails, he refused to confess. He was later placed on the rack (see Source D on page 92), where his arms and legs were pulled in opposite directions causing extreme agony, but still he did not confess. In the end, Campion was executed as a traitor, being hanged, drawn and quartered.

The use of torture

The point of torture was not to kill people, but to get them to confess. Torture inflicted pain, but was most effective if the increase in pain was gradual so that the victim always had something worse to fear. This is why prisoners were often left in their cells for a long time – they never knew when they might be taken to the torture chamber. Skilled torturers knew how to pile on the agony gradually, in an attempt to break the spirit of the toughest victims. According to the human rights organisation, Amnesty International, there are many countries in the world where torture is used today.

One priest who was tortured during Elizabeth I's reign, John Gerard, was hung by his arms from an iron bar. At first he used all his strength to hold up his body, but eventually he weakened and the weight of his hanging body gradually tore his muscles, dislocating his shoulders (see Source C). Gradually, however, the thought came to Gerard that the worst that the torturers could do would be to kill him. Since Gerard had 'often wanted to give my life for my Lord God', he said that, from that moment, 'the conflict in my soul ceased and the physical pain seemed much more bearable than before.' In this way, Gerard was able to face death bravely.

SOURCE C

... such a gripping pain came over me. It was worst in my chest and belly, my hands and arms. The pain was so intense I thought I could not endure it ...

In his *Autobiography of an Elizabethan*, *John Gerard describes the pain of torture.*

Many priests who were executed as traitors during Elizabeth's reign died with nobility, despite their gruesome deaths. For example, when on the scaffold, Edmund Campion showed no bitterness or fear, and wished Queen Elizabeth 'a long quiet reign with all prosperity'. He was one of 130 priests executed as traitors. The government said that these priests had betrayed the queen, but the priests would only confess to preaching their religion. They died bravely and to many people they were not traitors, but martyrs.

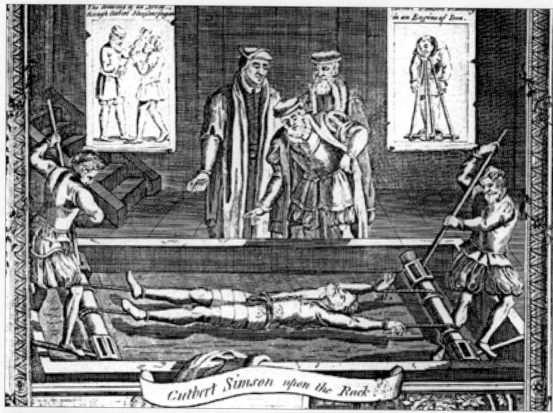

Cutbert Simson upon the Rack

SOURCE D

A contemporary engraving of a man being tortured on the rack in the Tower of London. This picture is taken from Foxe's Book of Martyrs *and shows the torture of Cutbert Simson in 1558.*

The case of Margaret Clitheroe

It wasn't just priests, or the people who had hidden them, who were tortured. Ordinary people also faced persecution. Margaret Clitheroe, a Roman Catholic who lived in the Shambles in York, was punished for not answering questions when she was interrogated. The law said that she must be crushed to death, so the door of her house was removed and put on top of her. Heavier and heavier weights were placed on the door until she died. By refusing to answer questions she saved her children from being tortured.

Activity time

1 Read the following statements:
   - Catholic priests were dangerous enemies and traitors to the queen.
   - Catholic priests were brave martyrs who died for their faith.

   Using the information in the Digging Deeper box, write two short pieces, presenting an argument to support each of the statements.

2 In Mary's reign Protestants were burnt at the stake and were called martyrs. In Elizabeth's reign Catholics were hanged, drawn and quartered and were also called martyrs.

   Can this statement tell us anything about attitudes to religion in the sixteenth century? Discuss your views in pairs.

The results of England's Reformation

While Elizabeth and her supporters continued to seek out resistance to Protestantism, and therefore to Elizabeth as England's Protestant queen, her problems continued to mount. Mary Tudor's husband, Philip II of Spain, had at first considered marrying Elizabeth, but by 1585 England and Catholic Spain were at war. This meant that Catholics were seen even more as the enemies of England and Elizabeth. In 1588 Philip II launched the Spanish Armada, a huge fleet of over 150 ships, in an attempt to invade and conquer England. The Armada's defeat was seen as a great victory for Protestant England and Elizabeth, and courtiers now celebrated by referring to Elizabeth as 'Gloriana'. She would be remembered as 'Good Queen Bess'.

By the end of Elizabeth's reign, the persecution of Catholics had succeeded in diminishing the traditional Catholic religion of the English people. Catholics lost their access to priests, and to the ceremonies and rituals on which Catholicism depended. Despite the bravery of the many Catholic priests who risked, and often lost, their lives, England was becoming a Protestant country. Bishops tried hard to educate the ordinary people in Protestant beliefs.

Perhaps Elizabeth's greatest advantage in making England Protestant was her good health: unlike her half-brother and half-sister, whose reigns were so brief, she ruled for 44 years. This gave Elizabeth time to make sure that her religious reforms survived beyond her death in 1603. For centuries after Elizabeth's death, Catholics and the Pope were seen as the enemies of England. Even today, England officially remains a Protestant country, and it was not until the nineteenth century that Catholics again began to enjoy freedom of worship.

Assessment section

Using the text you have just read and your own knowledge, answer the following questions:

1   Queen Mary

    a   How many priests did Mary burn?

    b   What was Mary's religion?

    c   What is Mary's nickname?

2   Queen Elizabeth

    a   How many priests did Elizabeth hang, draw and quarter?

    b   What was Elizabeth's religion?

    c   What are Elizabeth's nicknames?

3   Which religion did England have for over 400 years?

4   Some historians have said that 'History is written by the winners!' They mean that the opinions we form about historical characters, whether they were 'good' or 'bad', depend on whether they were on the 'winning side' in history. Use the evidence in this section to examine this view and present your own opinions about how we view people in history. You should include your answers to Questions 1, 2 and 3, and also think about the following:

    ● For hundreds of years schoolchildren learned the 'wicked deeds' of Bloody Mary because England was a Protestant country.

    ● They did not learn that Mary might have succeeded in making England Catholic if she hadn't died early.

    ● They learned the heroic deeds of Queen Elizabeth's reign, e.g. the founding of the Church of England, defeating the Spanish, the voyages of Drake, the plays of Shakespeare (see Chapter 6).

    ● They rarely learned about the cruelty of the persecution of Catholics during Elizabeth's reign.

5   The Spanish Armada is one of the most famous events of Elizabeth's reign. It is an exciting story. Research what happened to the Armada, and find out why it failed. You should use library books and history websites. Be sure to use more than one source of evidence. You can present either a written report with illustrations and maps, or you might choose to present your findings to your class using a computer and a digital projector.

Further reading

David Starkey, *Elizabeth* (Chatto and Windus, 2000)

Alison Weir, *Elizabeth the Queen* (Jonathan Cape, 1998)

4 The Stuart Crisis: Civil War to Glorious Revolution

The reign of the Stuart monarchs, Charles I and his son, Charles II, was one of the most turbulent periods of British history, which was to shape and direct much of our present-day government and monarchy. Parliament and King Charles I disagreed on a grand scale. The country was torn apart by furious fighting for four years, which resulted in the execution of King Charles I in 1649 (Source A). During this civil war, families were divided about which side they should fight for. It was a time when power moved away from the king and shifted to Parliament. As a consequence, much social change followed, including religious tolerance.

Transformation and transition

In this chapter we shall be examining the key themes of transformation and transition. The illustration on page 96 is a road representing the changes that transformed England and Britain, as it became known during this period. The people of England were on a journey which was to see many changes in their lives. There are a number of key issues in the period 1625–88. These are:

- religion
- politics

- military unrest
- social change.

SOURCE A

A contemporary painting of the execution of Charles I in 1649.

Each of these key issues – religious, military, political and social – affected the country at various stages of the Stuart rule and played an important part in the transformation of England, causing a movement of power from monarchy to Parliament and back again to monarchy.

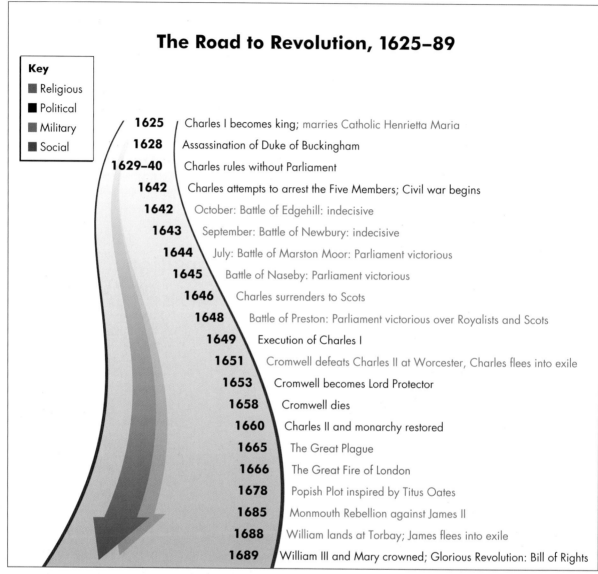

The Road to Revolution, 1625–89

Key
- ■ Religious
- ■ Political
- ■ Military
- ■ Social

1625	Charles I becomes king; marries Catholic Henrietta Maria
1628	Assassination of Duke of Buckingham
1629–40	Charles rules without Parliament
1642	Charles attempts to arrest the Five Members; Civil war begins
1642	October: Battle of Edgehill: indecisive
1643	September: Battle of Newbury: indecisive
1644	July: Battle of Marston Moor: Parliament victorious
1645	Battle of Naseby: Parliament victorious
1646	Charles surrenders to Scots
1648	Battle of Preston: Parliament victorious over Royalists and Scots
1649	Execution of Charles I
1651	Cromwell defeats Charles II at Worcester, Charles flees into exile
1653	Cromwell becomes Lord Protector
1658	Cromwell dies
1660	Charles II and monarchy restored
1665	The Great Plague
1666	The Great Fire of London
1678	Popish Plot inspired by Titus Oates
1685	Monmouth Rebellion against James II
1688	William lands at Torbay; James flees into exile
1689	William III and Mary crowned; Glorious Revolution: Bill of Rights

The road to revolution, 1625–89.

The Civil War, 1642–9

The reason why war broke out between Charles I and Parliament in 1642 is very complex and includes many short- and long-term factors (see pages 102–3). Historians do not agree among themselves about what exactly led to the Civil War. They do agree, though, on the fact that many of the causes were deeply rooted in the history of England.

Charles I's belief in the divine right of kings was one of the factors which gave rise to tension and misunderstanding in his dealings with Parliament. There were, however, other factors which created an unstable situation in England at this time.

Digging deeper

The divine right of kings

Charles I was brought up to believe that monarchs had a divine right to rule – that they were chosen by God to do so.

A painting of Charles I by Daniel Mytens, 1631.

The idea of 'divine right' was not new: it had been in existence for a number of years and was common throughout Europe at this time. However, Charles I's belief that he was only answerable to God and not to Parliament resulted in a rift between the king and Parliament. Parliament wanted more say in the running of the country and Charles would not allow this to happen. He only wanted to use Parliament to raise revenue for him to spend, through new and heavy taxes.

 ## Activity time

1   What do Sources A and B tell you about the type of king Charles might turn out to be?

2   Construct a mind map like the one below, using the sources in this section and your own knowledge, to show the main aspects of the divine right of monarchs and the problems it caused.

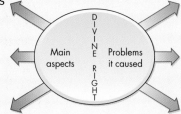

Religious problems

Religion had been a problem for Charles' father, James I. After Elizabeth's death in 1603, many Catholics had hoped for a better future with James as king. However, they soon became dissatisfied with his religious policies and this led to a Catholic called Robert Catesby trying to blow up Parliament and overthrow James I, in what is known as the Gunpowder Plot (see page 35).

When Charles came to the throne in 1625, he soon married a French princess, Henrietta Maria. She was Catholic and openly attended the Catholic Mass. This made Parliament and the people concerned that she would make Charles and any children they had Catholic, too; indeed the whole country might be converted to Catholicism.

Charles was in fact a devout Anglican (a member of the Church of England) but he was a cultured man who loved dignified services with beautiful music. He liked churches that had candles, pictures and statues. This was a very Catholic style of worship and one that many Anglicans, particularly Puritans (see pages 67–70) campaigned against. They wanted church worship to be very plain and simple.

Laud's religious reforms

Charles failed to understand how his subjects were feeling, and by 1633 he chose William Laud to become Archbishop of Canterbury. His reforms caused great concern amongst members of Parliament because they seemed to reverse all the changes made to Protestant worship during the Reformation in the mid-sixteenth century (see Chapters 2 and 3).

- Laud wanted services to be orderly and efficient.

- He made clergy (priests) wear vestments like Catholic priests and he ordered that the Communion table be railed off from the congregation. These changes have remained in Anglican churches to this day.

- His bishops punished those who disobeyed by fining them.

The illustrations on page 99 show the differences in the styles of church worship. Catholic churches were often ornate with statues, candles and priests wearing vestments. In contrast, Puritan churches were very simple with no decoration or religious symbols. Anglican churches were less severe, though still plain with no statues. Priests did not wear colourful clothes and used the Prayer Book instead of the Roman Missal. Many Anglicans rejected Laud's changes to their style of worship.

Opposition to religious reforms

Opposition to Charles and Laud grew. Meanwhile the Puritans gained in strength, making their followers live by a strict moral code. They made rules that said everybody had to go to church on Sundays and nobody was allowed to work on a Sunday. Even cooking or going for a walk were forbidden. People who broke these rules were fined or put in the stocks.

In 1637 a well-known Puritan called William Prynne wrote a pamphlet which condemned the power of the bishops. He, along with two others, was sentenced to stand in the pillory – a wooden construction with holes where

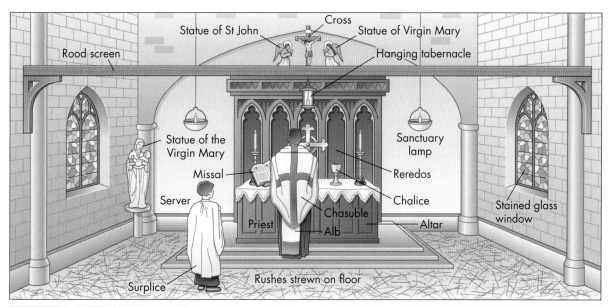

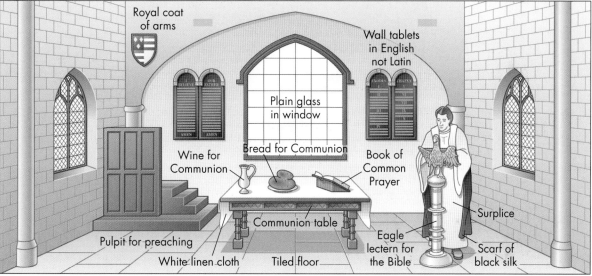

Inside a typical Catholic church (top) and an English Protestant church (bottom) in the 1600s. Archbishop Laud introduced changes to Anglican churches, such as the railing off of the communion table from the congregation.

the head and hands of offenders were placed. Here their ears were cut off, their cheeks were branded. Then they were imprisoned and fined £5000 each. This lack of tolerance on the part of the king and Laud made them even more unpopular.

Also in 1637 Charles and Laud ordered the Scottish Presbyterians (Scottish Protestants) to follow the rules of the bishops and to use the English Prayer Book. In St Giles' Cathedral in Edinburgh on the first Sunday the English Prayer Book was used, there was a riot (see Source F). This involved members of the congregation throwing their stools, books and other items at the priest. There was trouble elsewhere, too, as across Scotland Presbyterians refused to accept a new service and obey Laud's rules. The people were driven by a strong combination of religious beliefs and nationalism. This is known as the Scottish Rebellion (see page 138).

So Charles faced growing criticism on religious grounds with the Protestants and Puritans increasingly opposed to him.

The Arch-Prelate of St Andrewes in Scotland reading the new Service-booke in his pontificalibu assaulted by men & women, with Crickets stooles Stickes and Stones.

Political problems

From 1629 until 1640 Charles ruled without Parliament. This was known as the period of 'personal rule'. Charles was viewed by Parliament as a tyrant for a number of reasons:

- He used the Court of Star Chamber (see page 15) to punish his enemies without a fair trial.

- He wanted his chief minister, the Earl of Strafford, to use the army to crush any opposition to him.

- He raised taxes without Parliament's permission.

- The bishops who ran government for him were not from the traditional land-owning families.

- He wanted to rule without Parliament, because it held him back and did not approve of his fund-raising – raising taxes to finance his lifestyle.

Increasingly a rift developed between Charles and Parliament as the king was seen to be an absolute ruler (a dictator).

By 1640 Charles was forced to recall Parliament because he lacked money and faced problems in Scotland. This period was known as the 'Long Parliament' – due to the fact that Parliament was not officially dismissed for 20 years. The MPs, led by John Pym, began to take away some of the king's power by refusing to grant him taxes until he agreed to their demands. This caused much anger in Scotland and led to Charles making a humiliating treaty, because Parliament would not support his request for money which would help him raise an army to defeat the Scots (see page 138). The first demand was to get rid of the hated Strafford, who was beheaded for high treason. Charles thought long and hard over signing the death warrant of his closest adviser; it is supposed to be the only thing that he ever regretted doing. Archbishop Laud was imprisoned and eventually executed in 1645,

and the Court of Star Chamber was abolished. In November 1641, Parliament passed the Grand Remonstrance which condemned bishops and Catholics and Charles' ministers. Charles' reaction was to take an army of 400 men to Parliament on 4 January 1642 to arrest Pym and the four other rebel leaders of the House of Commons. Just before he arrived the Five Members of Parliament escaped by boat down the Thames. Charles said, 'Since I see all the birds are flown, I expect you to send them to me as soon as they return.' The Speaker would not be bullied by Charles and replied, 'I have neither eyes to see nor tongue to speak in this place, except as the House is pleased to direct me.'

SOURCE G

Charles orders the arrest of the Five Members in 1642, by Charles Cope, 1868.

War between the king and Parliament thus became inevitable. Riots broke out in London and within a week Charles and his family had fled from the capital to Nottingham. The soldiers that went to arrest the Five Members with Charles were called 'cavaliers' by their enemies as an insult. (*Cavalieros* were brutal Catholic troops from Spain and they dressed in courtly clothes.) This was the name given to royalist supporters in the civil war that was about to erupt. To add to the political unrest, there was the Irish Rebellion (see page 133) in October 1641 which arose because of the fear that the English Protestant Parliament might attempt to pass anti-Catholic laws. There were terrible massacres of Protestants in Ulster, and when Charles asked for money to raise an army Parliament was concerned that Charles would attempt to use it not only to put down the rebellion but also to stamp out any opposition to him at home. Pym demanded that Parliament should decide who led the army. This annoyed Charles.

Financial problems

Charles faced many financial problems throughout his reign. This led directly to disagreements with Parliament – often his financial problems were closely linked to religious and political issues, such as in the case of the Irish Rebellion. He needed money to run government effectively, to fight wars with Spain and France, to tackle uprisings in Scotland and to cover his own expensive lifestyle.

At the start of his reign MPs gave him only one-seventh of the money he requested so he decided to dismiss Parliament. This began the period of 'personal rule' which lasted from 1629 until 1640. Dismissing Parliament, however, did not solve the problem of needing to raise money.

Parliament normally gave the king the right to collect customs duties – taxes on imported goods. It had not done so before he dismissed it, but Charles ordered the collection of customs duties anyway. Another way he attempted to raise revenue was by issuing fines and forced loans. Some fines were reintroduced which hadn't been used since the Middle Ages. For example, poorer people were fined for pulling down unused cottages because it was said they were encouraging the peasants to leave the land and move to the cities.

Charles also had the right to sell monopolies which meant an exclusive right to manufacture and sell products like soap and wine. This greatly increased prices because it meant there was no competition and it annoyed merchants. Ship Money was the most hated of all the taxes. In 1634 Charles introduced a tax on coastal counties and in 1635 he extended it to all counties. The aim of the tax was to raise significant revenue for the Royal Navy shipbuilding programme. It had always been collected in wartime but this was now extended to peacetime. This angered many MPs and especially those people having to pay the taxes.

Charles and Parliament faced an ever growing dilemma. The king desperately needed money to rule and, as shown above, faced major financial problems. On the other hand Parliament firmly believed that it controlled the country's finances and therefore had overall control of the running of the country. The country split into two sides – Royalists, who supported the king, and Parliamentarians, who wanted Parliament to have a greater say.

Analysing the causes of the Civil War

As we have seen there were many issues leading to the outbreak of war in 1642. These can be put under the headings 'short-term factors' and 'long-term factors'. Analysing the issues like this helps us to understand why it was that power moved to Parliament and the king was executed.

What is a short-term factor?

A short-term factor is an event or series of events which takes place over a short period of time. Usually this would be about two to three years. These can also be called catalysts, because the impact of them can speed up the outcome of an event.

What is a long-term factor?

A long-term factor is an event or series of events which takes place over a long period of time, usually five or more years. These can also be called background factors because they tend to develop in importance over a long period of time.

Dividing events into short- and long-term factors helps historians to investigate the root causes of key issues and events. It also helps them to place the value or importance upon events and issues when forming an argument. Doing this also helps us to compare and contrast ideas, which then form the basis of analysis and explanation.

Short-term factors

Listed below are the short-term factors that led to the Civil War in 1642. They include political, economic and religious issues or events:

- the Irish Rebellion, October 1641

- the Grand Remonstrance, November 1641

- Charles attempts to arrest the Five Members, January 1642

- Parliament takes control of the army sent to Ireland

- Parliament splits into those who support Charles and those who do not by June 1642.

- Parliament and Charles begin to raise armies

- Charles loses control of London and declares war by raising his standard at Nottingham, August 1642.

Long-term factors

Listed below are the long-term factors that led to the Civil War in 1642. They include political, economic and religious issues or events:

- Ship Money – a new tax; old laws are reinstated to raise money for the king

- divine right of kings

- poor leadership by Charles

- Parliament demands more say in how the country is run

- Charles marries a Catholic which causes growing concern among Protestants

- from 1629 to 1640 Charles ignores Parliament which is calling for reforms including being allowed to meet on a regular basis

- Archbishop Laud and his religious reforms

- the Scottish Rebellion.

Question time

1   'The Civil War broke out in 1642 because of Charles I's belief in the divine right of kings.'

Write an essay, which includes analysis and evaluation of the short- and long-term factors which resulted in the outbreak of fighting between Royalists and Parliamentarians in 1642.

Main events of the Civil War

Having left London, Charles raised the king's standard at Nottingham on 22 August 1642, and the war began. This was a signal for all loyal supporters to join him. This was a civil war, a war between citizens of the same country. Some said that his defeat was inevitable because due to bad weather his standard soon blew down, which many took to be a bad omen.

Land held by king and Parliament in 1642 and the main battles of the Civil War.

SCOTLAND

Marston Moor (1644) ⚔ York

Preston

ENGLAND

Chester

Nottingham

Birmingham

Norwich

⚔ Naseby (1645)

⚔ Edgehill (1642)

WALES

Gloucester

Oxford

Bristol

London

Exeter

English Channel

N

0   100 km

50 miles

Key

■ Land held by the king

■ Land held by Parliament

Key people

- **Royalists or Cavaliers** – these were supporters of the king who fought for Charles I.

- **Parliamentarians or Roundheads** – these were supporters of Parliament's forces. The name 'Roundhead' came from the close-cropped way many of these supporters wore their hair – in contrast to the flowing hairstyles of noblemen at the court of King Charles.

- **Oliver Cromwell** – a Member of Parliament (MP) and a devout Puritan. He was a successful general of the Roundhead army – the New Model Army, formed in 1644 – which defeated the Royalists. During the period after Charles I's execution in 1649, known as the Commonwealth, Cromwell became the Lord Protector.

Organising the troops

There was no national army when the Civil War broke out so local gentry and nobles organised and paid for their own troops. For example, the Royalist Earl of Newcastle gave his soldiers tunics of unbleached white material, saying they would dye them with the blood of their enemies! Important cities like London had their own fighting troops called trainbands (trained bands). These were made up of local citizens trained and equipped by the authority.

One of the weapons used by foot-soldiers at this time was a pike. This had a long shaft about 4 metres (12 feet) in length with a sharp head like a spear. They were heavy so pikemen had to be tall and strong. These soldiers fought in squares and acted as a sort of fortified hedge against cavalry.

To fire a musket (a type of firearm) took nearly a minute; the process often went wrong. At the start of the war, muskets were so heavy they needed a stand. By the end of the war they became lighter. Another weapon in use was the cannon. These were inaccurate but frightening to the enemy! They could use up to 1300 kilogrammes (2860 lbs) of shot in a single battle. A heavy cannon train would slow down a whole army in wet and muddy conditions – this is one reason why armies often only fought in the summer.

Progress of the war

1642: The Battle of Edgehill

The king and his army began to march to London, but Essex's Roundhead army met him at Edgehill, about 30 miles from Oxford. The Royalist general, Prince Rupert, made a cavalry charge, but his troops got out of control and began to loot a neighbouring village. Meanwhile the two armies fought each other to a stalemate. This was the first major battle of the Civil War, and after it Oliver Cromwell, the leader of the Parliamentarians, withdrew to his home territory of Huntingdon to train his cavalry so that he could be a match for Prince Rupert. The battle was indecisive with neither side winning outright. However, the Royalists claimed the victory because they were able to continue their march to London. The king occupied Oxford as his headquarters from where he and his troops marched on to Turnham Green on the outskirts of London.

At Turnham Green the Royalists came face to face with the London trainbands who were determined, well trained and well-equipped. Rupert and the king had to withdraw to Oxford. Turnham Green was the nearest they ever got to London.

1643

The Royalists planned a three-pronged attack on London:

1 The Earl of Newcastle was to attack from the north. However, he was held up as he failed to capture Hull.

2 Sir Ralph Hopton was to attack from the south-west. He, too, was held up as he failed to capture Plymouth.

3 Charles I was to attack from Oxford. He was also held up as he could not capture Gloucester which was bravely defended by the Parliamentarians. Following a difficult siege, the city was relieved by Essex and the London trainbands.

At the First Battle of Newbury, the Royalist army attempted, but failed, to prevent Essex and the trainbands from returning safely to London from Gloucestershire. However, Prince Rupert captured the important port of Bristol and managed to keep the area round Oxford secure. Parliament lost Hampden who was killed at Chalgrove Field. The Parliamentarian leader Pym (see page 100) organised the war effort until his death in December. He made a pact with the Scots who were still unsettled after the Scottish Rebellion (see page 138). They had a strong army and, in return for their help, the Parliamentarians promised to set up a Scottish Presbyterian Kirk (church) in England. Charles made peace with the Irish chieftains so as to free up some of his army who were putting down the rebellion in Ireland. Meanwhile Oliver Cromwell's newly trained cavalry was gaining battle experience.

1644: The Battle of Marston Moor

The Scots marched south in the summer and joined the Parliamentarian army attacking York. At the Battle of Marston Moor, Prince Rupert was beaten for the first time and the Royalists lost control of the north. This was a key victory because Parliament was now turning the tide of the war in its favour. Along with Sir Thomas Fairfax, the commanding general, Cromwell was now training and developing his New Model Army on a national scale. This army consisted of well-trained and disciplined troops. A tax was levied on the counties where the men were raised so that they were more regularly paid and, therefore, less likely to desert.

SOURCE A

I had rather had a plain russet-coated captain that knows what he fights for, and loves what he knows, than what you call a gentleman ... if you choose godly honest men as captains of horse, honest men will follow them.

Cromwell talking about the soldiers in his New Model Army in 1644.

SOURCE B

No man swears, but he pays twelve pence; if he be drunk, he is set in the stocks or worse ... How happy it would be if all the forces were thus disciplined!

Cromwell speaking about the behaviour of his troops.

Cromwell cared for his troops, describing them as 'a lovely company'. But orders had to be obeyed at all times; if they were not, punishments were given out – for example, two deserters were publicly whipped in the market place in Huntingdon in April 1643.

1645: The Battle of Naseby

The New Model Army's first big battle took place in the summer of 1645 near Naseby in Northamptonshire, and it virtually decided the war. On the Parliamentary left, the cavalry was forced to flee by Prince Rupert's horsemen. But on the Parliamentary right, Cromwell and his cavalry proved to be indestructible. After scattering the king's cavalry he turned, as at Marston Moor the year before, to the centre and soon the whole of the king's infantry was crushed.

1646

After a series of Roundhead victories, the Royalists surrendered at Oxford, thereby ending the Civil War. Charles had escaped earlier and surrendered to the Scots, at Newark, who then sold him to Parliament (see page 139).

SOURCE C

The Battle of Naseby, from a print published in 1647.

Activity time

1 In you own words explain the following terms:
   - Roundhead
   - Cavalier
   - New Model Army

2 Make two columns headed Royalist Successes and Parliamentarian Successes. List the main events in their correct column and in chronological order.

3 Discuss your list of main events in pairs. Make a bullet point list of five key reasons why Parliament won the Civil War.

SOURCE D

There is always great difference in the relation of [speaking about] battles. It is certain that in a battle the next man can barely make a true relation of the actions of him that is next to him; for in such a hurry and smoke of a set field, a man takes notice of nothing but what relates to his own safety.

From Sir Richard Bulstrode's Royalist account of the Battle of Edgehill, 1642.

SOURCE E

I saw legs and arms flying apart.

Account of Colonel Slingsby, a Royalist.

SOURCE F

We came after our shot was spent to push of pike, and fought very gallantly having no relief from our horse [cavalry]. They attacked with great resolution and boldness, and in a very good order and we fought so long and so fiercely until all our powder and bullet was spent. Afterwards they joined and fell to hand-to-hand fighting, one upon the other, with the stocks of their muskets.

Sir William Brereton, a Parliamentarian, 1642.

SOURCE G

A whole file of men, six deep, with their heads struck off with one cannon shot of ours.

Account of Captain Gwynne, a Royalist.

SOURCE H

It was somewhat dreadful when bowels and brains flew in our faces.

Account of Sergeant Foster, a Parliamentarian.

SOURCE I

The cannon is a devilish machination to plague the sons of men.

Account of John Milton, who supported the Parliamentarians.

SOURCE J

I saw the field so strewed with carcasses of horses and men, the bodies lay slain about four miles in length, but most thick on the hill where the king stood. In the morning there was a mortifying object [terrible sight] to behold, when the naked bodies of thousands lay upon the ground and not altogether dead.

From the letter of a Roundhead soldier after Naseby, 1645.

SOURCE K

Our lying in the field hath lost us more than have been taken away either by sword or the bullet.

From a letter written by the Royalist Captain Rich, 1642.

4 Use the sources and your own knowledge to answer the following questions.

   a What is the value of Source D as evidence?

   b How informative is Source F about the way battles were fought?

   c Look at Sources E, G, H and I. Sources E, G and H are from eyewitnesses; Source I is from a famous contemporary writer, John Milton, who supported the Parliamentarians. Which is the least useful of these sources, and why?

   d What do Sources J and K tell you about casualties in the Civil War?

   e Do you think that Sources J and K are reliable? Explain your answer.

The impact of the Civil War on people's lives

If ordinary people lived in an area where there was no major fighting their lives were hardly affected by the war. However, most areas of England and Wales would have had armies passing through them, if not actually fighting. Once an army was in the area everybody was affected. Soldiers had a bad reputation for stealing goods and they were usually billeted on the local people. This was when local families had to house and feed soldiers – sometimes three or four in one house at the same time. The householder was supposed to be paid but sometimes this didn't happen. Horses were valuable property and were always in demand – one village in Cheshire lost 50 horses, probably all it had. Cattle and other livestock were also taken. This directly affected people's lives, especially in the villages near Charles I's headquarters in Oxford.

SOURCE A

A contemporary woodcut of Prince Rupert and Royalist forces attacking Birmingham in 1643.

The people of Carlisle were forced to eat rats and dogs and it is full of misery and desolation, as sword, famine and plague have left it.

A description of Carlisle by soldiers who captured the town after a siege.

I have lent money to both sides. Been plundered by both sides. Been imprisoned by both sides. A mad world.

From a letter written to the Earl of Middlesex in 1643, from the person in charge of his land in Gloucestershire.

I have had three horses taken from me, one after the other. Then my spade was taken to help build a fort, leaving me unable to grow my crops. I've got a family to support, the local taxes to pay and I have to feed and give shelter to a soldier.

Written by a farmer in 1644 near Ludlow in Shropshire.

Brother against brother

The war also had a major impact on families. Some people did not want to take sides with the king or with Parliament. They often did not want to fight at all but were forced to support one side or the other.

I do not like the quarrel and do heartily wish that the king would agree to what Parliament wants. But I have served the king nearly 30 years, and will not do so bad a thing as to abandon him. I would rather lose my life, which I am sure I will do [which is exactly what happened because he was killed at the Battle of Edgehill].

Sir Edmund Verney writing to a friend about his support for the king in October 1642.

Brother, what I was frightened of is true – you are against the king. It hurts me to think that Father and I are now your enemy. I am so troubled to think of you being on their side that I can write no more, only pray for peace.

One of Sir Edmund Verney's sons writing to a brother who was fighting on the Parliamentary side. Edmund had ten children and not all of them fought on the same side as him.

As in all civil wars, people were forced to take sides against each other and this included father fighting against son, brother against brother and sister against brother. Most people were affected by the Civil War; nearly one-quarter of adults in England took part in the fighting.

Activity time

Pick one character from the following list and, using the information provided, produce a written speech on 'side-taking' as if you were that person. Perform your speech to the class explaining which side your character fought on in the war and why.

1 Puritan member of the House of Commons
- The war was caused by the king ruling without Parliament for eleven years.
- Ship Money was taken instead of taxes that had been agreed to.
- The king's enemies were punished in his Court of Star Chamber.
- Fighting on this side to protect the power of Parliament, the people and the laws of England.

2 Member of the House of Lords
- The war was caused by the House of Commons trying to take away the king's power.
- Most of the nobility in the Lords supports the king.
- The king is able to rule without Parliament.
- Fighting on this side to protect the power of the king, the people and the laws of England.

3 Puritan preacher
- The war was caused by the king trying to force rituals and ceremonies on the Church of England.
- There is a demand for simple services, preaching from the Bible and an end to the power of the bishops.
- Fighting on this side to protect the Protestant religion – the king is no better than a Catholic.

4 Army officer
- The king had to fight two wars against Scottish rebels.
- In 1642 the Catholic rebellion in Ireland occurred.
- Who is to control the army being sent to Ireland?
- Fighting about who controls the army.

5 Country labourer
- A war was caused because the country is more organised and united than in the past: if there is trouble with Parliament in London it spreads across the whole country and can't be ignored.
- We fight whomever our local landlord tells us to fight, or because we've been forced to join one side or another.
- During the war, money, horses and other goods are taken and damage is done to property.

6 Country gentleman
- The war was caused because the king and his close allies (the Lords and wealthy gentlemen) attempted to keep merchants, townspeople and less wealthy gentlemen out of power.
- Fighting on this side to reduce the power of the very wealthy and powerful.

Digging deeper

Women in wartime

SOURCE G

A contemporary woodcut of a 'She Soldier'. Women played an important and varied role in the Civil War as camp followers, spies and even as soldiers.

Look carefully at Source G. What image of women soldiers do you get from this picture? How are women portrayed in it?

In 1642, women helped Parliamentary soldiers to enter Bristol; some women disguised themselves as men and fought alongside them in major battles such as Naseby. They were known as 'She Soldiers'. One famous She Soldier was called 'Mr Clarke' and joined the Parliamentary army with her husband. She behaved like one of the men soldiers, firing muskets, drinking, fighting and smoking. Legend has it that she even gave birth while fighting in the Civil War!

Another famous woman was Elizabeth Alkin who was known as 'Parliament Joan'. She was a Roundhead spy and wrote a number of pamphlets supporting Parliament as well as looking after wounded soldiers. Some women from wealthy families had to defend their homes and land if the enemy was threatening the area where they lived. One famous example of this was Brilliana, Lady Harley who lived in Brampton Bryan Castle near Hereford and was

on the side of Parliament. Her home was surrounded by the Royalists on 26 July 1642 and she was ordered to surrender. However, she refused, saying that she would not betray her husband's trust in her: 'I do not know that it is his pleasure that I should entertain soldiers in his house.' The Royalists attacked using cannons and the king himself wrote to Brilliana asking her to surrender so as to safeguard her and her children. Brilliana died after many months of siege due to poor health and the castle was captured by the Royalists. They looked after her three small children out of respect for her heroism.

However, women were not simply involved in the military side of war. Everyday life had to continue; households had to be maintained and farms kept functioning effectively despite the fact that many men were away fighting. Women not only kept their families together single-handedly but also kept a sense of order whilst the country tore itself apart with fighting. Their daily work in the home was affected directly by the war. For example, they had to know how to make almost everything that was needed in a home such as medicines, clothes and cooking.

The role of women during the Civil War was varied, important and should not be overlooked.

Activity time

Using the information above and your own knowledge write an extended paragraph to explain the different roles women played in the Civil War.

- Describe carefully what part women played in the Civil War.

- Give your own views on what women did in the war.

- Support your ideas and views with evidence from this chapter or from your school library.

Charles I and his execution, 30 January 1649

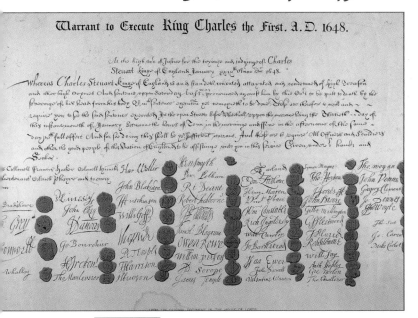

Warrant to Execute King Charles the First. A.D. 1648.

*The death warrant
of Charles I.*

The year 1646 saw the last fighting of the Civil War in Stow-on-the-Wold in Gloucestershire. The problem now facing the country was what to do with the king, and what would happen as a consequence of Parliament's victory. The members of the New Model Army under Cromwell wanted to have their say; they wanted to worship as they wished and be paid. They had the king imprisoned, first at Hampton Court and then on the Isle of Wight.

Members of Parliament were worried about the power of the army and could not see how they were going to go on paying for it. They also did not trust the Scots. The Scots wanted their reward for the help they had given Parliament in the Civil War and a say in English affairs. They wanted a Presbyterian Kirk (church) in England and to play a major part in it.

The king was defeated, had no army, but still believed that God would restore power to him. He was prepared to negotiate in order to regain power. At the same time as discussing peace terms with Parliament, he made a deal with the Scots (which they accepted because they thought that Charles would support them more than Parliament would). Fighting broke out again but the Royalists were not well organised and were easily put down by the army. The Second Civil War was very short – lasting June–August 1648. Fairfax defeated the king's troops at Colchester and Cromwell won victories in Wales and Lancashire. The king was held prisoner by the army which raised the question: what would they do with him now?

'That man of blood'

'That man of blood', as the king was called by the army, was to be put on trial, publicly condemned and then publicly executed. This was the view of the army leaders, but Parliament had to agree on this course of action. Many MPs, however, did not agree with this plan and thought it would be better for the country if the king were put back in power. In December 1648 Pride's Purge took place. Colonel Pride, one of the leaders of Parliament's forces, surrounded the Houses of Parliament with troops and would allow only MPs who were against the king, in other words in support of his trial, to enter. MPs who supported the king were not allowed to take part in the debate. This was called the Rump Parliament – only 80 of the 507 MPs were present. The Rump decided that Charles should be put on trial.

Many people wanted nothing to do with the trial, including the Lord Chief Justice. He was afraid of assassination, so an unknown London lawyer called John Bradshaw was appointed president of the court. Throughout the trial he wore a bullet-proof hat. Charles was accused of being 'a tyrant, traitor and murderer, and a public and implacable enemy of the people of England'.

Charles did not recognise the court of law at all and the charge against him read: 'He laughed in the face of the court.' The king still felt that as king he was the law – no one could appoint a special court like this without his permission and no one had the power to try him. Many people, including Fairfax who had recently fought against the king and defeated him at Colchester, now had sympathy with him. Cromwell did not, however, and said, 'We will cut off his head with the crown upon it!' As the king left the court, soldiers shouted, 'Execution! Justice!' but the watching crowd remained silent.

On 30 January 1649, the day Charles I was to be executed, he told a servant that it was his second marriage day and remained defiant in the face of death. It was a very cold morning so Charles wore two shirts as he did not want to shiver and appear scared. He said, 'I fear not death, death is not terrible to me.' He was taken to the Banqueting House in the Palace of Whitehall where a huge crowd waited. He was allowed to make a short speech and said, '... I am a martyr of the people. I have a good cause and I have a gracious God; I will say no more.' Soon after this he was beheaded.

Charles' execution was met with mixed feelings and in some respects his death did more for his cause than any other actions.

SOURCE B

Charles Stuart, late king of England, have by authority derived by Parliament been justly condemned and put to death for many treasons, murders ... and is hereby declared to be attainted of high treason.

From an Act of the Rump Parliament, 1649.

SOURCE C

The blow I saw given and can truly say with a sad heart, at the instant thereof, I remember well, there was such a groan by the thousands then present, as I never heard before and desire I may never hear again.

An eyewitness account of Charles I's execution, January 1649.

Activity time

1   Use your own knowledge and the evidence above, write a speech to be used as part of a whole class debate either supporting the execution of Charles as a traitor to the people or asking for his acquittal (release), seeing him as a martyr.

'The world turned upside down'

Now that Charles, the king, had been executed, the country experienced a number of major changes. England was now a republic, without a king, bishops or the House of Lords. It was called a Commonwealth. This was the Rump's doing. Because there was no longer a monarchy many people felt that the world had been turned upside down – this feeling was sometimes reflected in cartoons, such as in Source A, and in popular ballads.

SOURCE A

'The world turned upside down' – a cartoon published in 1647.

The Protectorate

Transforming England for the better?

In late 1649 and early 1650 England was changing very quickly. The lack of stability and the questions of how power should be managed in the country, now there was no king, put the new Commonwealth in a weak position. Cromwell also faced a number of problems from abroad. Europe was shocked by the news of the execution of Charles I, and Cromwell faced the possibility of a Royalist invasion via Ireland or Scotland from Charles II, son of Charles I. Charles II was heir to the throne and, although neither proclaimed nor crowned at this time, he came out of exile in Europe where he had been living for eleven years.

Cromwell also faced problems in Ireland. In early 1649 the Irish Catholics joined up with Protestant Royalists seeking to seize Ireland in the name of Charles II. Cromwell, as the newly appointed chief of the army, subdued the uprising with great force at Drogheda and Wexford (see page 134). Charles II avoided capture and travelled north to Scotland where, in June 1650, he rallied the Royalists and Presbyterians to fight the New Model Army at Dunbar (see page 139). In 1651, Charles II led the Scots south but was defeated at Worcester by Cromwell and again narrowly avoided capture.

The Rump and Barebones Parliaments

Cromwell's victories made him internationally famous. When, in 1652, the Rump Parliament (see page 113) declared a trade war on the Protestant Dutch, and attacked Portugal, Cromwell was furious. The Rump also taxed England heavily, but what angered Cromwell most was that it refused to carry out the legal and religious reforms the Puritans wanted. Then in 1653 members of the Rump Parliament discussed an Act that would enable them to prolong their own power. This was the final straw for Cromwell. He stormed the House of Commons with some soldiers and he proceeded to dismiss the Rump. He said, 'Be gone you rogues, you have sat long enough!'

A contemporary Dutch print showing Cromwell dismissing the Rump Parliament in April 1653.

As he was a strict Puritan, Cromwell decided to replace the Rump with a group of 140 godly Puritans, including some from Scotland and Ireland. They were not elected but were nominated or appointed. This was known as the Barebones Parliament after one of its members – Praise-God Barebones. It was also known as the Little Parliament. This Parliament demonstrated little skill in making laws to run the country effectively. It insisted on passing extreme religious laws such as getting rid of tithes (payments to churches). Its members often quarrelled and argued among themselves. By the end of the year, the moderate members had decided to return their power to Cromwell. The extremists were dismissed by Cromwell and those who refused to be dismissed were expelled by soldiers.

Cromwell as Lord Protector

Now that the Barebones Parliament no longer existed, England once again had no legal authority so the army drew up the Instrument of Government in December 1653. This gave Cromwell the power to run the country as Lord Protector, helped by a small council. It allowed Parliament to be called every three years when it could pass laws without needing the Protector's agreement. However, when Parliament was not in session, Cromwell and the council could pass any laws that they wished – these were called ordinances.

Cromwell ruled strictly in a Puritan style and these ordinances transformed society in many ways, for example:

- Swearing, duelling and cockfighting were banned.

- Selling goods on a Sunday was banned.

- There were fines for non-attendance at church.

- Unsuitable clergy (priests) were dismissed.

- The celebration of Christmas was banned.

- The legal system and Poor Laws were reformed.

- Trade agreements were drawn up and peace was made with European countries such as Holland and Portugal.

New groups emerge

So, for many people the world had been turned upside down. A major transformation to parliamentary control was in progress and Cromwell had been trying out different ideas as to how to rule the new republic, or Commonwealth as it was also called. Ordinary people also had new ideas as to how the country should be run and various groups emerged, such as the Levellers, Diggers and Quakers. Some of these ideas were not necessarily new but had been kept secret for years. The difference was that now, importantly, under the Protectorate, people felt free to talk about them, write about them and also to put them into practice. One of the most important groups at that time was the Levellers who felt betrayed by Cromwell and stated that he had not delivered the changes they had fought for in the Civil War, such as more representation in Parliament. The Quakers are still an active religious group in existence today. Of the following groups, the Levellers, Diggers and Quakers were the largest and most influential.

The Levellers

Led by John Lilburne, they believed in some revolutionary ideas, such as that the country should be ruled by a Parliament which should be elected every two years and that real power lay with the people. They said that Parliament should represent everyone, not just the rich, so everyone over the age of 21 was to be allowed to vote – but not women and servants (who they felt would be too easily influenced). They also wanted the different kinds of Puritans to be allowed to worship freely and law courts to work more fairly and cheaply. Some shopkeepers and apprentices in London were Levellers but most of their support came from ordinary soldiers and some officers in Cromwell's army. They promoted their ideas in pamphlets such as the *Agreement of the People*.

The Diggers

Led by Gerrard Winstanley, they believed that poverty could be solved if the land was shared and all men were equal so that no one person should rule over another. In 1649 a group of men and women took over the common land on St George's Hill in Walton-on-Thames. They believed that everyone had an equal right to share and farm the land. The experiment lasted for a year until local landowners saw them as a threat to their power and destroyed their homes and forced them off the land.

The Quakers

Founded by George Fox and his followers, they were also called the Society of Friends. They believed that all people were equal, calling one another 'thou' and keeping their hats on in the presence of their social superiors (viewed at the time as being disrespectful and too familiar). They were seen as dangerous because they might undermine authority. This led to them being persecuted. They had a vision of brotherly love where the spirit of God would inspire people and so there would be no real need for organised churches with set services. By 1700 there were some 40,000 Quakers in Britain and they also travelled abroad – for example, William Penn founded the colony of Pennsylvania in America.

The Ranters

They were a small group of people who believed they could do no wrong and were especially chosen by God. They did not follow the Bible, but they obeyed the Holy Spirit inside themselves.

The Muggletonians

This group was led by Ludowicke Muggleton and John Reeve. They believed in the coming of God's kingdom on earth and also that God had given them the right and power to decide who should be damned and saved.

The Fifth Monarchists

These people believed that Christ would rule the earth as the 'Fifth Monarch' having won the battle between good and evil. Their job was to make England suitable for Christ to rule and they wanted a Parliament of godly people, not elected MPs, because they saw it as more important to be God-fearing than to be a gentleman.

Reactions and opposition to Cromwellian rule

There were four key stages during Cromwell's rule when he experimented with his power. There has been a lot of discussion about the type of ruler that Cromwell was – for example, some historians view him as a dictator and tyrant whilst others do not, pointing out that he took the role of Protector and refused the role of king that was offered to him by Parliament in February 1657.

Stage 1: 1653 The Rule of the Saints (the Little or Barebones Parliament)

This Parliament lasted for just six months; nothing was achieved due to lack of agreement between its members (see page 116).

Stage 2: 1653 The Lord Protector

The power was handed back to Cromwell and he was given the official title of Lord Protector of England, Scotland and Ireland. He had to rule with a new Parliament. The old problems were still present – such as not enough money being voted to pay for the army. People were still unsettled and suspicious of Cromwell and his army. Parliament was therefore dissolved, there was a Royalist revolt and Cromwell had to use his army again to put it down.

Stage 3: 1655 The major-generals (Sword Rule)

England was divided into eleven districts and each one was controlled by a major-general whose job it was to keep the peace. They had to collect taxes and keep law and order. This caused resentment and unhappiness. The major-generals were strict Puritans who stopped people enjoying themselves. They were sacked in 1657.

Stage 4: 1657 King Oliver I ?

Another Parliament was called and the House of Lords was restored. Cromwell was offered the crown but refused it because he did not believe in the monarchy. The country still faced money problems.

In 1658 Cromwell outwardly appeared strong and effective after having been offered the throne; threats from supporters of the Royalist cause now seemed to have died down. He had successfully put down any opposition to the republic and continued to be a major political force at home and abroad.

Successes abroad

He was especially strong abroad:

- England had defeated the Dutch in a naval war and gained an alliance.

- Spain had been defeated near Dunkirk.

- Jamaica had been gained in the Caribbean.

- Sweden, Portugal and France became allies.

As the Earl of Clarendon, a Royalist supporter (also known an Edward Hyde), said at the time, 'His greatness at home was but a shadow of his greatness abroad.'

Successes at home

At home Cromwell also achieved many positive things.

- There was no religious persecution.

- Trade was flourishing.

- The law and education systems were reformed.

- For many ordinary people life was better, particularly after the six hard years of the Civil War.

However, military life and political troubles affected his health, and in August 1658 his favourite daughter, Elizabeth, died. Cromwell mourned her death and never really recovered. On 3 September 1658 he died having appointed his son, Richard, as the next protector. A period of chaos gripped the country as it soon became clear that Richard Cromwell was incapable of ruling, earning himself the nickname Tumbledown Dick (although it is possible that Richard inherited his problems, such as accumulated debt and the Spanish war, from his father). The army leaders were worried by the lack of leadership and recalled the Rump Parliament in May 1659, forcing him to resign. In October 1659 the army dismissed the Rump, suspicious of it. The Rump tried to assert its power over the army by dismissing some officers, but the army were having none of that. Finally, in 1660, General Monck who commanded the army occupying Scotland marched south to London. The House of Lords was restored along with the bishops of the Church of England and it seemed that the only solution was to invite Charles II back to England to claim his crown.

Activity time

1. Make a table to show Cromwell's good points and bad points as a leader, using the information and sources available in this chapter.

2. Read Sources C to F carefully. Using these sources and the table produced in Question 1, as well as your own knowledge, write an essay-style answer explaining whether you think Cromwell was a harsh or fair ruler. Be sure to back up your ideas with appropriate evidence. Write about one side of an A4 sheet.

SOURCE C

We have lost a Captain, a Shield, the Head, an Heir of Restraint, the Breath of our Nostrils, an Healer, a Shepherd, a Father and a Nursing Father, a Cornerstone, a Builder, a Watchman, an Eye, a Saviour, a Steersman and Rector, a Pilot and common Husband.

From the sermon of a Puritan preacher, George Lawrence, October 1658, following the death of Oliver Cromwell.

SOURCE D

His wisdom and piety in things divine, his prudence in management of the civil affairs and conduct of the military, and admirable successes in all, made him a Prince among the people of God...

An extract from an obituary to Cromwell in the Commonwealth Mercury *newspaper, 9 September 1658.*

SOURCE E

That the anti-Christ, the Babylon, the Great Dragon or Man of Sin Oliver Cromwell at Whitehall must be pulled down.

An extract from a sermon by London preacher, Mr Rogers, a Puritan extremist.

SOURCE F

The Government shall be in the Parliament and the People of England, and a single person qualified with such instructions as the Parliament shall think fit.

Parliament's view of Cromwell in 1654 – its members wanted more power and were critical of his position of authority.

Digging deeper

Samuel Pepys' view of history

Samuel Pepys, a government official working for the navy, began on 1 January 1660 one of the most famous historical sources available today – his diary. For about nine years he made entries about not just his own life but the great events of the time. This enables us as historians to gain a clear insight into the understanding of the key events of the times, such as the restoration of Charles II in 1660 and the move back to rule by monarchy.

SOURCE G

A portrait by an unknown contemporary artist of Charles II at the time of his restoration.

SOURCE H

23 May 1660. The king ... came on board ... we weighed anchor, and with a fresh gale and most happy weather we set sail for England ... he fell in discourse [started talking] of his escape from Worcester. Where it made me weep to hear the stories he told of his difficulties he passed through.

25 May 1660. And so on shore when the king did, who was received with all imaginable love and respect ... infinite crowd of people and the gallantry of the horsemen, citizens and noblemen of all sorts.

Written in May 1660 when Pepys was on board the ship that brought Charles II out of exile.

Charles II had put up with eleven years of hardship while in exile in Holland, which had made him cynical, questioning and negative. He was intelligent and interested in science, although not particularly hard working. However, he had the ability to get on well with ordinary people. One clear aim he had was to get back his throne. He knew he would have to rule with Parliament and co-operate with the ruling classes to do this. There were many problems facing him at this time and it was going to be difficult to please everyone.

2 May 1660. The king's letter was read in the House [of Commons], wherein he submits himself and all things to them ... The City of London have put out a Declaration wherein they disclaim their owning any other government but that of a king, Lords, and Commons.

9 May 1660. Certain news that the king was proclaimed yesterday with great pomp; a great joy to us all, for which God be praised.

25 May 1660. The king was received by General Monck with all imaginable love and respect at his entrance upon the land at Dover. The Mayor presented him from the town a very rich Bible, which he took and said it was the thing that he loved above all things in the world.

29 May 1660. This day it is thought, the king do enter the City of London.

31 May 1660. This day the month ends, and the world in merry mood because of the king's coming.

1 June 1660. Parliament ordered 29 May, the king's birthday, to be kept forever as a day of thanksgiving for our redemption from tyranny.

2 June 1660. Captain Holland tells me how every man goes to the Lord Mayor to set down their names, as such as do accept of His Majesty's pardon, and showed me a certificate under the Lord Mayor's hand that he had done so.

7 July 1660. To Whitehall to chapel where I heard very good music, the first time that I remember ever to have heard organs and singing-men in surplices in my life ...

Extracts from Pepys' diary.

Charles II did not want revenge against his enemies but it was agreed that those people who had signed his father's death warrant (regicides) should be punished. Some of the most important of his father's enemies were already dead, such as Cromwell, but this did not stop Charles! Cromwell's body was dug up and his head was stuck on a pole outside Westminster Hall for all to see. Those enemies who were still living were executed, such as Thomas Harrison who was one of Cromwell's major-generals. Many Royalists who had lost land in the Civil War got it back.

Question time

Read Sources H and I which contain extracts from Pepys' diary. Answer the questions which follow.

1   From the tone of his diary, do you think that Pepys was friendly, hostile or neutral to Charles II? Give supporting evidence from the sources to back up your ideas.

2   Suggest ways in which Pepys' diary is useful to historians studying this period. Give evidence from the sources to back up your ideas.

3   In what ways do we need to be careful about using evidence such as a diary when studying the past? Use the sources and your own knowledge to answer this.

4   How can we check the accuracy of Pepys' diary?

5   How reliable are diaries as evidence?

What was the Restoration?

By 1660 most people could see that the attempts to rule without a monarch had failed and there was the danger of another civil war. General George Monck therefore decided with Parliament to invite Charles I's son Charles to return to England from exile in Europe to become King Charles II. Charles was very intelligent and knew full well that he could only rule successfully and be a strong king by working alongside the nobles and gentry in Parliament.

This period is known as the Restoration because there was also a renewal of fun, the arts, light and life. There was a backlash against the strict Puritan lifestyle forced on the country by Cromwell (see page 116) and people started to enjoy themselves again; for example, festivals and celebrations started up again, theatres reopened, music, dancing, gambling and painting were once again enjoyed by ordinary people. Styles of dress became more extravagant – court ladies wore beautiful and ornate dresses. Coffee houses became popular in London as places to be seen. As well as this, in 1662, laws were made banning all religious services except those of the Church of England. Finally Charles II himself personified the Restoration by his own elaborate lifestyle, enjoying 'a mad range of pleasure'. He liked gambling and horseracing as well as having a number of mistresses, such as the famous actress Nell Gwynn. She became Charles' mistress in 1669, aged nineteen, and she had two sons by him. She was always very popular with the people, describing herself as 'the Protestant Whore'. She was sometimes painted partly nude which would never have been allowed under Puritan rule. On his deathbed Charles II said, 'Let not poor Nelly starve', and his brother, James II, honoured this instruction by giving her a pension of £1500 a year. Charles had fourteen illegitimate children (though none born to him and the queen legitimately). He certainly lived up to his nickname of 'the Merry Monarch'!

Two great events

There were two important events that affected London quite early on in Charles II's reign. They both had an enormous impact on the ordinary population.

The Great Plague, 1665

August	19,046
September	26,219
October	14,373

Approximate number of deaths from the Great Plague in London, 1665 (calculated from the Diseases and Casualties List for London of that year).

London was a more cheerful place under Charles II but it was also quite dangerous – disease was everywhere, the smell was disgusting and heaps of rubbish were piled high in the streets, providing a breeding ground for black rats. The fleas that lived on these rats carried bubonic plague. The deadly plague had never fully gone since the Black Death of 1348–9 and there were often repeated outbreaks. In 1665 there was a massive outbreak in London and nearly 70,000 people died. The disease was highly infectious and the victims often died within hours of catching it. Those that could, fled London. Houses where people had the plague were locked and barred; those inside were only allowed out at night when the carts went through the streets collecting the dead and the famous cry was heard, 'Bring out your dead.' By the end of 1665, even though a cure had not been found by doctors, the plague ebbed away due to brown rats driving out the black rats. The brown rats did not carry the plague.

The Great Fire of London, 1666

Between 2 and 6 September 1666, a fierce fire swept through London, England's most densely populated city. The summer of 1666 was extremely hot and by autumn the timber-framed buildings were bone dry. During the early hours of 2 September a fire broke out in the house of Thomas Farynor, a baker in Pudding Lane. Farynor and his family escaped by jumping from an upstairs window, but their servant refused to jump and was burnt to death, becoming the first casualty of the Great Fire. A strong easterly wind blew the fire into neighbouring Thames Street and the fire soon spread – even buildings on London Bridge caught fire. By Monday 3 September, the fire had reached the centre of the city and people started to flee London. The fire burnt itself out on the fifth day, but by then most of the older part of the city of London had been destroyed, making thousands homeless.

There was no fire brigade at the time. Chains of men passed leather buckets of water from hand to hand to put out the fire – even King Charles and his brother, James, were involved. Other people used small hand pumps called 'squirts' and long hooks to pull the thatch off the timber houses. Charles II ordered that London be rebuilt in brick and stone. The architect, Sir Christopher Wren, drew up plans and designs for a new city with wider streets, proper sewers and squares. This never completely happened because people who had lost their homes wanted them replaced exactly as they had been. However, Wren did design and have built about 60 new churches, including St Paul's Cathedral which had been a casualty in the fire. It took 35 years to build. A tall column called the Monument now marks the spot where the fire began.

Religion in Charles II's reign

Although England appeared to be a much merrier place under Charles II religion still posed a serious problem. There was a feeling of deep suspicion towards Roman Catholics in Parliament and around the country. This was not helped by the fact that Charles' Portuguese wife, Catherine of Braganza, was Catholic. The Church of England continued to get stronger and in 1673 a Test Act was passed which stopped Catholics from holding government jobs or posts in the army or navy.

As time went on and Charles failed to produce a legitimate heir, it became apparent that his Catholic brother, James, might inherit the throne. Anti-Catholic feeling deepened and, in 1678, a clergyman called Titus Oates informed the Privy Council of a plot by Catholics to kill the king and put James on the throne. This developed over a period of years until finally Oates was revealed as a liar. In May 1685, Oates was sentenced to pay a large fine and every year was locked in a pillory and flogged.

Charles II's death, 1685

When Charles II died in 1685 he left no legitimate children to inherit the throne. It was therefore his brother James, Duke of York, who took the throne. James was a Catholic and in the first year of his reign there were rebellions, such as Monmouth's Rebellion. This uprising soon failed due to lack of effective support and weak leadership by the Duke of Monmouth himself who was Charles II's illegitimate son. James showed absolutely no mercy to the rebels; Judge Jeffreys held the Bloody Assize (court) where 300 were executed and 800 were transported to the West Indies.

James ruled along similar lines to his father, Charles I, believing in himself as a king appointed by God and ruling by divine right (see page 96). He now set about giving freedom to Catholics. This set the scene for future problems.

The Glorious Revolution

James II's downfall

There were a number of key reasons why James II lost the throne in the Glorious Revolution of 1688:

- In 1685 James pushed ahead with plans to give full rights to Catholics and negate the Test Act of 1673.

- He wanted to transform England back to a Catholic country; this desire was summed up in his statement of 1687 that 'all his subjects as members of the Catholic Church'.

- In 1687 James dissolved Parliament, which was made up of members of the Church of England.

- In 1688 James' Catholic wife, Mary of Modena, gave birth to a baby boy. Some of James' opponents, such as the Bishop of London, believed that the queen had not really been pregnant at all and that the boy had been smuggled into the royal bed in a warming pan!

The birth of a son to Mary of Modena meant that there was a male, Catholic heir to the throne who would continue James' policies, as the next claimant to the throne had been James' Protestant daughter, Mary, through his first marriage to Anne Hyde (see family tree on page 140). There was concern that James was a Catholic; he was particularly open about it after his second marriage. Before the birth of his son, there had been great relief that, whatever happened, his heir would be a Protestant. There was now a sense of shock at the birth of a son who would be above his half-sister in the line of succession and was Catholic. Obviously this pleased the Catholics!

Why was the revolution 'glorious'?

A revolution often involves fighting, battles and bloodshed on a grand scale; however in 1688 this was not the case! As a group of senior members of Parliament were opposed to James' policies and to the 'warming pan baby' becoming the next Catholic king, they sent a message to Mary's husband, William, in Holland. William landed with an army on 5 November 1688 at Torbay in Devon. Instead of marching quickly to face his invader, James hesitated because his most trusted general, John Churchill, and his younger daughter, Anne, had both deserted him.

William marched towards London. James was allowed to escape down the Thames towards France with his wife and baby son. On the way he carried out a feeble act of defiance by throwing the Great Seal, needed for all official documents, into the river. In this way, James was forced to give up his throne without bloodshed – there were no battles and no executions.

England was now ruled jointly by William and Mary. However, the problem remained as to who exactly would rule the country – Parliament or the monarchy? It was still to be decided how much power each side would have.

The consequences of the Glorious Revolution

The main impact of the Glorious Revolution was that Parliament now held the key to power. It was to decide how the monarchy was to reign and, in the years immediately following the Glorious Revolution, Parliament passed a series of laws, headed by the Bill of Rights of 1689, some of which form the basis of how we are governed today.

1689: The Bill of Rights

The main points were:

- The crown could only be inherited by a Protestant.
- MPs could say what they wanted – i.e. they had freedom of speech.
- Parliament had to agree to all taxes being imposed.
- The king was not allowed a standing army during peacetime.
- The monarchy was not allowed to interfere with trials.
- Parliament was to make all laws.

Parliament also passed a number of laws which set the foundations for the future:

- An annual sum of money was to be given to the monarchy – called the Civil List.
- There was to be freedom of worship.
- Press censorship was ended.
- Expenditure was to be controlled by Parliament
- In 1694 the Triennial Act was passed which stated that Parliament was to be elected at least every three years.

The balance of power

A major consequence of the revolution was that a balance of power was created between the monarchy and Parliament.

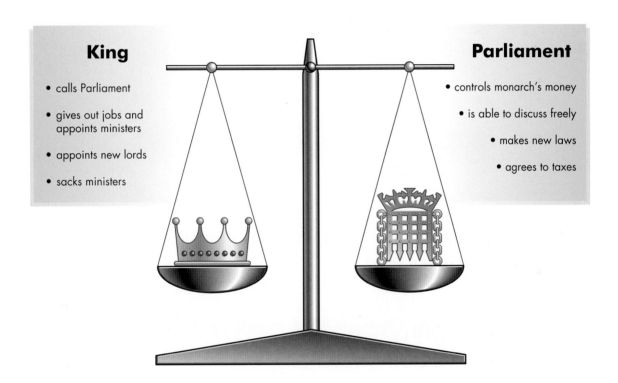

King
- calls Parliament
- gives out jobs and appoints ministers
- appoints new lords
- sacks ministers

Parliament
- controls monarch's money
- is able to discuss freely
- makes new laws
- agrees to taxes

For the first time in English history there was a balance of power between Parliament and the monarchy, which remains today.

As a direct consequence of these events, Parliament was given increased power in the running of the country. There was a triumphant transition to joint parliamentary and monarchical rule, the first time this had ever happened in the history of England. In essence, this has remained up to the present day.

Assessment section

Choose one of the following questions and answer it in an essay. You could also do your own research using your school library or the Internet to help you with your answer.

1 'To what extent was the Civil War a turning point in English history?'

   Use ideas and information from this chapter and your own knowledge to answer this question.

2 'How far did life in England change under Cromwell's rule?'

   Use ideas and information from this chapter and your own knowledge to answer this question.

3 Consider the following terms:
   • transformation / transition
   • divine right of kings
   • regicide
   • Protectorate / Commonwealth
   • Restoration
   • Glorious Revolution

   Write a short paragraph about each term to explain what it means.

4 Organise a class debate on the motion 'This House believes that Charles I should not have been executed'. Write a speech either proposing the motion, or opposing it.

Further reading

Dr Anne Millard, *Britain Through the Ages: Stuarts* (Evans Brothers Ltd, 1995)

The Making of the UK: Stability and Unity

Today England, Wales, Scotland and Northern Ireland are reigned over by one monarch and by one main Parliament. This unity is symbolised by the title 'United Kingdom of Great Britain and Northern Ireland', or UK for short. In the seventeenth century this was not the case and what happened then has determined how we are today.

So what brought about this unity? When considering this issue historians ask various questions. What did each side stand to gain? Was it agreed in order to secure lasting peace or was it arranged for financial reasons? Did the English Parliament support the idea of unity in order to have greater powers over the other countries?

England, Scotland, Wales and Ireland, 1485.

Independent
Most land ruled by local lords and chiefs (some of whom were English)

SCOTLAND

Independent
Ruled by James IV

N
↑

IRELAND

ENGLAND

WALES

Ruled by Henry VII

Independent
but acknowledged the new Tudor king Henry VII due to his Welsh lineage

The kingdom united

In this chapter we shall look at the process of unification and how each country – England, Wales, Scotland and Ireland – became involved in a course of political action. The reasons for unification are many and varied and involve such factors as land, religion, future peace and stability and trade. We shall look at each country individually and consider its history and reasons for unification and ask whether, even today, they are totally satisfied with the outcome of this historical process.

Look carefully at the maps on this page and page 130 and make a note of the differences between them.

By 1750 the Kingdom was effectively United – Acts of Union had taken place with both Wales and Scotland.

SCOTLAND

Ruled by British King

Ruled by British King

IRELAND

ENGLAND

WALES

Ruled by George II

Ruled by British King

N

The United Kingdom, 1750.

Ireland – a solveable problem?

Control of the land

English monarchs had been ruling Ireland since the early Middle Ages (1155), calling themselves 'Kings of Ireland'. But, at the start of the sixteenth century, most of Ireland was controlled by the Irish people themselves, except for a small area around Dublin called 'the Pale', which was still run by the English. At this time, the area 'beyond the Pale' was controlled by local lords and chiefs who ruled the rest of Ireland as if they were kings. These lords had inherited land from their ancestors, some of whom had been Norman barons, who had been given land in the twelfth century following the Norman Conquest. Henry VII aimed to increase English control over Ireland with the passing of Poynings Law in 1494 (see page 15).

The Irish people had their own culture – language, poetry, customs and laws. Local chiefs were often at war with each other, which made life very unsettled for many people. Most ordinary people were farmers who kept cattle or grew crops. The English did not understand the Irish; they thought of them as uncivilised and barbaric. Similarly, the Irish hated the English (see Sources A and B).

SOURCE A

The Irish live like beasts ... are more uncivil, more uncleanly, more barbarous in their customs ... than in any part of the world.

An English view of the Irish in the sixteenth century.

SOURCE B

The greatest murderers and the proudest people in all Europe and I am surprised that God tolerates them so long in power ... I shall say no more, because I should use all my ink and paper on this subject.

An Irish view of the English in the sixteenth century.

Religious differences

Another area that was to cause great conflict between England and Ireland was religion. The Irish rejection of the Reformation of the Church during Henry VIII's reign (1509–47) brought with it many problems. Although in 1534 there was a revolt against English rule and changes in the Church, by 1541 the Irish were forced to accept Henry as king. Nevertheless, most people remained Catholic. During the reign of Henry's son, Edward VI (1547–53), the Reformation gathered pace. The first of a series of English laws were put in place. These tried to make people agree to the beliefs of the Church of England and went against the Catholics (see Chapter 3). There were very few Protestants in Ireland; it was mainly a Catholic country and so the Protestant changes could not be enforced.

The French, who were mainly Catholic too, hoped to work with the Irish in any future battles or conflicts with England. The French did what they could to encourage the Catholics in Ireland and, with the accession of the Catholic Mary I in 1553, France encouraged the Irish even more, as they gained more support for their Catholic cause and their beliefs from the English crown.

Under Elizabeth's reign the Religious Settlement (see page 88) was accepted by an Irish Parliament but again it could not be enforced. At the same time a strong force of Jesuit missionaries from Europe worked hard in Ireland and it remained a Catholic country. With this background the English people's natural mistrust of the Irish was to turn into hatred due to the problems of religion.

The seizure of land

Another issue that fuelled this already growing hatred between the Irish and the English was land inheritance. English settlers had been sent to Ireland by Elizabeth I in the sixteenth century. There were many uprisings by the Irish against these English settlers towards the end of her reign.

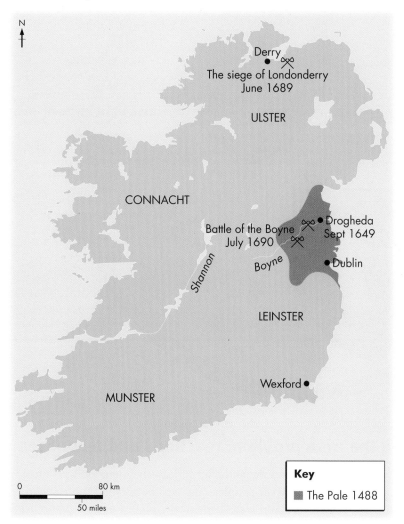

A map of Ireland showing 'the Pale' and the sites of major battles.

N

Derry
The siege of Londonderry
June 1689

ULSTER

CONNACHT

Battle of the Boyne
July 1690
Drogheda
Sept 1649

Boyne
Dublin

Shannon

LEINSTER

Wexford

MUNSTER

0   80 km

50 miles

Key

■ The Pale 1488

In 1607, during the reign of James I (1603–25), the English decided to send 'civilised' Protestant people to inhabit Ireland and bring about change there. This is called the Plantation of Ulster. English and Scottish farming families were given small plantations of about 1000 acres. These farmers introduced new farming methods: cattle were sold off and crops grown instead. The Irish were employed as labourers on the land they had once farmed themselves. This change in farming meant that ownership of land changed during this time. In 1603, 90 per cent of land was owned by Roman Catholics; by 1750, they owned only 5 per cent. By 1640, over 30,000 Protestant Scots and English were living in Ireland. The English Parliament's land policies also affected the ratio of Catholics to Protestants in Ireland. In 1600 more than 90 per cent of the population was Catholic, but by 1750 this figure had dropped to about 75 per cent.

The cycle of hatred.

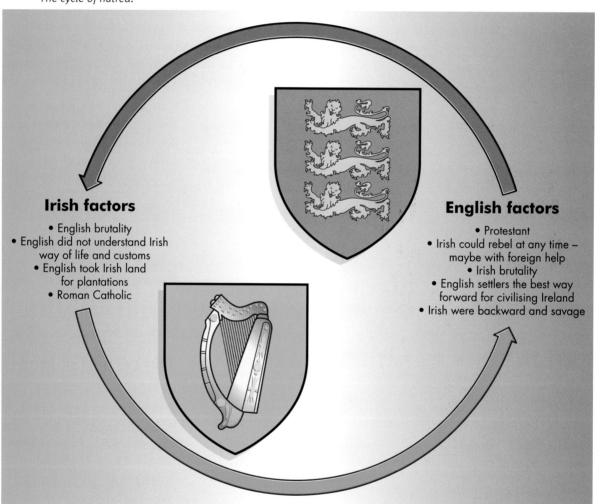

Irish factors
- English brutality
- English did not understand Irish way of life and customs
- English took Irish land for plantations
- Roman Catholic

English factors
- Protestant
- Irish could rebel at any time – maybe with foreign help
- Irish brutality
- English settlers the best way forward for civilising Ireland
- Irish were backward and savage

Settling the Irish problem: reactions and responses

As we have already seen, the English believed that they needed to control and civilise Ireland and the Irish people. This was because of the issue of religion and the fact that Ireland was strategically placed and could be used for a possible European invasion of England. During the seventeenth and eighteenth centuries there were various attempts to stabilise Ireland.

James I's policies (1603–25)

During the early part of James I's reign, the question of what to do with the rebellious Irish was a difficult problem for him. What were his choices and what were his aims? What risks would he be prepared to take in his attempt to sort out the difficulties there?

Activity time

1   Think about how you would have solved the problems facing James, and what would have been the consequences of your intended action. Consider these options:

- Subdue the rebellious Irish with force (e.g. a strong army presence).
- Take over their land and send Protestants to convert them.
- Come to a compromise (both sides agreeing), which would allow the Irish to keep their land, but on condition that they would become Protestants.

You may want to discuss this as a class or in groups. Then read the following account of what actually happened below. Do you think that James I's policies would help secure a lasting peace in Ireland?

James I and his advisers put in motion the Plantation of Ulster in 1607 (see page 132). This occurred after the Earls of Tyrone and Tyrconnel, who had been defeated by the Earl of Essex following a rebellion, fled to Europe in 1607. The English government thought that the Irish were both uncivilised and dangerous. They believed the only way to bring Ireland under control was to send Scottish and English Protestants to settle there. The English government seized the lands belonging to Tyrone and Tyrconnel, and then proceded to sack the Irish Catholic landlords and replace them with Protestants. These new landlords arranged for Scottish and English Protestants to settle on the land which had previously been farmed by Irish Catholics.

The Irish Catholics resented this Ulster Plantation. This did not solve the problems in Ireland and led to more trouble in the future.

Charles I's policies and the Irish Rebellion of 1641

In 1641 the Irish Rebellion took place. The Irish Catholics in Ulster feared that the English Protestant Parliament was about to pass anti-Catholic laws. Nearly 3000 Protestant settlers were killed as the Irish Catholics attacked Protestant farms and murdered their owners. Thousands more were driven into hiding.

When news of this rebellion reached London there were rumours that there was a Catholic plot to destroy Parliament. Charles I hoped that England would unite against the Irish Rebellion and that his argument with Parliament would fade into the background. The king asked Parliament for money to put down the uprising but it would not give it to him. Parliament thought he would use the army to stamp out any opposition to him at home. The Irish problem remained unsolved until 1649.

Cromwell's policies

When Oliver Cromwell took over the running of England in 1649 he decided it was time to put a stop to the Irish uprising for good. He, along with a significant number of Puritans, was of the view that Charles I and Henrietta Maria had been behind the massacre of Protestant settlers in 1641. They believed that Charles had been a secret Catholic. This view was strengthened after Charles' execution in 1649, when Irish Catholics and Royalists joined forces and rebelled against Parliamentary rule.

A Parliamentarian army defeated the rebels before Cromwell arrived in Ireland.

SOURCE C

The Irish uprising of 1641; a contemporary Protestant playing card depicting the massacre of Protestants on the bridge at Portadown by Irish Catholic rebels.

This did not stop Cromwell marching up and down the east coast besieging towns and killing Catholics. A number of massacres took place and these are still remembered today by the Irish with much bitterness. Cromwell believed that it was the will of God that he should kill the Irish: 'Blood and ruin shall befall them.' The worst of the massacres occurred at Drogheda, north of Dublin, in September 1649. Over 2000 people died when Cromwell and his troops laid siege to the town which had refused to surrender. Wexford was another town where many inhabitants were massacred.

SOURCE D

In the heat of action I forbade to spare any that were in arms in the town: and I think that night they put to the sword about two thousand men ... I ordered the steeple of St Peter's Church to be fired. One of them was heard to say in the midst of the flames '... God damn me, God confound me; I burn I burn'. I am persuaded that this is a righteous judgment of God upon these barbarous wretches, who have soaked their hands in so much innocent blood; and that it will prevent the shedding of blood for the future.

Oliver Cromwell writing about Drogheda on 17 September 1649.

SOURCE E

According to Thomas Wood, when the people took refuge in the churches, Cromwell's soldiers pursued them up the towers, holding the children before them as shields. After which, they went into the vaults to slaughter the women hidden there.

From Ireland Story *by Desiree Edwards-Rees (1967).*

At first all Catholic priests who were caught were instantly killed. Later Cromwell sent captured priests to a special camp on a Scottish island as punishment. Cromwell also gave orders for hundreds of Irish rebels to be sent to work as slaves on the sugar plantations in the Caribbean. Irish landowners lost their land to soldiers and Protestants. Protestants controlled all of Ireland even though most of the people living there were Catholic.

When Cromwell had crushed the rebellion, a third of the people of Ireland were dead and two-thirds of the land was owned by English Protestants. Irish resistance had been quashed but an even deeper hatred was created and even today, to many Catholics, Cromwell is known as 'the curse of Ireland'.

Question time

Look carefully at Source C.

1 What message does the picture give to the people living at the time?

2 What message and information does it give to an historian studying this period? Explain your answers carefully using Source C and your own knowledge.

3 Using Sources C, D and E, reply to the following statement in as much detail as possible:

'In the seventeenth century, the English treated the Irish harshly.'

Consider whether this statement is a fact or an opinion.

James II (1685–8) and William III of Orange (1688–1702)

When James II was on the throne from 1685 to 1688, Irish Catholics enjoyed more freedom than they had done in over 300 years. James appointed the Earl of Tyrconnell as Lord Lieutenant of Ireland. He was an Irish Catholic. Catholics could now worship freely and hold senior appointments, such as that of judge; they could also sit in the London Parliament as MPs. By 1688 James had amassed a large Catholic army in Ireland led by a Catholic general. The Irish saw it as a chance for revenge.

When James II lost his English throne in 1688 (see page 126) he first travelled to France where King Louis XIV, a Catholic, helped him raise an army. James landed in Kinsale along with his large French army and joined forces with his Irish Catholic supporters. He called a Parliament in Dublin and it soon passed laws, which reversed the settlement imposed on Ireland by Cromwell in 1649. Land was to be taken back from the English and Scottish Protestant settlers. Protestants were angry and scared – they retreated into the fortified city of Londonderry.

The Siege of Londonderry, 1689

James II and his armies attacked Ulster in the north of Ireland, where Protestant settlers lived alongside Irish Catholics. There he laid siege to Londonderry.

The Protestants had fortified the city heavily in case of such an attack by James II and his supporters, having been concerned about the large Catholic army for some time. As James II and his army approached, the Protestants shut the doors in the city's walls and refused to allow James II and his troops to enter. James II was determined to take the city. He planned to starve Londonderry into submission as he camped his troops outside the city gates and prevented all supplies from reaching the Protestants. King William III sent ships and supplies to the city to help the people of Londonderry, but James had blocked off the harbour. In an attempt to stay alive the Protestants were reduced to eating rats, mice, dogs, candles and drinking the blood of horses! Finally, William's ships broke through the harbour barrier and brought in food and ammunition, bringing the 105-day siege to an end. Fifteen thousand Protestants had died from starvation and nearly all the city's children had died. The Protestants' motto during the siege was 'No surrender'. This phrase is still used by Protestant loyalists in Northern Ireland today.

It is interesting to note that Londonderry was called Derry until it was colonised by the City of London under James I. It then became Londonderry and to this day few Catholics like to use the longer name because it reminds them of the control the English have over the city.

The Battle of the Boyne, 1690

Following the Siege of Londonderry, William decided that some firm action was necessary to defeat James II and so on 14 June 1690 he landed in Ireland with some 15,000 troops. On 1 July he confronted James II's army at the River Boyne. William had a larger army which also contained Dutch Blue Guards who were some of the best soldiers in Europe at that time. The battle was fought all day until, in late afternoon, James II admitted defeat and fled the battlefield; William suffered only light casualties. Shortly afterwards James fled Ireland for France. So, as far as the Protestants were concerned, 'King Billy' had prevented a 'Papist' take-over. The Irish Catholics were defeated finally at Aughrim in 1691.

In the aftermath of the Battle of the Boyne, English troops soon took control of the rest of Ireland. The Protestant English were now in control and Ireland was a conquered land. William had been prepared to allow Catholics to practise their religion and keep their land but Parliament had its own view. The Catholics were treated harshly and, although rebellion was over for the time being, the grievances over religion and land remained.

By 1714, Catholics owned only 7 per cent of the land. No Catholic was allowed to be a lawyer, soldier or MP. They were forbidden to attend Mass, to attend Catholic schools or to send their children abroad to be educated. Schools and universities in Ireland were officially Protestant. Catholics were not even allowed to own a horse that cost more than £5! Thus the Battle of the Boyne was a very important event for Protestants and to this day pictures of 'King Billy' can be seen on walls and banners in Protestant parts of Northern Ireland. Today, the Orange Order is an organisation of Northern Ireland Protestants. Members call themselves Orangemen after William of Orange and still march to commemorate the Siege of Londonderry in 1689 and the Battle of the Boyne in 1690. Catholics in Ulster march to protest against the injustices that followed.

SOURCE F

The Battle of the Boyne in 1690.

Activity time

1 Today, Irish Protestants and Irish Catholics regard the Battle of the Boyne in 1690 as an important event in Irish history. Explain why you think this is so.

2 Using all the information you have just read about the policies of Parliament and the monarchs of England with regard to Ireland, assess the English attempts to control Ireland by answering the following question:

'Which person contributed most to the problems by 1700 – James I, Charles I, Cromwell, James II or William III?'

Construct a spider diagram for each person to aid you in your analysis and then explain the reason for your answer.

Unity with Scotland

Up until 1603, England and Scotland were totally separate countries. Each had its own monarch, Parliament, Privy Council and Church (Kirk). However, when Queen Elizabeth died without leaving an heir to the English throne, her cousin (and the son of Mary, Queen of Scots), James VI of Scotland, also became James I of England. From then on the two countries were to have the same monarch, but they shared little else.

James I (1603–25): King of Scotland and England

As James I was monarch of both England and Scotland, he promised the Scots that he would return to Scotland every third year. However, in his 22-year reign, he returned there only once! During his reign, the Scots were treated as foreigners – for example, merchants were made to pay import taxes on goods they brought into England. The Scots were not given trading rights with the ever-expanding English empire. In fact, the English actively prevented the Scots from obtaining an empire.

Charles I and the Scottish Rebellion, 1637

Some people – especially Puritans and other Protestants – believed (wrongly) that Charles I was a secret Catholic. He was an Anglican but, with the help of Archbishop Laud, began to reintroduce a Catholic style of worship in England (see page 98). Charles ordered the Scottish Presbyterian Kirk to use the Prayer Book of the Church of England. The discussions for the introduction of the new Prayer Book were held only with the Scottish bishops. They did not involve the General Assembly of the Kirk, the group that appointed all the ministers and key members of the Kirk.

In 1637 riots broke out during church services, including one at St Giles' Cathedral in Edinburgh, over the use of the new Prayer Book (see page 99). By 1638 a National Covenant was drawn up and signed by thousands of people. They became known as the Covenanters and promised to defend their Kirk against Charles I and his bishops. The Covenanters amassed an army and marched into England. This is called the Scottish Rebellion. Thus Charles I faced an expensive war – something he really did not want! Charles I appealed to Parliament to raise money for an army, but Parliament refused his request. Instead the king negotiated a somewhat humiliating treaty with the Scots which meant giving into them and their demands.

The Civil War (1642–9)

In order to gain support during the Civil War in 1643, Parliamentarian John Pym negotiated with Scotland, promising that if Parliament won the war it would set up a Presbyterian Church in England similar to the Scottish Kirk. The Scots were sympathetic to the Parliamentarian cause, mindful of Charles I's treatment of them over the introduction of the new Prayer Book in 1637. The Scots were also keen to use the situation of the Civil War to gain as much as possible for their own purposes and would go to any lengths to achieve their aims. With Scottish support, Parliament defeated the Royalists at Marston Moor in July 1644. The Royalists suffered further defeats and in 1646 Charles I gave himself up to the Scots when he heard news of the surrender of his main stronghold in Oxford. Parliamentarian troops now had the upper hand and the war was over. Charles and Scotland were unable to secure a treaty, which resulted in the Scots handing over Charles to Parliament in February 1647. In fact, they sold the king to Parliament for £400,000. The money was used to pay the outstanding wages of the soldiers of the Scottish army.

Whilst under the protection of the army, Charles managed to escape to the Isle of Wight. Up to this point, Cromwell had been trying to negotiate a deal with Charles. Cromwell discovered that he had signed an alliance with the Scots and felt betrayed. Charles had made a deal with the Scots in 1648 in much the same way as Pym had done in 1643 – in other words Scotland agreed to invade England and fight, this time for Charles, in return for an English Presbyterian Church. With the rise of the New Model Army, the Royalists and Scots were defeated at the Battle of Preston in August 1648, in what has become known as the Second Civil War. What factors made the Scots get involved? For the Scots, it was primarily a question of religion – they were prepared to fight to keep their own religion and customs.

Cromwell

When Charles I was executed in 1649, the Scots were angry because their treaty with the king was now invalid. They allowed his son Prince Charles, the future Charles II, to be taken to Scotland and he was crowned king of Scotland in 1650. This annoyed Oliver Cromwell and the English Parliament so Cromwell's army invaded Scotland, defeating the Scots at the Battle of Dunbar. The following year, 1651, Scotland retaliated by sending an army to England, which resulted in the Battle of Worcester. Again Cromwell defeated Scotland and Charles fled to Holland.

Scotland was then occupied by English troops to ensure that law and order were maintained there. The Scottish Parliament and the General Assembly were closed down. Important decisions were now being made by the English Parliament. This understandably angered the Scots, who also hated having English soldiers on their streets. However, with the invasion of English troops, there were some benefits because many merchants grew prosperous. They were now allowed to trade freely with other British ports and with overseas ports.

Charles II (1660–85) and James II (1685–8)

When Charles II was restored to the English throne by Parliament in 1660, he was also restored to the Scottish throne. He immediately allowed the Scottish Parliament to meet again. Even though many Scots objected to rule from England, many felt that having Charles Stuart (descended from the Scottish King James VI) back on the throne was much better than being ruled by the English Parliament.

During the rule of James II the Scots were able to uphold their own laws, Parliament and Kirk. When James II was deposed and sent into exile and the English Parliament called on William of Orange and Mary to take the throne (see page 126), some Scots were very angry.

William III (1688–1702)

When William and Mary began their reign in 1688, Scotland was a divided country, made up of Highland and Lowland peoples who were divided into clans (see map on page 141).

- **The Highlands** – The clansmen were loyal above all to their chiefs and were unwilling to submit to anyone else. Many of them were Catholic. Feuding and the rustling of herds of cattle were rife. Many of them were Jacobites so their support was given to James II and his son, James Edward Stuart.

The Stuart family tree.

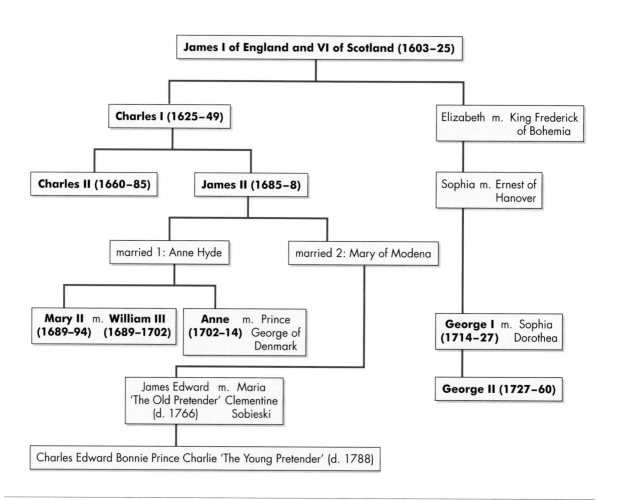

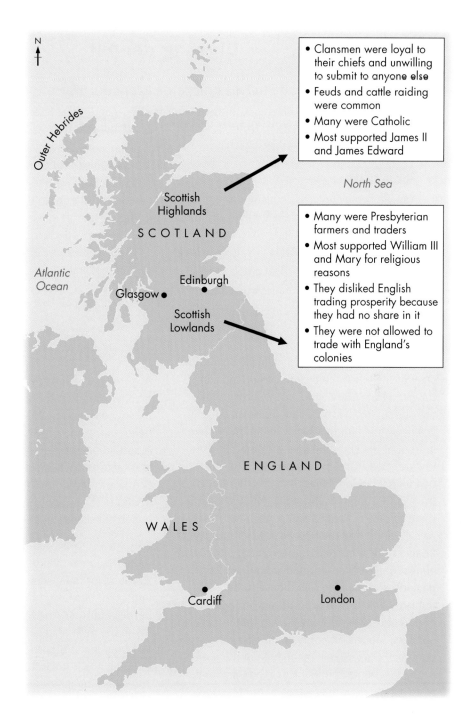

The Highlands and Lowlands of Scotland, 1688.

- Clansmen were loyal to their chiefs and unwilling to submit to anyone else
- Feuds and cattle raiding were common
- Many were Catholic
- Most supported James II and James Edward

- Many were Presbyterian farmers and traders
- Most supported William III and Mary for religious reasons
- They disliked English trading prosperity because they had no share in it
- They were not allowed to trade with England's colonies

- **The Lowlands** – Many of the Lowland clansmen were Presbyterian. They were farmers and traders who supported William III and Mary, largely for religious reasons. They resented England's prosperity as well as the fact that they were allowed no share in it and were not allowed to trade with England's colonies.

Highland clans were close to rebellion when William III became king in 1688. In order to enforce law and order and avoid future rebellions, William forced all Scottish clansmen to swear an oath of loyalty to him by 1 January 1692. This act was to have tragic consequences for one clan (see Digging Deeper on page 142).

Digging deeper

The Massacre of Glencoe, 1692

Look at Source A and then read the story of the MacDonald clan of Glencoe.

SOURCE A

You are hereby ordered and authorised to act against these Highland rebels who have not taken the benefit of our indemnity, by fire and sword and all manner of hostility; to burn their houses, seize or destroy their goods or cattle, plenishings or clothes and to cut off the men.

From a letter sent by William III to the Secretary for Scotland on 11 January 1692.

On 29 December 1691, Maclain MacDonald, the chief of the MacDonald clan, a Highland clan, travelled from Glencoe to Fort William to take the oath of loyalty to William III. However, the governor told him that his oath had to be taken in front of the sheriff at Inverary some 60 miles (80 km) away. On 2 January, a day after the deadline, MacDonald reached Inverary having travelled through a snowstorm. No one was there to take his oath because the sheriff was away, celebrating the New Year. MacDonald was unable to take his oath until 6 January. This was almost one week after the deadline. William decided that the clan would have to be punished in order to exert his authority over the Highlanders. Therefore William ordered that 120 soldiers, the vast majority coming from the rival Campbell clan, should be billeted in the homes of the MacDonalds in Glencoe. The Campbells were actually sworn enemies of the MacDonalds but they were accepted into the MacDonalds' homes as Highland custom stated that feuding had to end when hospitality was being given.

For two weeks the Campbells lived in the homes of the MacDonalds until they received the order telling them to massacre the MacDonalds (see Source B).

SOURCE B

You are ordered to attack the rebels, the MacDonalds of Glencoe, and put all to the sword who are under 70 years old. You are to secure all exits so that no man escapes. You are to do this at exactly five o'clock. This is by the king's special command, for the good and safety of the country, that these rebels be cut off root and branch. See that this is done without fear or favour. Or else, you may expect to be dealt with as a traitor.

From a letter written by Major Robert Duncanson to Captain Robert Campbell of Glenlyon, 1692.

At 5am on 13 February, the killing of MacDonald men, women and children started. Some managed to escape the massacre but froze to death in the snow as they fled over Cannoch Moor: 38 bodies were found. As a result of the massacre and William's part in it, the Highland Scots saw how cruel the English were. This added to the support which the exiled James II and his descendants received in later years.

Why was this massacre so important? Whilst there had been rivalry between the clans in Scotland for many years, this massacre is important because it demonstrates a huge betrayal of trust. The MacDonald clan chief had taken the oath of allegiance to William and the MacDonalds of Glencoe trusted the Campbells to follow the Highland tradition of hospitality. The king's minister in Scotland had been involved in the planning and the king's Scottish forces had carried out the massacre but the Highlanders questioned William's own involvement. Those that carried out the massacre were never punished so feuds and mistrust continued.

The Darien Disaster, 1698–1700

Further problems arose between the English and the Scots because of the failed attempt by the Scots to set up a colony in Darien near Panama. The hope was that it would become an effective base from where they could trade and make profits in the silk and spice industries. It would also enable the Scots to develop further colonies with which to trade. However, the reality was that the climate was humid and hostile and not really suited to a European colony. It was full of swamps and jungle – breeding grounds for mosquitoes which bit the colonists, causing many to die of fever. In addition it was part of a larger area controlled by Spain; England had at first backed the scheme, but withdrew because Spain was an ally in the war against Louis XIV of France. Many ordinary Scots had invested heavily in the scheme. All their money was lost because it was a total failure.

Following the deaths of many of the colonists and hostilities from the Spanish, the colony was abandoned in 1700. The vast majority of the colonists who tried to settle there either died in shipwrecks or of fever. The Scots blamed William and the English government for failing to support them. While at the outset, many English people were keen to invest in the new company, the powerful East India Company, unhappy with a potential Scottish rival for trade, had pressurised the English government into not allowing English investors to put money into the Scottish colony. The English were not interested in helping to share their trade in the colonies.

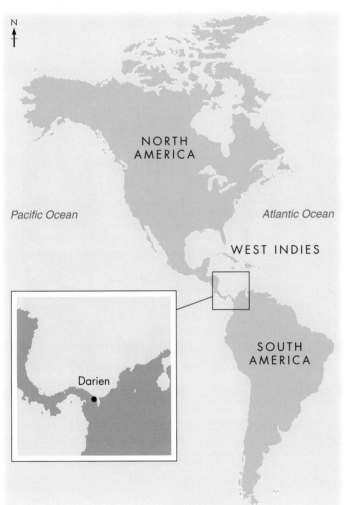

The position of the Darien colony in South America.

Question time

1. Why do you think William III was unpopular in Scotland? Refer to the Massacre of Glencoe and the Darien Disaster in your answer.

The Act of Union, 1707

In 1702, upon the death of William III, Queen Anne succeeded to the throne and ruled until 1714. She was the sister of William's wife, Mary, and the daughter of James II. She had seventeen pregnancies but none of her children lived to adulthood. Who would rule when she died? The absence of an heir made the English Parliament look to the House of Hanover in Germany – descendants of James I – to take the throne after Anne (see family tree on page 140). Scotland, while it shared the same monarch, was still a separate country. Many Scots, particularly Jacobite supporters, wanted to choose their own monarch regardless of what the English wanted, but some saw that there were positive aspects to a closer union between the two countries. The Scots would be able to trade freely with England and its colonies if it united with England. For the English, if Scotland were part of a United Kingdom, the government in London would never have to worry that France would attempt an alliance with Scotland.

SOURCE C

A contemporary engraving showing Queen Anne signing the Act of Union, 1707.

SOURCE D

For the English the union will make no change. They will keep the same Parliament, the same taxes, the same laws, and the same courts. But the Scots will have to pay the English debts, now and in the future. Scotland will lose the right to manage its own affairs. For the Scots the union will be a complete surrender.

From a speech made by Lord Belhaven to the Scottish Parliament, 1706.

The month before the Act of Union, 31 whales were found dead on Kirkcaldie Sands. The local people said this was a bad omen and that nothing good would come of the union. However, the Act of Union came into effect in May 1707, and 45 Scottish MPs and sixteen Scottish peers entered the Parliament in London. A new British Parliament was elected with 513 MPs from England and Wales and the 45 from Scotland. There were demonstrations and riots against the union in Glasgow and Edinburgh. Church bells were heard to ring out the tune 'Why should I be sad on my wedding day?'

There were various reasons why people had misgivings about this union of the two countries. Many English merchants didn't want to share their trading rights and privileges with the Scots. Many Lowland Scots were Presbyterians and hated the Catholic Highlanders and many English people didn't want to support the Presbyterians. In the Highlands rebellion was plotted. Given all this, how long would the union survive?

What was agreed with the Act of Union?

The Scots agreed:

- There would be one United Kingdom Parliament.

- Scotland would send Lords and MPs to Westminster.

- George of Hanover would be king of the whole of the United Kingdom when Anne died.

- Scotland would use English money and English weights and measures.

The English agreed:

- Scottish merchants had equal trading rights in Britain and with the colonies so could trade on the same terms as English merchants.

- The Scots would keep control of their own Church (Presbyterian Kirk) and keep their own law courts.

SOURCE E

For Scotland, the union brought nothing but good. The farmers of the Lowland learnt new skills. Glasgow, which had been just a fishing port, grew into a rich and mighty city. Peace changed the wild men of the Highlands into peaceful herdsmen. The only thing the Scots lost was their old hatred of England.

From a book by the English historian, J.R. Green, 1874.

SOURCE F

How the first Union flag was developed from the Scottish and English flags.

Activity time

1   Design a poster *either* to persuade English people that they will benefit from union with Scotland *or* to persuade Scottish people that they will benefit from union with England.

2   Read Sources D and E carefully and, using your own knowledge and the information in this section, answer the following questions:

    a   What did Lord Belhaven think about the Act of Union?

    b   What impact did he expect it to have on England and Scotland?

    c   What did J.R. Green consider to be the results of the Act of Union?

    d   Compare Sources D and E. Which view do you think is more accurate?

    e   Do you think England or Scotland gained most from the Act of Union? Divide your answer into long-term and short-term gains.

Further signs of instability

The Jacobite Rebellion of 1715

The Act of Union of 1707 was more the work of the Lowland Scots than the Highland Scots. Many Lowland Scots disliked the Highlanders, because of their strong clan system and their chiefs, more than they hated the English. Many of the Highlanders were Catholic whilst the majority of Lowlanders were Presbyterian. The Highlanders stayed loyal to the Catholic king and drank toasts to the 'king over the water', meaning James Edward Stuart, the son of James II, who was in exile. They felt he was the rightful heir to the throne and plotted to gain him the crown. These Scots were called Jacobites from the Latin *Jacobus* meaning James.

In 1715 the Jacobites believed that the time had come for James Edward Stuart to claim the throne. Queen Anne had died and as she had no children there was no obvious heir in England to inherit the throne. The Jacobites believed that the Catholic children of King James II could now claim what was rightfully theirs (see the Stuart family tree on page 140). Parliament did not agree. It had stated at the Act of Union that the throne would pass to the House of Hanover on Queen Anne's death, so the crown was given to Prince George. As king, George I was not popular in England and there were riots on his arrival in London. He was German and didn't speak any English. This meant that most of the running of the country was left to his chief minister, Robert Walpole. The supporters of James II and his son, James Edward Stuart, were ecstatic – was this the time to put the Stuarts back on the throne?

The Earl of Mar, one of the Scottish Lords in the new Parliament, had supported the Act of Union in 1707, but by 1713 he wanted the Act repealed and independence for Scotland. Rebellion seemed the only way forward. At Braemar on 6 September 1715, he set up the Jacobite standard (flag) and called upon all people loyal to James Edward Stuart to support him. The Highlanders' reaction was amazing. By the end of September, Mar controlled the whole of the Highlands – over 5000 clansmen had joined his cause and more were arriving each day. Mar established his headquarters at Perth and, by the beginning of November, he had gathered a force of over 9000 men, ready and willing to fight for the cause of James Edward Stuart.

The Duke of Argyll was waiting for Mar outside Stirling ready to fight against him in the name of King George. The two sides fought each other on 13 November 1715 at Sheriffmuir. The fighting did not produce a fixed result and both sides retreated peacefully. They never fought again. James Edward Stuart arrived in Scotland in December and spent six weeks in the country. Mar persuaded James Edward, known as the Old Pretender (from the French, *prétendre*, meaning 'to claim'), to return to France because he was fearful that the Duke of Argyll would capture him. The rebellion was over for the moment – at least until 1745.

The Jacobite Rebellion of 1745

The 1745 Jacobite Rebellion was a more serious threat to the English crown than the uprising in 1715. King George I had died and his son, George II, had been on the throne since 1727. By 1745, the Hanoverians had been ruling Britain for some 31 years. There were many factors that led to the 1745 rebellion:

- Most Scottish Catholics believed that James Edward Stuart, the Old Pretender, was the rightful king of Scotland and England.

- Charles Edward Stuart, son of James Edward Stuart, believed his father was the rightful king and that he had the right to put his father on the throne.

- Rebellion in Scotland was not a new thing – since France was at war with England, it seemed likely that France would support this Jacobite rebellion. In 1744 France had planned to invade England and Louis XV (the French king) had invited Charles Edward to join the invasion.

- There was discontent because the Scots did not like having to pay taxes to the government in London.

- Following the 1715 uprising, a number of Scots had joined forces with James Edward Stuart in creating opposition to the Hanoverians in Europe.

- The Scots were now funded by Aeneas MacDonald, a wealthy banker living in Paris, and could afford to raise an army.

- Highlanders called Charles Edward Stuart the 'Young Pretender' or 'Bonnie Prince Charlie'; they had a figurehead.

Raising an army

So in July 1745 Charles Edward Stuart landed at Eriskay, a small island off the west coast of Scotland. He had with him his political, financial and military advisers and he was determined to put his father back on the throne.

Bonnie Prince Charlie and his advisers quickly travelled to Glenfinnan on the mainland of Scotland and on 19 August 1745 raised the Stuart flag, proclaiming his father James Edward Stuart to be king. He already had 200 men with him and was gaining support all the time; soon he had men from many different clans – the Frasers, the Camerons and the Mackintoshes. This resulted in an army of some 4000 men who were prepared to fight for the Jacobite cause.

Control of Edinburgh

In September 1745, the Jacobites marched towards Edinburgh, the Scottish capital. Many of the Scots living in Edinburgh were sympathetic to the Jacobite cause and Bonnie Prince Charlie soon controlled the whole city except the castle. A clash with the government troops was inevitable and took place on 21 September at Prestonpans, east of Edinburgh, when Bonnie Prince Charlie led 5000 Highland clansmen against General Cope's troops. Here Bonnie Prince Charlie secured a victory after furious fighting and great bravery displayed by the clansmen, especially the MacDonalds. Some horrific injuries were sustained – arms and legs were cut off and heads split open! Jacobite casualties were light but 3000 of the government's troops had been killed.

The British troops were chased away and even threw away their standards and abandoned their horses. Nearly 1500 prisoners were taken by Bonnie Prince Charlie.

Scotland was basically under his control now and Bonnie Prince Charlie had to decide whether to advance into England or consolidate his power in Scotland. He disagreed with his advisers and decided to push into England, believing the English Catholics would join him, giving his cause more money, soldiers and a better chance of putting his father on the throne. As we shall see this was to prove a big mistake!

South to Derby

Charles and his troops marched south into England and reached Derby, some 138 miles from London. Only 300 English supporters had joined his army and none of them were important or wealthy Catholics. Charles' advisers told him to turn back but Charles wanted to push on to take London and the crown. What they didn't know was that King George II had packed his bags and was ready to leave. The Jacobite advance had caused great fear amongst the English people and there had been a financial panic, with people beginning to withdraw their money from the banks – this is known as a run on the bank. However, at the same time, the Highlanders were feeling unsettled at being so far south, as well as being concerned for their farms at home. They soon realised that the English Catholics had not supported them as they had hoped they would, so how could they be successful?

Captured Highlanders posed for the painting of the Battle of Culloden by David Morier, 1746.

Return to Scotland

Feeling demoralised, Bonnie Prince Charlie and his troops turned around and marched back to Scotland, pursued by English soldiers. They were freezing and starving. Bonnie Prince Charlie was disappointed at the lack of support from Catholics in Cumbria, Lancashire and Cheshire. He was also very disappointed at the decision to return to Scotland. On 19 December, they reached the Scottish border and split up to confuse the English. The main party went to Glasgow and then on to Stirling. At Falkirk, the Jacobites defeated a small government force. All the time, small groups of men and individuals were deserting the army and returning to their families who depended on them. Charles headed for safety in the Highlands, where clans loyal to the Jacobites sheltered him.

The Battle of Culloden, 16 April 1746

George II's son, the Duke of Cumberland, along with a highly trained and well-disciplined army was close on the heels of the Jacobites and Bonnie Prince Charlie. Cumberland's key aim was to destroy them so that the Stuarts would never threaten the throne of Great Britain again. He caught up with Bonnie Prince Charlie at Culloden Moor not far from Inverness. They didn't fight immediately because Cumberland and his men first celebrated his birthday! The Jacobites waiting on Culloden Moor made some serious errors.

One of Charles' best commanders, Lord George Murray, suggested that the Jacobites should cross to the soft ground over Nairn Water. There the ground would be ideal for the Highlanders' fighting techniques and would be hopeless for Cumberland's cavalry charges.

Bonnie Prince Charlie ignored the advice and ordered his troops to stand and wait for battle on the flat springy ground of Culloden Moor, which was perfect for Cumberland's well-trained cavalry. Meanwhile Cumberland's men were relaxing and celebrating his birthday in Nairn. So the Jacobites had to wait for nearly three days without food; their supplies were nearly 6 miles away in Inverness.

The Jacobites were starving, exhausted, outnumbered two to one and poorly equipped. Cumberland's troops massacred the Jacobites – at the end of the battle 1200 Jacobites were dead with the loss of only 76 English. Cumberland and his troops were merciless and chased the fleeing Jacobites, hunting them down and slaughtering them. Because of his cruelty after Culloden the Duke of Cumberland became known as 'Butcher'. Culloden was the last battle to be fought on British soil.

SOURCE H

This picture, painted in 1746, shows the Duke of Cumberland, the general who defeated the Jacobites at Culloden.

Impact of the Jacobite rebellions

Despite the fact that the battle was now over, Cumberland's troops devastated the Highlands by raping, killing, capturing and plundering at will. They were searching for Bonnie Prince Charlie but never found him. He had become a hunted man and was always on the move, often in disguise and protected by loyal Highlanders. He hid successfully until he escaped by boat to France in September 1746. The British government now attempted to smash the Highland clan system. It passed laws which destroyed the power of the clan chiefs, and it forced clansmen to surrender their weapons and stop wearing clan tartan. The clan system and Bonnie Prince Charlie thus became a romantic and treasured memory.

While the Jacobites had been defeated, Scotland was to gain from the union with England in other ways. By the end of the eighteenth century, there were successful linen and cotton industries in the Lowlands. Glasgow had become a prosperous port and Edinburgh a centre of trade and learning. Many Scots became famous engineers, inventors, teachers and doctors working in Britain and throughout the world.

Digging deeper

Bonnie Prince Charlie: the romantic prince

What sort of man was Bonnie Prince Charlie? Why did he become such a legend?

After the defeat at Culloden, in April 1746, Charles fled westwards with his followers. Over the next five months, he roamed through the Highlands and islands getting about by means of horse, boat, but largely on foot. He moved from one helping hand to another with a price tag of £30,000 on his head. First he spent ten weeks in the Hebrides (small islands west of Scotland – see map on page 141), moving from island to island and back again with King George II's naval patrols close on his heels. He passed nights at seas and in the open fields. He suffered from illness and starvation, becoming 'ill-coloured and overrun with the scab'.

By July 1746, Charles was back on the mainland and he spent the next two months seeking safety, living in caves, woods and in the mountains. He must have walked long distances but did not give up which gained him much support from the clans. The clansmen remained very loyal and risked their own lives to support him. Finally, on 19 September, he sailed to France – his fourteen-month adventure since he first arrived in Scotland in July 1745 was finally over. He lived for another 42 years but became a drunkard. He said: 'I should have died with my men at Culloden'.

Bonnie Prince Charlie had all the natural hallmarks of a romantic hero. He possessed not only good looks, but a personal charm and appeal. He was athletic, a golfer and an expert with the crossbow. He played the violin well and loved dancing. Despite the crushing defeat of Culloden, the legend of the dashing prince who had come so close to winning the throne for the Stuarts lived on. The romance was strengthened by the reign of terror conducted by the 'Butcher' Duke of Cumberland against the clans after the battle (see page 150), and by the daring adventure of the prince's five months as a fugitive.

Question time

1   Explain why you think Bonnie Prince Charlie is portrayed as such a romantic hero.

2   Did the Jacobites stand a real chance of winning? Give reasons for your opinion.

3   Look at Source G on page 149 and Source H on page 150. They are both pictures of the Battle of Culloden in 1746. Bearing in mind that the captured Highlanders posed for the artist in Source G, and that the artist of Source H was paid £200 a year by the Duke of Cumberland, explain how accurate a portrayal each gives of the Battle of Culloden. Give reasons to support your ideas.

Union with Wales

The Glyndwr Rebellion, 1400–9

This rebellion is named after its influential leader, Owain Glyndwr. He was an important Welshman connected to the ruling Welsh families. He lived during the time of Henry IV (1399–1413), long before the period we are studying in this book.

There was unrest in Wales at this time, due to the harshness of English rule. Many battles followed over a period of years and there were notable successes for Glyndwr against Henry IV's armies. In 1404, Owain was crowned as the Prince of Wales and the first Welsh parliament was held. Within a few years a treaty had been signed with France. The rebellion failed in the winter of 1408–9 as the English surrounded Harlech Castle where Owain and his family lived. It was a harsh winter and many communities starved or froze to death. The French sailed back to France and Owain surrendered in 1409 due to famine and sickness in his family.

After the failure of the Glyndwr Rebellion, it was inevitable that Wales would be ruled by England. When Henry VII came to the throne in 1485 he was accepted by the Welsh because of his Welsh ancestry. It was apparent that those in power in London at this time were seeking to create a united kingdom of Great Britain that would include Wales. This view was strengthened when Henry VII's daughter married James IV of Scotland. These policies of closer union continued under the reign of Henry VIII.

The Act of Union, 1536

When Henry VIII broke with Rome (see Chapter 2) he felt ready to show how strong and powerful he was as the rightful king of Wales as well as of England. In 1536, the Act of Union was passed. It provided for the political unification of Wales to England. It sent forth the message that the English government wanted to 'utterly extirpate all and singular the sinister usage and customs differing from the [English laws]'. In other words, England wanted the Welsh to speak and act like the English; getting rid of the Welsh language and customs! As a result of the Act of Union, London was the capital of Wales and it was not until 1955 that Wales got its own capital city in Cardiff.

SOURCE A

An Act for Laws and Justices to be administered in Wales in like form as it is in this realm hath ordained [ordered], enacted and established that his [Henry VIII's] said country or dominion of Wales shall stand and continue forever from henceforth incorporated, united and annexed to and with his realm of England.

Extract from the title for the Act of Union of 1536.

The Act of Union was welcomed by many in Wales and especially by the gentry. They were able to extend their business interests and gained certain freedoms (see Source B).

SOURCE B

Persons born or to be born in the said Principality of Wales shall have and enjoy and inherit all and singular Freedoms, Liberties, Rights, Privileges and Laws as other the King's subjects have, enjoy or inherit.

From the Act of Union, 1536.

SOURCE C

Of late, [they] are applying themselves to settle in towns, learn mechanics, engage in commerce, cultivate the soil, and undertake all other public duties equally with other Englishmen.

Humphrey Llwyd, famous Welsh writer, writing of his fellow Welshmen in 1572.

The impact of the Union

Apart from the individual advancement of ambitious Welshmen flocking to London, the Act gave all the king's subjects, including Welshmen, equal rights and privileges. It also secured a lasting peace and it authorised the appointments of many Welsh gentry as justices of the peace. It gave Wales representation in Parliament, and it settled the border between Wales and England through the creation of new boundaries – Wales was divided into thirteen counties. Finally it abolished any legal distinction between citizens of Wales and those of England. So the benefits gained through the Act of Union made further rebellion largely unnecessary.

SOURCE D

No country in England so flourished in 100 years as Wales hath done since the government of Henry VII to this time; in so much as if our fathers were now living they would think it some strange country inhabited with a foreign nation so altered is the countrymen, the people changed in heart with and the land altered in hue without, from evil to good, and from bad to better.

George Owen, a famous Welsh cartographer (map-maker), writing in 1603.

SOURCE E

… by means whereof that entire country in a short time was securely settled in peace and obedience, and hath attained to that civility of manners and plenty of all things, as now we find it not inferior to the best parts of England.

The poet Sir John Davies of Hereford (1529–1626) in 1605, comparing the peaceful nature of his native Wales with that of Ireland.

Initially the Act of Union was a heavy blow to Welsh culture. The speaking of Welsh was frowned upon in England and all Welsh officials were made to speak English. And, as we have seen from the sources, the rich Welsh landowners behaved as if they were English. Indeed Welsh gentlemen looked upon Welsh as a less important language – they married into English families and sent their children to English public schools.

As England became more Protestant, the new religion in Wales helped maintain the Welsh language. In 1567 a new Welsh Prayer Book was published, followed in 1588 by the introduction of a Bible in Welsh. Over the next century many Non-conformists continued to speak Welsh, passing on their culture to their children. Even though only half a million people lived in Wales at the beginning of the eighteenth century and many were very poor, their rich culture continued to survive.

Even though the Act of Union provided many benefits for the Welsh and was one of the most important documents in the history of Wales, it was passed without consultation with the Welsh people. The Act abolished any distinction between English and Welsh law and it also made English the official language of the courts. This restricted many Welsh people from participating in the courts because they couldn't speak English.

Despite the Act being an attempt by the English to absorb the nation of Wales and so diminish the Welsh culture, the people of Wales continued to maintain their identity: everyone living in Wales still considered themselves Welsh.

SOURCE F

A page from the Bible in Welsh, published in 1588.

Question time

1   Why do you think that this Act of Union with Wales was passed? Explain your answer carefully.

Think about the following points when constructing your answer:

- Geographically, Wales is very close to England.

- Many of the earlier rebellions such as the Glyndwr Rebellion (1400–09) had failed.

- There was much inter-marrying between the English and Welsh lords and nobles.

- The Act offered opportunities for individual advancement for hundreds of ambitious Welshmen in terms of buying land and furthering business interests.

With reference to Sources C, D and E on the impact of the Act of Union, answer the following questions in as much detail as possible:

2   How successful do you think the Act of Union was for both the Welsh and the English?

3   How did it compare to the situation in both Scotland and Ireland? Use examples from all three countries to explain your answer.

How far was Britain a United Kingdom by 1750?

By 1750 Britain was moving forward and had come a long way since 1485. However, what did the people of Britain think about Union and other changes that had taken place since 1485? Was the kingdom really united? The following assessment section will help you decide.

5 Assessment section

1 In groups carefully read these typical views of different people from across the United Kingdom (see below) comparing their ideas in 1485 with those in 1750.

2 Choose *one* group and write a speech to be given to the class, which represents that group's views about Union or other changes that have taken place in Britain – be sure to include extra evidence and information from this chapter and your own knowledge.

IRISH

1485 The King of England has little influence and life continues without interference.
1750 Catholics are second-class citizens in their own country. Much of their land has been given to Protestant settlers. They have been ruthlessly put down by Cromwell and William III.

WELSH

1485 Henry VII is Welsh. Expectations are high for greater rights and more freedom.
1750 Welshmen now have the same rights as Englishmen. Many rich Welshmen are allowed to be MPs, judges, merchants and courtiers.

SCOTS

1485 Scots do not trust the English and see them as the old enemy. The Scots work to keep the English out of Scotland.
1750 Many Scots resent losing control of the country but feel they have done well from the Union, particularly now they can share English trade in the expanding empire.

CHURCHMEN

1485 Up until now the Pope in Rome has been head of the Catholic Church in England. It is powerful and rich, well respected and brings people close to God.
1750 The Protestant Church of England is now the official religion in England. It does not want to share power with other Christian churches, especially the Catholics.

MPS

1485 Parliament is called when the monarch decides. It is there to advise the monarch and raise taxes when the monarch needs money.
1750 By law, monarchs cannot govern without the support of Parliament. Parliament cannot be ignored.

NOBLES

1485 Nobles are rich and powerful. They have influence over the monarch.
1750 Nobles are gaining wealth. They are making more money out of better farming techniques and investing this in newer industries.

3 'How united was the United Kingdom by 1750?'
Use ideas and information from this chapter and your own knowledge to answer this question.

4 Answer the following essay question:

'What were the difficulties in unifying England, Scotland, Wales and Ireland?'

In your answer, identify any common themes.

5 In a class discussion consider why Bonnie Prince Charlie has become a romantic folk hero. Does he deserve this title?

6 Write an essay to say whether or not you agree with the following statement:

'Irish problems date back to the period of Cromwell.'

7 Consider the following events:
- the Battle of the Boyne
- Cromwellian rule
- the Siege of Londonderry.

Write a paragraph about each event to explain why it is still remembered in Ireland today.

The Renaissance and the Scientific Revolution

During the Renaissance period, which began in Italy in the fourteenth century, there was a major shift in ideas and thinking. Writers, artists, scientists and scholars looked at things in a fresh new way – the word 'renaissance' comes from the French meaning 'rebirth'. The result was a period of exceptional creativity. The Renaissance led the way for the Scientific Revolution of the seventeenth century.

	15th century	16th century	17th century
Thinking (philosophy)	Machiavelli (1467–1527)	Francis Bacon (1561–1626)	Thomas Hobbes (1588–1679)
Science	Copernicus (1473–1543) Gutenberg (1397–1468) Caxton (1422–91) Leonardo da Vinci (1452–1519)	Vesalius (1514–64) Brahe (1546–1601) Harvey (1578–1657) Kepler (1571–1630) Galileo (1564–1642)	Hooke (1635–1703) Newton (1642–1727) Boyle (1627–91)
Architecture	Brunelleschi (1377–1446) Bramante (1444–1514)		Wren (1632–1723) Bernini (1598–1660)
Art	Michelangelo (1475–1564) Leonardo da Vinci (1452–1519) Raphael (1483–1520) Dürer (1471–1528)		

A timeline of the Renaissance and the Scientific Revolution.

What was the Renaissance?

From the fourteenth century onwards there were many advances and developments made in science, medicine and art. The Renaissance began in Italy, spreading and influencing other parts of Europe, reaching England by about 1500. People looked towards Italy as the centre of new learning. People who travelled were drawn to Italy; if traders wanted luxury goods they went to Italy – for example, in the fifteenth century Florence was one of the most famous and beautiful cities in the world.

There was a great influx of new ideas and new ways of looking at the world and a revival in art and learning. This coincided with the beginning of what is known as the Modern age in Europe. In the Middle Ages, people had looked to the Church as the source of all knowledge to guide and direct them. During the Renaissance, the Church still played an important part in people's lives, but scholars and intellectuals also looked back at the lives and teachings of the Ancient Greeks and Romans. The study of their writings and works of art was seen to be like a great adventure and a voyage of discovery. The study of Greek was fashionable and new – rather like the use of the Internet today!

Europe at the beginning of the sixteenth century.

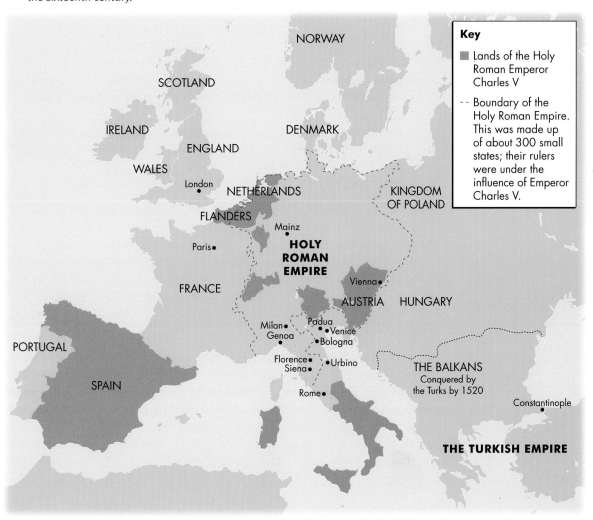

This new learning caused great changes in Britain as well as across Europe. People developed a sense of being individuals who created their own destinies. New techniques and theories were developed in art, architecture, poetry, philosophy, science and music. The concept of the 'Renaissance man' was born out of the idea that Man was limitless in his capacity for development whether physical, social or artistic.

The spread of new ideas

Because of the great influence of the Greek and Roman cultures during this period, people began to question some of the traditionally held views and many new ideas and thoughts were debated in the universities around Europe. It became fashionable for kings and queens to take on board some of these new ways of thinking. With the invention of the printing press around 1450 in Mainz, Germany (see page 161), and increasing literacy (the ability to read and write) amongst the population, the seeds were sown for future change. Established trade and sea links also meant that ideas developed in Italy, for example, could easily be printed and then sent to other parts of Europe.

The Italian city states

The Renaissance began in northern and central Italy. In the middle of the sixteenth century, Italy was divided into about 200 city states. Each city state was made up of a powerful city that controlled the weaker towns and countryside that surrounded it. The city states raised their own taxes, made their own trade laws and built fortifications and defences. Some of these cities, such as Florence, were republics where the people had power and a say in how the city state was run and there was no monarchy. They were run by elected councils and the members were drawn from the peasants and lower classes as well as the upper classes and nobility. This type of government was very similar to that of Ancient Greece and Rome.

Whilst the power in these republics was very much in the hands of the citizens, wealthy merchants, churchmen or soldiers were often the leaders. The leaders of the city states were called *signori* and they had huge power which many passed on to their families. Among some of the most powerful ruling families were the Medici in Florence and the Visconti and Sforza in Milan. There was a great deal of rivalry between these families and they continually looked for ways to increase the power of themselves and their city states.

One of the most famous of the *signori* was Cosimo de'Medici. He became a patron of the arts (someone who gives backing and assistance, usually financial aid). Patronage was often given to glorify God as well as improve a patron's city because it enabled cathedrals and churches to be built and decorated. It was also given to gain popularity with the people. By building magnificent monuments to themselves, patrons showed off their own wealth and the glory of their city states to outsiders.

Machiavelli (1469–1527) and theories of government

The citizens of northern Italy were very proud of their city states. They supported their leaders and believed that they would bring them wealth, power and prestige in return. This was different from the rest of Europe at this time, where people's main loyalties were to their local lords and the Church. The leaders of the city states were interested in ideas about how they should govern. They especially believed that citizens should owe their main loyalty to the city states rather than to the Church. Therefore rulers studied theories of government by writers like Niccolò Machiavelli – the father of 'political science'.

Machiavelli was born in Florence and served the city state in several key jobs. He wrote a book about politics and government called *The Prince* in 1513; it became very famous and the ideas in it were followed by many leaders including Henry VIII (see page 20) – and still are today! In his book, Machiavelli advised rulers to make their states powerful by doing what worked best, as opposed to being good or moral. Rulers, Machiavelli believed, should be feared rather than loved by their people. If necessary they should be dishonest in their dealings with other rulers. As we discussed earlier, in modern usage the word 'Machiavellian' has come to mean cunning and ruthless behaviour.

SOURCE A

Machiavelli, the father of political science, painted by an unknown contemporary artist.

SOURCE B

A prince should be a fox, to know the traps and snares: and a lion to be able to frighten the wolves.

This quote from Machiavelli's book The Prince, *1513, shows the qualities he thought a ruler needed to be powerful.*

Machiavelli's ideas were widely adopted in Italy and also in other European states. However, his ideas did not lead to peace, nor did they make the city states powerful. The rulers were great rivals and spent a lot of time and money plotting against and fighting each other. In the end these wars weakened Italy.

Education

Education was an important aspect of the Renaissance – indeed the beginnings of the Renaissance were called 'the new learning' by scholars who had studied the Ancient Greeks and Romans. Children were not forced by law to go to school in the Tudor and Stuart periods. If they did attend, in most cases their parents had to pay fees. As the Renaissance progressed and as the new learning spread, more and more books became available due to the invention of the printing press, and popular ideas about education began to change. It is important to note that up to this time books were mostly written by monks and would therefore have had a certain religious viewpoint in them. The invention of the printing press allowed scholars with all sorts of different views to make them public.

Schooling in England

One of the oldest schools in London is St Paul's, which was refounded in 1509–12 by John Colet. Its particular aim was to spread the new learning through the study of purer Latin and Greek, which had not been taught at all in medieval schools. School hours were very long, usually from 6am until 5pm, with two breaks, one at 9am and dinner at noon. By 1700 in England most children in towns got some schooling. The sons and daughters of nobles had private tutors and part of their studies included spending three to five years abroad with their tutors on a 'grand tour'. While travelling they learned to speak French, studied works of art and buildings as well as the laws of European countries.

The gentry and merchants sent their sons to grammar schools. Here they learnt to read, write and speak Latin; they progressed to university at Oxford or Cambridge. Often this was followed by studying law at the Inns of Court in London. Girls were expected to marry at an earlier age than boys, so the daughters of the gentry stayed at home. They were taught to read, write, sew and to manage the home by their mothers.

The children of craftsmen and labourers attended the parish and charity schools where they learnt to read and write and do simple mathematics. A lot of time was spent on scripture (studying the Bible) and there were not many books or much equipment. School children had to learn long passages by heart and would often be beaten if they forgot anything! There were only two holidays of about two weeks each at Christmas and Easter. The majority of children left school to start work when they were ten or eleven years old.

The impact of the printing press

If we were to choose one invention during this period that was to change the world and be a major factor in the Renaissance and the spread of new ideas, it would have to be the invention and development of printing. The printing of books led directly to the increased and faster circulation of books and ideas throughout Europe. Consequently the influence the Church had over people's lives decreased because it could not control the ideas they picked up through their readings.

The Chinese had invented printing using blocks of wood, over 700 years before the first printing press went into production in Europe in around 1450. Over time, they developed their printing methods and started using movable letters. However, this invention was slow to reach Europe. Up to this time, most books were produced by monks. The books were beautifully hand-written and illustrated (decorated), with fine pictures and colours. They were written on vellum (animal skin) – a book of 200 pages would need the skins of about 100 sheep. As a result, books were very precious and rare, and were used only by the wealthiest people in society.

Why didn't the invention of printing, as begun in China, not happen in Europe until the middle of the fifteenth century? There were two main reasons:

- Many people, particularly those who led the Church, felt that books should be written by monks, so that only 'godly teaching' would be passed on to readers.

- Because printing was an unknown business, many traders felt that they could not invest money in machinery, paper and workers' wages – they were not sure whether they could make a living from it.

What changed in the fifteenth century causing Europeans to make printing presses?

- People learnt the skill of making paper quite cheaply from wood bark and vegetable fibres. Travelling merchants brought back the technique from China where it had been invented.

- New paper mills sprang up as a result of this newly acquired skill and people grew rich from the profits.

- Due to the growth of schools (see page 160), more and more people needed books to read. The demand for books was greater than the number being produced at this time so men saw that printing books was fast becoming a profitable business opportunity.

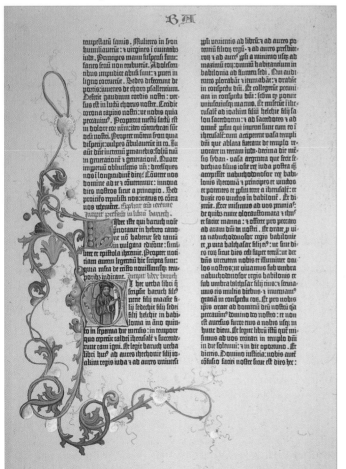

A page from one of the 48 surviving '42 line Bibles' printed by Gutenberg. After the text was printed, the pages were decorated by hand.

Gutenberg (c.1397–1468) and Caxton (1422–91)

In 1438 a German craftsman named Johann Gutenberg and three partners contracted to develop printing techniques. By 1450 Gutenberg had refined his techniques enough to convince a Mainz merchant, Johann Furst, to sponsor his work. So it was that in 1450 the first printed version of the Bible was produced (see Source A) using the new method of printing with movable type invented by Gutenberg. Unfortunately Furst later sued him for debt and consequently seized and used his printing facilities!

The printing process consisted of a mould in which thousands of letters of equal sizes could be cast from hot metal. Gutenberg learnt this skill in metalwork from his uncle, who was a master of a mint where money was made. Lines of letters were laid out and locked firmly together in a frame by wooden wedges in order to make up a whole page of words.

This page of movable type was then fixed into a printing press, possibly one developed from a wine or cheese press (see Source B). A piece of paper was then placed over the inked type and held in place by a paper holder. The paper, paper holder and type were then slid into the press, where a large, flat, wooden plate was lowered on to the paper by turning a huge wooden screw on the printing press. This pressed the paper firmly down on to the inked type to print the page. A press of this kind could print about 300 pages a day.

Other businessmen quickly followed Gutenberg. William Caxton set up the first English printing press in 1476, in the precincts of Westminster Abbey.

He was a travelling London mercer (cloth merchant), who picked up the skills of printing from his visits to the Netherlands (Holland) and Germany. He was successful in producing a series of books in English, including some of his own translations, which appealed to the taste of the court and gentry. One famous book printed at this time was Chaucer's *Canterbury Tales*, in 1484. The first ever printed 'English' newspaper appeared on 12 December 1620 in Amsterdam! It was called the *Corantos* meaning 'foreign'. Even so it was very popular, though when it was eventually introduced in England it was banned.

The printing of books and pamphlets became common over the next century. More and more people began to voice new ideas and wished to pass on their views to a wider and more literate public. In this way the development of the printing press was a major factor in the Renaissance movement. Up to this point the Church was, by and large, the main producer of written documents, controlling what was read. With the invention of printing the opportunities for the spread of new ideas and free speech grew, but for those people who criticised governments and prominent people life could be dangerous. Even today some governments around the world control (censor) the 'press' (the name given to newspapers, periodicals and anyone working as a journalist).

The growth of the press

As we learned in Chapter 4 by the 1640s there were major problems between Charles I and Parliament and many journalists saw this as their chance to speak out or communicate the problems of the day. One of these was Samuel Pecke who from 1641 began to produce 'news books' which reported parliamentary debates from the House of Commons, giving long and graphic accounts of parliamentary business. It was from this time that newspapers began to produce news from home, instead of reporting only news from abroad.

The press and propaganda in England

During the Civil War in England (1642–9), newspapers came into their own. The MP John Pym realised just how important they could be in spreading Parliamentarian propaganda (views and opinions supporting Parliament's cause). Fleet Street, the centre of newspaper production and journalism in London, kept up an amazing output of news-sheets throughout the war. The Royalists, too, had their own newspaper called *Mercurius Aulicus*, which kept alive the Royalist cause.

After the war, Cromwell banned all news-books, except those written by his supporter, the Puritan Marchamont Nedham. Similarly, when Charles II was on the throne (1660-85) he passed a Licensing Act that halted the flood of newspapers which had greeted him in 1660 when he returned to England to be crowned king. This was a form of censorship. In 1665, the *Gazette* was founded and it was the only newspaper permitted. This caused journalists to produce handwritten sheets in order to air their views; these were supplied to subscribers and coffee houses. It wasn't until 1702 that another publication, the *Daily Courant*, was able to survive as a newspaper in its own right.

By this time the flow of newspapers had grown because William III was more accustomed to the freedom of the press in Holland and so he put an end to censorship. Politicians now hired writers to put their views across to the public, and this was to create a group of professional journalists such as Daniel Defoe (author of *Robinson Crusoe*) and Jonathan Swift (author of *Gulliver's Travels*). Another journalist, Sir Richard Steele, wrote a pamphlet called *The Crisis* in 1714. This was in favour of the Hanoverian succession and he was subsequently expelled from the House of Commons! A number of politicians complained greatly about this expulsion and halted attempts in Parliament to tax newspapers out of existence.

SOURCE C

This eighteenth-century cartoon, titled 'This Man's got the whip hand of them all', attacks the freedom of the press to criticise anyone they want.

Question time

1 Why did the invention of the printing press take so long to come to England?

2 What do you think the Church thought about this new invention and why?

3 In what way did the invention of the printing press have an effect on the Renaissance?

4 Why did the writing of pamphlets become so popular during the Civil War? Why wasn't it outlawed?

5 Why do you think it was that the Church and kings and governments tried to outlaw news-books and newspapers?

The arts during the Renaissance

Drama in England

Since the Middle Ages, the only kind of drama people ever saw was the mystery play, in which local people would act out stories from the Bible in the streets of their town. This changed in the Renaissance. With the spread of new ideas and religious reforms these plays became unpopular – Queen Elizabeth herself frowned upon them. Because of these changes in attitude, many new playwrights began to emerge; they experimented with new kinds of plays, including comedies.

Elizabeth I's love of music and drama encouraged new playwrights such as Ben Jonson (1573–1637), Christopher Marlowe (1564–93) and William Shakespeare (1564–1616). Elizabeth often commanded players to come to her palace and perform for her. Shakespeare, the most famous of all playwrights, developed a new kind of verse drama. His plays gave a vivid picture of Elizabethan life and also explored important issues in depth. Until the last part of the sixteenth century, actors had toured the country in groups, performing from place to place. From 1575 onwards many new playhouses were being built in London. The most famous were the Swan Theatre (Source C) and the Globe Theatre. The latter of these theatres was where the young William Shakespeare's plays were performed.

Not everyone welcomed the growth of playhouses and the rise in the number of actors. There were many different opinions at this time.

SOURCE A

This picture of the playwright William Shakespeare, by an unknown contemporary artist, is probably the most accurate to have been produced.

SOURCE B

Great disorders and inconveniences have been found to ensue [caused] to this city by the inordinate [excessive] haunting of great multitudes [crowds] of people – especially youths – to plays, interludes and shows. These cause frays [fights] and quarrels, and also evil practices of incontinency [immorality] in great inns, having chambers [rooms] and secret places adjoining to their open stages and galleries ...

Declaration by the Common Council of London in 1574.

This picture was drawn by an eyewitness and is the only contemporary illustration of the inside of an Elizabethan theatre.

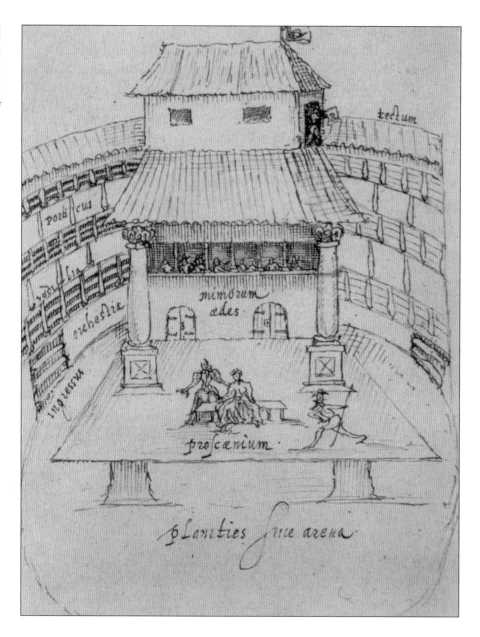

SOURCE D

Look but upon the common [public] plays of London, and see the multitude [crowd] that flocketh to them and followeth them. Behold the sumptuous [expensive] theatre houses ... but I understand they are now forbidden because of the plague ... and the cause of the plagues is sin, if you look to it well; and the cause of sin are plays. Therefore the cause of plagues are plays.

Thomas White in a sermon, 1578.

SOURCE E

Rich young men with nothing to do are always at the theatre. That is where they mix with the tramps, thieves, and tricksters who meet there to plot their crimes. And the plays they see are full of wickedness and cheating. Those who watch are soon persuaded to copy what they see. Apprentices and servants waste their time at the theatre, neglecting their work. People who should know better go there instead of to Church. On top of all that, theatres can make you ill – it is easy to catch an infection in the crowd.

From a letter written by the Puritan Lord Mayor of London in 1597.

SOURCE F

Going to the theatre does young people no harm. If they don't go they might get up to worse mischief elsewhere. Most of the plays set a good example – they tell about the brave actions of the men of the past. And if you do see cheats and liars on the stage, they always come to a bad end.

Thomas Nashe, a writer, in 1592.

SOURCE G

Daily at two in the afternoon, London has two, sometimes three, plays running. Those which play best obtain most spectators. They play on a raised platform so that everyone has a good view. There are different galleries where the seating is more comfortable and therefore more expensive. Whoever care to stand below only pays one English penny. But if he wishes to sit, he enters by another door and pays another penny. If he desires to sit in the most comfortable seats which are cushioned, where he not only sees everything well but can also be seen, he pays yet another. During the performance food and drink are carried around the audience. The actors are expensively dressed; it is the English custom for Lords or for Knights to leave almost the best of their clothes to their servants. It is [not suitable for them] to wear [these], so they offer them for sale to the actors.

T. Platter describing a visit to the playhouse in his Travels in England (1599).

SOURCE H

It is considered that the use and exercise of such plays, not being an evil in itself, may with good order and moderation be suffered [allowed] in a well governed state … as Her Majesty is pleased that sometimes to take delight and recreation in the sight and hearing of them, so order is fit to be taken for the allowance [permission] and maintenance [money] for such persons as are thought meetest [best] in that kind …

In 1600 the Privy Council (advisers to the queen) stated that plays were acceptable – this was due to the rise of great playwrights, such as Marlowe and Shakespeare.

Activity time

1   When interpreting the past, historians need to use contemporary sources (those created at the time) and analyse them in order to create their own ideas and arguments. Using the above sources, your own research from the Internet, and any other sources you find, write an essay about the Elizabethan theatre which is constructed using the following sub-headings:

a   **Playhouses in the sixteenth century**
Say what playhouses were like in the late sixteenth century.

b   **Reactions to the new playhouses**
What were the various reactions to the growth of playhouses. Say if they were acceptable or not and why.

c   **Playwrights**
Explain who the key playwrights of this period were, and give examples of their work. (This is a research question.)

d   **Summary and conclusion**
Be sure to include your views on the theatre, summing up your ideas and analysing the short- and long-term impact of theatres.

Painting and sculpture

Some of the most obvious changes brought about by the Renaissance are in painting and sculpture. During the Middle Ages (the period of history before the Renaissance), the subjects of paintings looked flat and lacked any feeling of movement. Sculptures were often shallow carvings, called bas-reliefs and were used to decorate walls and other stonework. Medieval artists focused on the religious meaning of their work and did not try to make their subjects appear life-like. Many Renaissance works of art show subjects taken from the Bible. This was because they were to decorate cathedrals and other religious buildings. However, Renaissance artists also began to paint non-religious subjects and they wanted to show people and nature in a more realistic way. Painters like Michelangelo (1475–1564), Raphael (1483–1520), Leonardo da Vinci (1452–1519) and Dürer (1471–1528) learned new techniques to make accurate drawings of people, animals and plants. Leonardo da Vinci even drew cut-up bodies so that he could learn the shape of the muscles under the skin and paint more realistic figures.

Artists like Raphael adopted a new style in their work. Paintings now had perspective, which meant that objects in a picture looked the same in relation to each other as they did in real life. The rise of perspective gave the impression of distance and a feeling of depth to the painting. The Renaissance painters also developed the technique of using light and shade to make subjects appear solid.

SOURCE I

'Betrothal of the Virgin Mary' by Raphael, 1504.

As well as developing a new style, artists used new materials for the first time; for example, oil-based paints, which were made by mixing powdered pigments with linseed oil. Oil paints became popular because they dried very slowly, remaining soft and workable for many months. This meant that painters could take more time and trouble over their work.

In the Renaissance period, artists experimenting with new materials began to sculpt figures applying the rules they had learnt about painting. Previously, sculptures had been made only by stonemasons. In bas-reliefs artists used perspective to make the scenes more life-like. A famous example of this is the 'Gates of Paradise', made by Ghiberti in 1452 for the Baptistery in Florence (Source J). These were paid for by the Medici family (see page 158).

Renaissance sculpture went a step further! Inspired by Ancient Roman statues dug up from ruins, artists began to carve figures which could be viewed from any position – in the round. These sculptures stood upright on their own. They caused a sensation at first and appeared to symbolise the Renaissance

The 'Gates of Paradise'
by Lorenzo Ghiberti,
1452. This forms part of
a bronze relief from the
east gates of the
Baptistery in Florence.

ideas of human independence and individuality. One of the most famous sculptors was Michelangelo, who began painting and sculpting at the age of twelve. He carved huge life-like statues in marble (Source K), which demonstrated physical strength and spiritual power.

SOURCE K

Michelangelo's famous sculpture of 1498, the Pietà, in Rome.

The Renaissance also influenced architecture because it renewed interest in the Classical style (the style of the Ancient Greeks and Romans). Architects in Florence started this process – one of the most famous was Filippo Brunelleschi (1377–1446). He was one of the first to bring the laws of perspective (see page 168) into practical use in the design of buildings. Most of his work was done in Florence – for example, the Foundlings Hospital and the cupola of the Duomo (cathedral). This great octagonal dome dominates the cathedral and the city (see Source L). The Renaissance style of architecture, remarkable for its strong but graceful appearance, spread throughout Italy, following the work of Brunelleschi.

St Peter's Basilica in Rome

One of the most impressive Renaissance churches is St Peter's Basilica in Rome, the biggest Christian church in the world. It was modelled on a Roman basilica and was started in AD 325. In 1506, Pope Julius II decided to rebuild it and had the original church demolished. The cost of rebuilding was very great and some of the money was raised through the selling of indulgences, something that Martin Luther criticised John Tetzel about in Germany (see page 40).

SOURCE L

A photograph showing the cupola (dome) of the cathedral (Il Duomo) in Florence.

The original design for the new church was drawn up by Donato Bramante (1444–1544). His plan was for a symmetrical church in the form of a Greek cross (a cross with four arms of equal length), topped with a magnificent dome. When Bramante died in 1514, new plans were drawn up but no building took place until 1547 when Michelangelo took over the project. He changed the design of the dome, reduced the size of the basilica and added a portico. Michelangelo died in 1564 just before the dome was built and it was finished by Giacomo della Porta. He stuck to Michelangelo's plans with only a few minor changes. Work continued after the Renaissance and in 1629 Bernini continued in a Baroque style. The basilica contains some of the most famous pieces of Renaissance art such as Michelangelo's sculpture, the Pietà (see Source K).

Poetry and music

In poetry and music, the fresh ideas of the Renaissance also found expression. One of the most famous figures in the development of opera towards the end of the sixteenth century was an Italian composer called Claudio Monteverdi (1567–1643). He used new techniques such as increasing the number of instruments in the orchestra. His innovations made a great impact on the development of music after this period. Two of his most important works are *Orpheus* and *The Coronation of Poppaea*.

One of the most famous poets of the Renaissance was John Milton (1608–74). His classic masterpiece is *Paradise Lost*. In this poem Milton used great imagery and justified the ways of God to man. The work of Milton is studied in schools and universities today and he is regarded as one of the greatest of the English poets.

Digging deeper

Leonardo da Vinci 1452–1519: Renaissance man

Leonardo da Vinci is regarded as one of the most famous painters of all time. He was born near Florence and spent most of his working life in the city. He was not just an artist; like many Renaissance figures he was interested in a variety of subjects. As well as being a great painter, he was an accomplished anatomist, engineer, mathematician, musician, naturalist, philosopher, architect and sculptor.

The majority of his scientific ideas remained hidden in his notebooks and have not had the same impact as his paintings, for which he is best remembered.

The anatomist

Leonardo da Vinci was very interested in anatomy and made over 30 dissections of human bodies to find out more about the structure of the body. The Church took a negative view of this, believing that when people died they would need their whole bodies in the afterlife. Da Vinci could have been

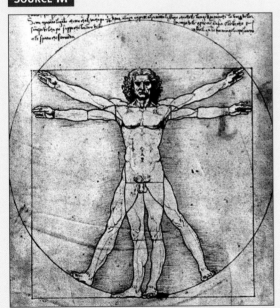

SOURCE **M**

Anatomical drawings from Leonardo da Vinci's notebooks.

imprisoned or even executed as a result of his dissections. Evidently he was prepared to go to these lengths in order to further his own learning and understanding.

Da Vinci was familiar with the new methods of scientific learning, particularly with regards to his dissection work, and said: 'An experiment should be made many times, so that no accident may occur to hinder or falsify the proof.' His studies of the human body also helped him in his artistic work.

Da Vinci as an artist

Da Vinci painted slowly; some of his paintings were never finished. Only fifteen of his paintings still survive today. On account of his versatility (being capable of doing many things well), he was the personification of the Renaissance man – someone who pursued many interests and whose talents were far reaching. By the age of 25 he had gained a great reputation and the patronage of a Florentine ruler – Lorenzo the Magnificent. Because Leonardo da Vinci quite often failed to complete projects, he frustrated Lorenzo and his other Florentine patrons. They viewed him simply as if he were just an ordinary artist producing work to order. However, he strongly objected to their attitude towards him and looked on himself more as an inspired creator. So da Vinci left Florence for Milan in 1482 and worked at the court of Sforza where he was given a much freer rein in structuring his time and work. Eventually he moved to France and was under the patronage of the French King Francis I until the artist's death in 1519.

Leonardo was a strict vegetarian and would go to the market and buy caged birds so that he could then set them free.

The 'Virgin of the Rocks', c.1506.

The above picture is typical of da Vinci's work as a Renaissance artist. In the 'Virgin of the Rocks', painted in about 1506, da Vinci uses light and shade very skilfully which helps to create perspective – taking the viewer far into the picture. The figures in the painting are solid and life-like. His understanding of rock formations as a scientist has been used to create the distant and mysterious background.

Activity time

1 Research da Vinci and other Renaissance artists, using the library and Internet. Create a fact-file of key works of art and include pictures if you can.

2 From your fact-file, produce a timeline which highlights the dates and events of major artistic achievements.

Astronomy and the Church

As we have seen, the Renaissance brought with it a tide of change. For centuries, scientists and philosophers had accepted the work of Ancient Greek and Roman philosophers such as Aristotle and Plato, which they interpreted in the light of Christian belief. But, with the advancement of new ideas, many scientists, such as Sir Francis Bacon (1561–1626), believed that a new approach to scientific theory was called for. This approach was based on factual evidence rather than belief (see page 175).

In the same way, Renaissance astronomers now used the new scientific methods of experimenting and observation to study the skies. It was their sensational discoveries which shook European beliefs about the world.

Greek ideas

The ancient Greek philosopher Pythagoras (c.570–495 BC) proved that the Earth was round and Aristarchus suggested that the Earth and planets revolved around the Sun. However, these ideas were replaced by Ptolemy's theories of the universe written in about AD100. Ptolemy was an Egyptian mathematician, astronomer and geographer who believed that the planets and stars all revolved around the Earth. This 'geocentric' theory fitted well with the Church's ideas of the heavens being a circle, because it was the 'perfect' shape. It also fitted with the idea of the Earth (God's creation), the Church and God himself being at the centre of the universe. It wasn't until the beginning of the Renaissance in Europe that scientists and astronomers started to challenge existing theories about the orbit of the planets. One person who began to doubt Ptolemaic theory was Copernicus.

Nicolaus Copernicus (1473–1543)

Copernicus was a Polish–German astronomer. He founded modern astronomy when, in 1543, he published his book *The Revolution of the Heavenly Orbs*. In it he said people should assume that the Earth moved around the Sun. This 'heliocentric' theory, which put the Sun not the Earth at the centre of the heavenly stage, aroused fierce religious opposition.

Later scientists went on to prove scientifically that Copernicus' theories were correct. The Danish astronomer, Tycho Brahe (1546–1601), began to make measurements of incredible accuracy, which was a major achievement considering that the telescope had not yet been invented! Brahe calculated the position of over 800 stars and made careful observations of the movement of Mars. When Brahe died in 1601, his pupil, Johannes Kepler (1571–1630), who took over his work, discovered that not only did the planets revolve around the Sun but that they moved in elliptical (oval) orbits. This further shattered the old idea of the perfect circular motion of the heavens.

The work of Galileo (1564–1642)

In 1610 the Italian mathematician, scientist and astronomer Galileo became one of the first people to build and use a telescope to observe the sky. Invented by him, he managed to observe the Milky Way, the Moon and the orbit of planets in the solar system. He concluded in his book of 1610, *The Starry Messenger*, that his scientific observations showed that Copernicus' theories, 67 years earlier, were indeed correct. This was to cause a negative reaction from the Catholic Church because these discoveries undermined the teachings of the Church, and attacked the idea that the Church and God were at the centre of a perfect universe. They also contradicted stories in the Bible. This resulted in the seizure of Copernicus' book which was placed on the Church's list of 'forbidden' books. The Church accused Galileo of heresy, and threatened him with torture unless he denied everything. Legend has it that, after making the oath in Source B, Galileo whispered, 'And yet it [the earth] does move'.

It seems incredible today that a scientist should make such a statement, denying his own findings through the scientific research he had conducted. Yet it reveals the strong influence that the Church and religion had on people at this time. In 1633 Galileo went through a trial conducted by the Church, which led to him being under house arrest for the last eight years of his life! Galileo and his work continue to be of interest to people today – see, for example, Dava Sobel's book, *Galileo's Daughter*.

This period of invention and discovery and the swing towards a new understanding of the universe greatly challenged the teachings of the Church. The new scientific methods were to prove scientists' theories and justified the growth in scientific learning, even though challenged the established teachings of the Church. In fact the Church began to adjust its teachings so they were in line with some of the more widely accepted scientific theories of the day. This period of history truly was a *renaissance* or rebirth of learning.

> **SOURCE B**
>
> I, Galileo, do swear that I have always believed, do now believe and with God's aid shall believe hereafter, all that which is taught and preached by the Church. I must wholly forsake the false opinion that the Sun is the centre of the world and moves not, and that the Earth is not the centre of the world and moves.
>
> *Galileo's statement at his trial in about 1633, in response to the Church's accusation of heresy.*

Question time

1   What beliefs in the Church were challenged by the theories and scientific discoveries of the Renaissance scientists described above?

Make a chart like the one below to help you analyse the information in this section. Allow yourself plenty of room for writing. Then write a short essay-style answer to the question.

Scientist	How did they approach scientific problems?	Did they challenge the beliefs of the Church and if so how?	How did they tell the world about their findings?
Ptolemy			
Copernicus			
Brahe			
Galileo			

The scientific revolution in the seventeenth century

As well as a flourishing of the arts and philosophy, scientific inventions and discoveries were an important feature of the Renaissance, as people began to ask questions and challenge traditionally held beliefs. During the Scientific Revolution in England in the seventeenth century, the scientist William Harvey (1578–1657) proved that the heart continually circulates blood around the body. Isaac Newton worked on new ideas in maths, physics and astronomy, discovering gravity and its affect on the Sun and planets. And Christopher Wren (1632–1723) was a scientist but is perhaps best known for his architecture – he rebuilt St Paul's Cathedral in London in a classical style, drawing on many of the ideas of the Romans and Ancient Greeks in the design of this cathedral as well as his later buildings.

As we have seen by looking at astronomers on pages 173–4, scientists changed the way they approached their experimentation. They began to base more of their understanding on observations made during their experiments, rather than giving explanations based on what they were told to believe or on magic and superstition. This approach to science is very much the same today: one of observation and experimentation. In the seventeenth century the English philosopher and statesman, Sir Francis Bacon (1561–1626), argued that the scientist's first task was observation followed by experimentation. This new approach was the start of modern science and was one of the most important changes to take place between 1600 and 1750.

During this time many important instruments were invented – for example, the telescope, microscope and thermometer. In 1662 Charles II granted a Royal Charter to honour the Royal Society which had been set up in 1660 by a group of scientists including Sir Christopher Wren. All the top scientists belonged to it, as they still do today.

Question time

1 Using the information above, explain in two paragraphs what the Renaissance was and why it was so important. Include in your answer the broad impact that the Renaissance had upon Europe, e.g. through science, discoveries, the arts, education and learning.

Isaac Newton (1642–1727)

The fierce reaction of the Church over the findings of scientists from Copernicus in 1543 through to Galileo in 1633 did not discourage other young scientists from continuing to develop new methods of scientific investigation. Forty-five years after the death of Galileo, the English physicist and mathematician, Sir Isaac Newton, published what has been termed the best scientific book ever written. The book, published in 1687, was called *Principia Mathematica* and laid down the laws of motion and gravitation. It was the first complete and accurate explanation of what was happening in the heavens and was accepted as one of the greatest scientific works of the age.

Isaac Newton became a professor of mathematics at Cambridge University in 1669. He was a strong Protestant believer who was able to accept the new scientific theories and findings. He is mostly remembered for his law of gravity. The story goes that after watching an apple fall from a tree he began to wonder why it fell straight down and did not just stay where it was, or move sideways. His theory of gravity, developed in 1686, showed that all objects attract each other, depending on their mass and distance apart. Therefore the huge Earth pulls a small apple towards it by a force called gravity. This force of attraction happens whether it is a tiny object or a planet and so it is a law of science. Newton's scientific laws explained a great deal about how the universe worked and yet did not clash with his Christian beliefs. Although in 1705 he became the first scientist to receive a knighthood in recognition of his work, he had a very humble opinion of himself and his findings.

Advances in medicine

Look carefully at Source B which shows Charles II attempting to cure people of skin diseases by simply touching them. Between 1660 and 1682 Charles II touched over 92,000 people with skin diseases! It was due to the Renaissance that great strides were made in the understanding of science and medicine. Today scientists approach problems in a structured way rather than following what they are told to believe or believing in magic.

SOURCE B

Charles II touching people to cure their skin diseases – scrofula – known as the King's Evil. This picture is an engraving by Frederick van Hove (1628–98). Charles and many of his doctors believed he was able to cure sufferers just by touching them because he was the king.

This approach was developed during the Renaissance and sometimes got scientists, such as Galileo, into trouble with the Church (see page 174). The five steps to follow when solving scientific problems are:

1 **Observe** what happens.

2 **Develop** a theory.

3 **Devise an experiment** to test the theory. Repeat the experiment to ensure the same outcome.

4 **Observe and measure the results** of the experiment.

5 **If the results do not fit**, return to step 2 and develop a new theory.

During the Renaissance, there were several key scientists who sparked off a scientific revolution in the field of medicine.

Andreas Vesalius, founder of modern anatomy

Vesalius (1514–64) was a Flemish anatomist who wrote a book in 1543 called *De Humani Corporis Fabricia* (On the Fabric of the Human Body). This became the foundation stone of modern anatomy and was based on actual dissection work and examination carried out by Vesalius.

SOURCE C

Vesalius' drawing of the human skeleton, 1543.

Robert Hooke and the microscope

Robert Hooke (1635–1703) was a professor of geometry, an astronomer and designer of the compound microscope and marine barometer. He also discovered how metals behave when they are stretched. He almost discovered the laws of gravity and its effects on the planets before Newton (see page 176), but his mathematics was not good enough! He studied the way metals behave and we still call his description of this 'Hooke's Law'.

Leeuwenhoek, a Dutch scientist, had demonstrated how microscopes could be used effectively in many areas of science but he had only an instrument with one lens. Hooke invented a much more powerful microscope with several lenses which was called the compound microscope. He described his invention and other pieces of equipment, and made detailed drawings from his observations of objects such as the flea in his book, *Micrographia*. However, Hooke was bad tempered and often argued with other scientists. He was very worried that someone else might steal his discoveries, so he often left his work in code. As a result of his secrecy and bad temper, he did not always get the credit for his discoveries!

Digging deeper

William Harvey (1578–1657)

What was William Harvey's contribution to scientific discovery?

William Harvey studied at Cambridge University and, having decided to follow a career in medicine, he went to study at the respected medical school at Padua, Italy, in 1599. It was here that the lecturers used dissection to explain how the human body worked.

On his return to England, Harvey practised medicine and became a lecturer in anatomy. He also became doctor to Charles I. He worked to discover how the heart and blood worked in the body. Prior to this, scientists in Europe were believers in the teachings of Galen, who was a Greek doctor from the second century. Galen taught that the blood was moved from the heart to all the different parts of the body, where it was used up. He also taught that the liver was the producer of new blood. It was during Harvey's lifetime that scientists again began to question Galen's views. William Harvey's approach to Galen's teachings was to be more scientific; he began to experiment and measure scientifically how the blood moved around the body. These are some of the ways in which Harvey experimented in order to discover how the blood circulated:

- He pushed thin wire down veins.

- He cut up live cold-blooded animals, such as frogs, to watch how their hearts worked.

- He made attempts to pump blood past valves inside the veins. When he failed he realised that blood only flowed in one direction.

- He took measurements of how much blood the heart pumped.

Eventually Harvey was able to calculate how much blood was pumped out of the heart per hour. He discovered it came to three times the weight of an adult. He then concluded that, as the body could not make that amount of new blood every hour, people have a fixed volume of blood in the body which circulates around it. Harvey's experiments had proved that the heart pumped blood to the body through arteries and the blood returned to the heart through veins. Unfortunately, at that time, knowing how the heart worked was not of use in healing people, although this theory proved that people could not have too much blood, so the practice of 'bleeding' patients to make them well made no sense. However, as medicine developed and anaesthetics and antiseptics started being used in the nineteenth century, Harvey's discoveries proved vital in medical surgery.

SOURCE D

It is proved by the structure of the heart that the blood is transferred through the blood to the heart, as in a water pump. It is proved that there is a transit of blood from the arteries, to the veins, and from this is shown that the perpetual movement of the blood in a circle is brought about by the heart.

William Harvey speaking about his discovery that blood circulates around the body in 1628.

SOURCE E

I have heard him say that after his book on the circulation of blood came out he lost a great many patients and 'twas believed he was crack brained.

John Aubrey, a friend of Harvey, speaking in the 1630s.

SOURCE F

Harvey's illustration of 1628, showing how valves in the veins allow blood to flow in one direction and not the other. In Figure 2, if the finger is pressed along the vein from O to H, the vein empties and does not refill. The valve at O stops the blood. Therefore it has to be a one-way valve, only allowing blood to move towards the heart. The vein only refills when the finger is removed from H.

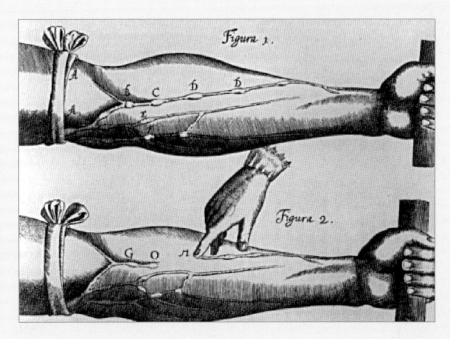

Question time

1 Copy and complete the charts below, which list evidence (reasons) *for* and *against* Harvey's new theories for blood circulation. Use Sources D to F and the text to help you.

2 Using the lists and your own knowledge, answer the following essay-style question:

Explain the benefits that William Harvey brought to scientific research and knowledge of the circulatory system.

EVIDENCE AGAINST showing that people didn't totally believe in Harvey's theories

EVIDENCE FOR showing that Harvey's work was to become successful

Links to modern technology

We can see that during the 1600s many important discoveries were made in the world of science and medicine. Scientists began to use experiments and factual evidence to discover how the human body worked and to find ways in which sick people might be treated. These findings had short- and long-term effects because it was some time later that doctors and surgeons had the knowledge to understand illnesses and discover cures for diseases. For example, William Harvey's discovery (see above) had a limited impact for some 200 years, until the 1800s when more was known about germs and anaesthetics.

Up until then surgery was so basic that many patients died during or after an operation! However, Harvey's discovery about blood circulation represented an important leap in medical understanding in the 1600s.

In today's society we take science for granted. It is expected that experiments are carried out in order to discover how things work – observations are made, recordings taken, and experiments checked and double-checked. New technology creates advanced machines and computer systems that enable us to push the boundaries of knowledge more and more in our understanding of the world (the Internet and the information 'super highway' are examples of this).

This new way of thinking affects our world – cloning animals and even humans, genetically-modified crops, space stations, cancer research, AIDS research are all examples of how our world is changing rapidly due to discoveries in science.

Some of these discoveries improve our lives and some do not. Some questions will never be answered. The changes that began this modern way of examining and understanding the world began during the Renaissance and the process continues today. For example, the Royal Society was established in 1660 to encourage scientific research and in 1676 the Royal Observatory at Greenwich was founded to learn more about the planets and the universe. Thus we can trace back to the Renaissance some long-term causes of the Scientific Revolution in the seventeenth century:

- The rediscovery of Greek and Roman ideas in the Renaissance led to a questioning of the ideas held during the Middle Ages about the body, health and the universe.

- The printing press helped to spread new ideas (see page 160).

- Improved metal-working led to better tools and equipment.

- New and more life-like art and sculpture allowed people to examine more critically how things were created (see page 168).

- Improved glass-making techniques led to the manufacture of higher quality magnifying lenses.

- Previously held views that the dead should be left alone in order to secure a safe passage to heaven changed, and, later in the period, permission was granted for more dead bodies to be examined.

- The expansion in education led to a more literate society and increasingly the Church had less influence over people's lives.

- The rise of Protestantism in the early sixteenth century (see Chapter 2) led to the questioning of some religious views and traditions held by the Catholic Church. People became more open to ideas about their world.

Question time

1. Why was there a growth in scientific understanding and discoveries in the seventeenth century? You should consider causes and effects of the Scientific Revolution.

Express your answer in the form of a spider diagram, like the one below.

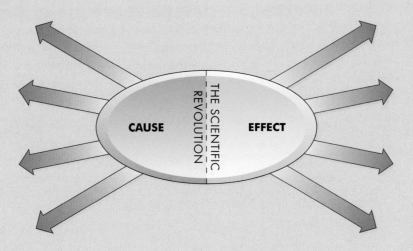

Trade, exploration and voyages of discovery in the sixteenth and seventeenth centuries

Italy – the key centre for trade

The Renaissance helped establish a number of trade routes and encouraged new commercial ideas. In the fifteenth century Italy was well positioned to become a key centre for European trade with the east, because it attracted many scholars, bankers, merchants and trades people. It became the banking centre of Europe and the rest of the known world. As these people prospered, so did Italy. It is important to remember that at this time it was not a united country. The Pope as head of the Catholic Church ruled the land around Rome; cities such as Venice, Milan and Florence were independent city states (see page 158). Successful traders wanted the best for themselves, their families, and their towns and cities. They had the money to buy beautiful things and support the arts. Wealthy families acted as sponsors to scholars and artists, providing them with work and a living, so cities such as Florence became centres of learning and the arts.

It was not just Italy that prospered – during the Renaissance period, Britain gained a great deal of land, wealth and prosperity as new colonies were established and trade routes were opened, increasing the trading opportunities for British merchants.

Trade in the East

Trade was not limited to Europe alone. For Europeans, the East – countries such as India and China – was seen as a great mystery and exciting and the goods to be found there were much in demand. For example, in England there was a market for spices such as ginger, pepper and cinnamon. Also cottons, silks and delicately coloured porcelain were much sought after in Europe. The search for gold spurred explorers to go to far-flung places. By the end of the fifteenth century there was not enough gold in Europe to satisfy the needs of the rich and wealthy; they wanted gold objects to decorate their homes as well as needing gold to produce high-value coins. Trading ports in Europe became rich and powerful as they made great profits from bringing these goods from centres in the eastern Mediterranean and the Black Sea.

Journeys of discovery

At this time knowledge of the world was rapidly expanding as people journeyed more and new peoples and cultures were discovered (see Source A). This process was aided by recent inventions like the compass, logline (see page 183) and maps.

Why did voyages of discovery take place? There are a number of factors, namely:

- the desire for trade

- spreading religion

- the desire for increased wealth and power

- the desire for adventure to discover the unknown

- technical advances

- empire building and to establish control over other countries.

Travelling to the East presented an exciting challenge to Renaissance explorers, but what was the East actually like at this time? Europeans had a good idea what China was like because the thirteenth-century explorer Marco Polo (c.1254–1324) had been there and had written about its wealth and riches. They also knew about India, or the Indies, but were not sure of the exact location. They were confident about the luxury goods they would find there and there were stories of a mountain of gold. They had also heard stories about strange peoples (see Sources A and B) and fearful monsters, as well as unknown dangers like the sea boiling in the hotter areas or being so solid with weeds that it could trap a ship forever! Danger seemed always to be around the corner.

SOURCE A

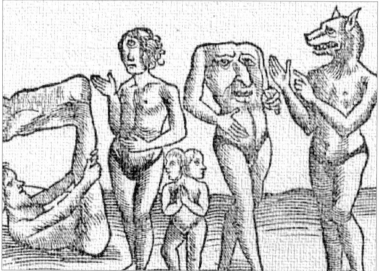

Drawing showing the 'Strange Races of Men' by the explorer Sebastian Munster from his 1540 map.

In another isle are men without heads, and they have eyes in either shoulder, and their mouths are round-shaped like a horseshoe amidst their breasts. Yet there is another isle where the folk have but one foot, and that foot is so broad that it will cover all the body and shade it from the sun.

Written by Sir John Mandeville, whose book called The Travels of Sir John Mandeville, *became increasingly popular in the 1400s and 1500s.*

O most excellent gold! Whoever has gold has a treasure which gives him the power to get what he wants. It lets him do what he wants in the world and even helps souls into heaven.

Columbus, the famous Italian explorer and sailor, summing up the reasons for his voyages to Queen Isabella and King Ferdinand of Spain in 1492.

Setting sail

A sixteenth-century caravel. This was a type of ship suited to long voyages. In this picture a battle is fought between European explorers and native peoples.

For centuries, European sailors never ventured far from land so that they wouldn't lose sight of familiar landmarks. In the open sea it was vitally important to be able to navigate effectively because accurate maps did not exist. Dead reckoning was used by sailors, which meant that a compass told them what direction they were going in and a logline allowed them to make a rough calculation as to their speed. This logline was a piece of wood with a rope attached to it. On the rope knots were made at regular intervals. When the wood was thrown into the sea, the rope would unwind as the ship sailed forward and, by counting the knots, sailors could make a rough calculation of their speed. A knot is still used today as a nautical term for miles per hour. Sailors would also use a cross-staff or quadrant as a further check to measure the position of the pole star and other stars in relation to the horizon. John Harrison (1693–1776), a clockmaker, greatly aided navigators by solving the longitude problem. He devised a timepiece which would keep accurate time, enabling sailors to plot their position at sea. You can learn more about Harrison in a book by Dava Sobel called *Longitude*.

The explorers used ships called caravels. They could travel quite quickly because the big square sails caught the wind well and the triangular lateen sail at the back made it easy to tack (move in a zig-zag direction) when sailing directly into the wind. These ships were set deep enough into the water so they didn't capsize easily. They were just large enough (approximately 21 metres long and 6.5 metres wide) to take the crew needed to deal with all the complicated rigging, the necessary stores and the guns, which could be fired through the ports (holes) cut into the high sides.

What problems did the sailors face?

One problem, which was never really solved by the explorers, was how to keep the crew healthy. The crew had to put up with many hardships and dreadful conditions whilst on board ship. Below decks it was very cramped, dirty and dark; often the sleeping space was not much more than a metre high; rats and lice were common-place. In bad weather, water seeped in through the wooden planks and it was not possible for the sailors to go on to the open deck; the work was extremely dangerous because adjusting the sails in a storm was a hazardous operation. In a dead calm, on the other hand, the crew soon became bored because there was nothing to do to keep them occupied.

As the ship was made from wood, fire was a constant risk and a sailor's diet became worse and worse as the long journey progressed. Hot food was cooked on a fire in a box of sand, when the weather allowed. However, water stored in barrels soon went off and wine turned sour. Food also went stale and rotted or the ship's biscuits became infected with weevils. Lack of fresh fruit and vegetables meant sailors often suffered from diseases such as scurvy. When they went to places where no other Europeans had been before it was dangerous to land and restock with food and water because the inhabitants might be hostile.

This is a typical set of stores for an exploration. It is based on a voyage that was carried out at this time with a crew of 280 men.

- 9700 kg of biscuits
- 258 kg of salt beef
- 238 dozen dried fish
- 200 barrels of sardines
- 508 kg of cheese
- 770 kg of fish
- 216 kg of oil
- sacks of beans, peas, lentils, flour, honey, onions, figs, salt
- 2310 kg of gunpowder.

An explorer had to have a lot of money to fund a trip. He needed several ships, stores, equipment, and the crew had to be paid enough to persuade them to travel! An investor was needed to back the operation.

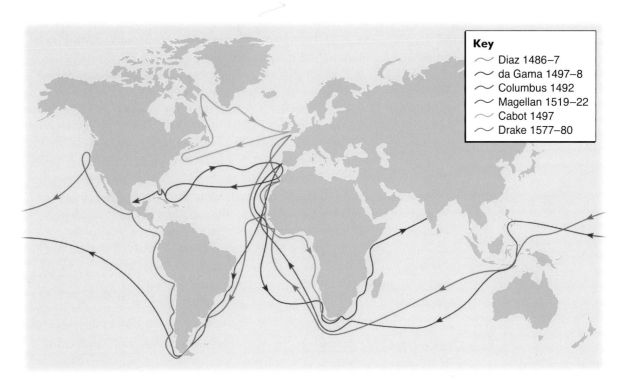

Key

~ Diaz 1486–7
~ da Gama 1497–8
~ Columbus 1492
~ Magellan 1519–22
~ Cabot 1497
~ Drake 1577–80

The routes taken by some of the great Renaissance explorers.

Who were the great explorers?

Spain and Portugal were great naval powers in the fifteenth and sixteenth centuries; they wanted to enlarge their empires. They led the way in exploration with Christopher Columbus (1451–1506) discovering the islands of the Caribbean – the West Indies – in 1492. In 1497 the Portuguese navigator Vasco da Gama sailed round Africa and discovered the southern sea-route to India and the east. This opened up the East India trade route and led to the development of the Portuguese empire.

The English also wanted a route to the east but did not want to compete with Spain and Portugal for the southern seas. John and Sebastian Cabot led English expeditions in 1497 and 1509 in search of the north-west passage to China. They sailed to the northern coasts of North America and reached Newfoundland. Martin Frobisher in 1576 and Henry Hudson in 1610 also explored the northern route to the east but failed to find a passage because of icebergs and pack ice. They did, however, succeed in opening up to Europeans what we now know as Canada. From 1553–4 Hugh Willoughby and Richard Chancellor explored the route to the east via Norway and Russia. Willoughby died trapped in ice but Chancellor reached the coast of Russia and helped develop trade with Moscow.

Privateering

During the reign of Elizabeth I (1558–1603) English merchants and nobles began to see the advantages of England's island status because it provided relative security from invasion. They looked westwards across the Atlantic for adventure as well as an opportunity to become rich. At this time privateering became a very profitable occupation.

Privateers were ships owned by English trading companies and courtiers like Sir Walter Raleigh. They had plenty of space for cargo and were well armed with cannons. Their goal was to seize the cargo of other ships in much the same way as pirates except that they had to give some of their profits to the queen as well as to the ships' owners. Spanish treasure ships were their main targets. Elizabeth encouraged this because England was at war with Spain. In the 1580s and 1590s there were some 100 privateering voyages each year and large cargoes were unloaded at the docks in Bristol, London and Southampton. Valuable items such as sugar, china, silk, pearls, emeralds, gold rings and chains, sapphires and silver coins were seized. As well as travelling round the world in his ship, the *Golden Hind,* from 1577 to 1580, Sir Francis Drake was one of the most famous and successful privateers. He led many daring raids in South America and was very influential in the war against Spain during Queen Elizabeth's reign, by attacking the Spanish navy in its own harbour in Cadiz in 1587, sinking ships and burning supplies. It took the Spanish a year to recover from this attack known as the 'singeing of the King of Spain's beard'.

Many of the surprise attacks on the Spanish by Drake and other privateers took place in the Caribbean. Spanish ships, laden with gold, silver and other treasures from Mexico and Peru, passed through this area on their way back home. By 1585, small settlements, or colonies, began to develop, giving the English a convenient trading base in the region and also places out of which the privateers could operate. North America and the Caribbean continued to flourish as part of England's trading empire and by the middle of the seventeenth century colonisation here, and in other parts of the world, was well established.

Examples of colonies gained by the English in the seventeenth century:

- **1655** Cromwell captures Jamaica

- **1660** Charles II given the Indian city of Bombay as a wedding present

- **1664** New York taken from the Dutch

- **1704** Gibraltar won from the Spanish

- **1688–1713** Britain gains Newfoundland, Nova Scotia and Hudson's Bay following wars with France.

Question time

1 Do you think that Sir John Mandeville (see Source B on page 183) was himself an explorer? Explain your answer.

2 What problems did the Renaissance explorers face?

3 What factors led to the increased desire to explore the world in the sixteenth and seventeenth centuries?

4 Which factor do you consider to be the most important reason behind exploration?

5 Which inventions helped sailors and explorers?

6 Assessment section

1 Religion was an important part of life during the Renaissance period. In class, discuss the ways in which the beliefs of the Church were challenged by key thinkers of the time. Once you have discussed this write your findings in your exercise book.

2 Answer the following essay question:

'In what ways was there a major shift in ideas and thinking during the Renaissance?'

3 Use the Internet, CD-ROMs, your library and textbooks to research one scientific discovery and one artistic change of the period 1485–1750. Present your findings in an illustrated essay.

4 In pairs, research one of the following areas which changed so much during the Renaissance:

- science

- music

- architecture

- art

- exploration.

Explain how your area of focused study has or has not had an impact on our world today. Use this argument in a class debate.

Further reading

Dava Sobel, *Galileo's Daughter* (Fourth Estate, 1999)

Daval Sobel, *Longitude* (Fourth Estate, 1996)

Tim Wood, *The Renaissance* (Hamlyn Books, 1993)

Famous Faces – Portraits in History (Hodder and Stoughton, 1994)

7 A Changing Society 1485–1750

Today we are very familiar with rapid changes in the way we live. Technology advances almost daily. Mobile phones, videos, personal computers, the Internet – few of these would have been familiar items in our homes just 25 years ago. From talking to your parents and grandparents you can find out how different life was when they were children. By the time you are in your early twenties you will probably be able to remember how different things were when *you* were very young.

Did people notice rapid changes in their lifetimes during the sixteenth and seventeenth centuries? From the moment when Henry VII won the crown at the Battle of Bosworth Field in 1485 to the failure of the Jacobites at Culloden 260 years later, the people of Britain witnessed many dramatic changes in the way their country was ruled.

The sixteenth and seventeenth centuries were turbulent, with riots, rebellions, uprisings and even the execution of the monarch and overthrow of the crown. The power of kings and queens weakened in this period while that of Parliament, the aristocracy and wealthy merchants grew. A great deal of blood was spilt in the conflict between the different religions, although by 1750 there was growing tolerance.

But there was another side to life in England during these centuries. The disturbances were not unusual, but they were not the normal experience for most people. From the end of the Wars of the Roses in 1485 to the eighteenth century, there were very few serious outbreaks of rebellion or war, and most parts of England and Wales were becoming much more peaceful than they had been in earlier periods. In the last chapter you read about the growth of new ideas in science and medicine.

But did the daily lives of people change in this period? This chapter will look at the homes of the nobles and gentry, the merchants and farmers, labourers and townspeople. We shall try to find out how they lived, what they wore, and what they ate and whether or not the daily lives of people changed between 1485 and 1750.

Nobles and gentry

Apart from during the Civil War in the 1640s, the monarchy had tight control over the nobles. Most stayed loyal and began to use their wealth to make their lives more comfortable rather than to raise armies. Many noble families (the aristocracy) still had castles as homes, but these had been built in the Middle Ages and were unsuitable for the more peaceful country that England was becoming. Henry VIII (1509–47) had set the style by building or rebuilding many palaces, which were designed not as fortresses, but to show off his magnificence and wealth.

Houses of the nobility

By the end of the reign of Elizabeth (1558–1603), English nobles were copying the monarchs, and many of their great houses have survived. For example, Bess, the Countess of Shrewsbury, was busy rebuilding the houses which belonged to her family. In Derbyshire, she built Hardwick Hall (Source C), the front of which seems almost to have been built of glass, so large are the windows – clearly, Bess of Hardwick had little fear of attack since her house was quite unsuitable as a fortress. Instead of battlements on the roof, Bess built an intricate balustrade decorated with her initials. The great windows allowed light and air into the rooms.

The houses themselves were usually built of stone, but the new material of brick was now also widely used. Builders were learning new styles for carving the stone and bricks into elaborate patterns copied from royal palaces. They had also learnt how to build staircases that went straight up, rather than spiralling like the staircases of castles. The stairs could now become grand features of the houses, allowing ladies and gentlemen to display their upstairs rooms more easily. On beautiful plaster ceilings the coat of arms of the noble family was often displayed to show off its ancestry.

When the French ambassador came to England to try to arrange a marriage between the Duc d'Alençon and Elizabeth I, he was invited to stay with Lord Burghley at his country house called Theobalds.

SOURCE A

The handsome and delightful hall is so ornamental and artistic that its equal is not to be met with. For, besides other embellishments, there is a very high rock of all colours made with real stones, out of which gushes a splendid fountain.

The French ambassador expressing his astonishment at the impressive hall at Theobalds, the country house belonging to Lord Burghley, in 1578.

SOURCE B

In another hall is depicted the kingdom of England, with all its cities, towns and villages, mountains and rivers. And also the coats of arms of every squire, knight, lord and noble who possess lands.

As he moved through the house there was more to impress the French ambassador at Theobalds.

As he looked up, the ambassador could see that the ceiling was decorated with the signs of the zodiac, and he was told that at night this could be used to identify which stars were in which sign. Lord Burghley's interior designers had obviously given his hall a make-over. On each side were six carved trees, complete with birds' nests, leaves and fruit, so life-like that the ambassador was almost taken in.

Outside, Burghley had made changes, too. There was still a moat surrounding the house but the ambassador noted that this had been expanded into a pleasure lake, so that guests could be taken for boat rides among the shrubs of a beautiful garden. Burghley's gardener had been busy collecting a great variety of trees and plants, and there were also fountains of marble, and a summer house in which were white marble statues of the twelve Roman emperors.

SOURCE C

Hardwick Hall in Derbyshire, the home of the Countess of Shrewsbury.

Inside, the great houses of the nobles were becoming much more comfortable. The stone walls were often hung with tapestries, or panelled with oak to make the rooms warmer. Carpets were imported from Turkey. Cushions, and chairs, almost unknown in the Middle Ages, were becoming more common.

Perhaps one of the really important new inventions of the sixteenth century with regard to houses was the chimney. In earlier times fireplaces had been in the centre of rooms even in great castles. Now, using brick chimneys to carry the smoke and soot away, they could be built on side walls. They could even be built in upstairs rooms. Imagine what an improvement this must have been to Tudor homes! For many wealthier people this meant they could now have a room with privacy upstairs, rather than having to sleep around the open hearth downstairs in order to keep warm. On the roofs the architects found another opportunity to show off their decorative skill, building tall, elaborately shaped chimneys.

Beds were a new feature of the Tudor period. Until then it had been usual to sleep on a straw mattress on the floor. Logs had been used as a bolster to support the head, but now mattresses and pillows were filled with goose down; the mattress itself was placed on a bed and supported by a framework of ropes. Curtains were hung round the bed to keep out draughts.

There were changes at mealtimes too. Before the Tudor age, plates and spoons had been wooden, whereas now they were more commonly pewter, tin, or, in wealthier homes, silver. Glassware could now be seen on the tables of the rich, who might also be using another recent invention – the fork. These changes seemed remarkable to people in Elizabethan times (see Source D).

There are old men yet dwelling in the village which have noted three things to be marvellously altered within their remembrance. One is the multitude of chimneys whereas in their young days there were not above two or three. The second is the great improvement of lodgings, for said they our fathers, yea, and we ourselves also, have lain oft upon straw pallets [mattresses], on rough mats covered only with a sheet and a good round log under their heads for a bolster. The third thing they tell of is the exchange of vessel, as of wooden platters into pewter, and wooden spoons into silver or tin.

The clergyman, William Harrison, explains how life was getting better for many people under Elizabeth I in A Description of England *written in 1577.*

Changing styles of architecture and design meant that the aristocracy continued to rebuild their houses and redesign their gardens to keep up with fashion. By the eighteenth century, money from trade had made many aristocratic families very rich indeed. The Palladian style became very fashionable for country houses in England. It was based on the designs of an Italian architect, Andrea Palladio (1508–80): houses had symmetrical plans and rooms were designed with balanced proportions, imitating classical Roman styles. The rooms were elegant, and richly furnished with gilded mirrors, fine furniture of walnut or mahogany and paintings of ancestors. Robert Walpole, prime minister in the 1730s, spent £15 a day on candles to light his home, at a time when a labourer earned about 4 shillings a week. He also ordered 1200lb of chocolate (for drinking) each year!

The role of the nobility

It was not just the homes and gardens of the aristocracy that were changing. The way they behaved and how they thought of themselves was quite different by 1750 from what it had been when Henry VII had come to the throne in 1485. At the end of the Wars of the Roses nobles and knights saw themselves above all as warriors, and their interests and their pastimes were mostly related to war: hunting, jousting and wrestling. In 1750 a gentleman might fight a duel, he loved hunting, and would be knowledgeable about military matters, but to these interests were now added many more peaceful ones.

The nobility and gentry were now more educated and cultured, and were enthusiastic to learn of the new developments in astronomy, navigation and medicine. In the seventeenth century, following the inventions of Galileo and Hooke (see pages 174 and 177), they often purchased microscopes, telescopes and globes. Samuel Pepys' friend, Mr Spong, enthusiastically told him that he had made himself a microscope and 'He doth discover that the wings of a moth is made just as the feathers of a bird.'

Some gentlemen were keen on botany, or agriculture, while others were fascinated by history. They built libraries in their homes, and they liked to collect works of art. The Duke of Devonshire built a museum in his home at Chatsworth, in Derbyshire, to display the many statues and paintings he had gathered from all over Europe.

The lower classes

Yeomen

Home improvements were also taking place in the houses of those below the rank of the nobles and gentry. In many parts of southern England, better-off farmers (yeomen) were rebuilding their houses in brick, with tiled roofs and chimneys. Timber and thatch were still often used, but these new houses were now sturdier, with a timber frame replacing the crucks which had been used earlier. These were curved tree trunks split from top to bottom which were leant against each other to make the framework of labourers' cottages. Sometimes the spaces between the timbers were filled with brick, although wattle and daub – a mixture of clay, horse-hair and animal dung which was used as a plaster over walls – was still used. Inside they would have seemed very bare by our standards. There was just one room with little furniture, usually a long trestle table with benches or stools and sometimes a chair or two. The few windows may well have had no glass in Elizabeth's reign, just an oiled linen cloth to keep out the rain, or possibly shutters. The houses were generally well maintained and gradually improved by their owners throughout the period from 1550 to 1750. New rooms were added, as well as glass windows and stairs rather than ladders; more fireplaces and oak-panelled walls were among the other popular home improvements made. Many of these yeomen houses have survived and are still lived in today (see Source A).

SOURCE A

Many yeomen houses from the sixteenth and seventeenth centuries are still in use as homes today, for example Gawsworth Hall.

Labourers

For the poorer peasants, and for those in many parts of Britain away from the south-east, change came more slowly. Labourers' cottages were usually poorly built of timber and thatch; they did not last long before they needed rebuilding but they could be put up quickly. Inside they would be bare and smoky, with an open hearth for the cooking. Animals shared the accommodation with the cottagers. At one end a cow might be in a stall and chickens would scuttle across the floor while, hanging from a beam above the fire, would be the remains of the pig, preserved by the smoke. There was little improvement to the homes of the poorest cottagers in this period (see Source B).

Home life

The kitchen

In Tudor times, only the largest houses had separate kitchens, and sometimes these were very large, just as they had been in castles. This was because a nobleman's household might have well over 100 people sharing the food. Bess of Hardwick's husband, the Earl of Shrewsbury, regularly had over 150 people dining in his house during Elizabeth's reign! Elsewhere, in smaller houses, food was prepared and cooked in the one room where the family lived. Farmers and country gentlemen were largely self-sufficient, with home-bred meat, fruit and vegetables grown in their own gardens, home-baked bread, and ale and beer brewed in their brewhouses. Farm labourers were much worse off.

SOURCE A

The kitchen at the Tudor manor house of Cotehele in Cornwall, c. 1800.

Most food was prepared by boiling it in an iron pot suspended over the fire. The same pot could be used to prepare a two-course meal of, say, meat, dumplings and vegetables followed by a suet pudding, with the various ingredients put in at different times and kept separate by string net bags. The kitchen must have become very hot and smoky while all this was going on, and if there was a fall of soot the whole meal would be ruined! The results, however, could be impressive.

... had for dinner a neck of mutton and potage [soup], a piece of powdered beef and cabbage, a leg of goose broyled, a rabbet, a piece of apple tart, cheese, apples and peares.

A meal described by a seventeenth-century squire called Henry Ferrers.

SOURCE C

The frontispiece of the Dictionarium Domesticum (1736) which explains the kitchen chores of a housewife.

Baking could be done in several ways. Some housewives used flat stones heated up in the fireplace, or baked in an iron pot either hung over the fire or placed in the fire and covered with the embers. Bread, cakes, puddings, fish and stews could be cooked in this way. Although it was not possible to see how the food was cooking, women became skilled at listening to find out how the meal was progressing.

In the larger houses of the gentry and the better-off yeomen, ovens were built into a side wall, or in the corner of the fireplace. Sometimes villages had communal ovens, or bakehouses, often built in the open air, where perhaps once a week women would gather to do their baking. Wood was burned in the oven for several hours to heat the bricks. It would then be raked out. Loaves would go in first, followed later by cakes, pies and buns which needed a shorter cooking time. The wealthier people ate wheaten bread, while country labourers ate loaves and puddings made from barley. Oatcakes were popular among northerners and in Wales, and dark rye bread was still found in the north though only eaten by the poorest people in the south.

Another method of cooking was spit roasting, where a piece of meat or poultry was held in front of the fire on a spit supported by stands. A pan underneath the meat caught the dripping fat. The spit had to be turned so that the meat cooked evenly. At first this was a job often given to children, but later animals were used, either dogs or geese. The dog would be put on to a treadwheel in a cage which turned continually with the weight of its body. Later, mechanical devices were invented to keep the spits turning.

SOURCE D

... excellent in kitchen service. They so diligently look to their business, that no drudge can do the feat more cunningly.

A description of a particular breed of dog used to turn spits (1576).

Activity time

1. What changes took place between 1500 and 1750 in the way houses were built?

2. a Which people gained from these changes?

   b Which group of people saw little change in how their houses were built?

3. From Source C on page 194 identify the following:
   - butter making
   - baking
   - brewing
   - the kitchen
   - the still-room for washing up
   - bee keeping
   - the pigeon cote (house).

4. Using the information in this section, write a description of the daily work of servants in a kitchen like the one at Cotehele in Source A on page 193.

Eating and drinking

In Tudor times there were sumptuary laws, passed at the beginning of Henry VIII's reign, which set out how many separate dishes should be served at one meal. A cardinal might have nine, while anyone with an annual income of £40, or goods worth £500, could serve three, not counting soups. These would have been rich landowners or merchants: £500 of Tudor money would have been worth over £2 million today. At wedding feasts, anyone could serve three dishes above his normal limits. The laws were an attempt to stop humble people from copying their betters!

During Elizabeth's reign, meals were eaten quite early. Breakfast consisted of cold meats, cheese and ale and was eaten between 6am and 7am. Dinner, the main meal of the day, was between 11am and noon; a light supper was served at around 6pm. During the seventeenth century, mealtimes gradually became later and by the middle of the eighteenth century fashionable Londoners were dining as late as 7pm with breakfast between 9am and 10am and supper becoming a late-night snack. To fill the gap between breakfast and dinner, afternoon tea became the custom, served with bread and butter or buttered toast. Country people tended to keep to their earlier hours.

- Avoid clapping your fingers in your mouth and licking them, although you have burnt them in the carving.

- Do not baul out aloud for anything you want ... but whisper softly.

- Do not fill your mouth so full, that your cheeks shall swell like a pair of Scotch bagpipes.

- It is uncivil to rub your teeth in company, or to pick at them after meals with your knife.

From Hannah Wooley's 1682 guide to etiquette (good manners).

Customs at the table

At the start of the period, food was served on a trencher – a piece of hard-baked, coarse bread cut into an oblong shape. For important people, a knife and spoon were provided. The diners rinsed their hands after sitting at the table because most foods were taken by hand from the serving dishes – guests helped themselves to whatever was within reach. Finer, white bread was cut into finger shapes and used to mop up sauces and gravy. Soups were eaten from shared bowls with spoons and bread. Meat and vegetables were placed on the bread trenchers with sauces, and eaten with the fingers. At the end of each course the trenchers were collected and given to the poor.

Pottery or pewter dinner plates gradually replaced trenchers; forks became popular during the seventeenth century although many people – including Louis XIV of France – continued to eat with their fingers.

Meals

Meals were served in courses with savoury and sweet dishes set out in a geometric pattern. A typical meal was served in three courses. The first two had a main centrepiece such as a soup or a roast. The third course of fruit and confectionery (sweet dishes) was laid out in the same way.

SOURCE F

I gave them for Dinner a Leg of Mutton boiled and Capers, a boiled Fowl and a Tongue, a batter Pudding, a fine Turkey roasted, Fried Rabbit, Tarts, Custards and Jellies. Almonds and Raisins, Oranges and Apples after. Port wine, Mountain [a wine from Malaga], Porter and Ale.

Parson Woodforde, an eighteenth-century clergyman, describing in his diary a meal which was prepared when the squire and his family paid a visit.

In the sixteenth and seventeenth centuries vegetables were rarely eaten as a side dish, but were mainly used for soups, broths or sauces. However, by the 1700s, they were becoming more popular as an accompaniment to meat. The discovery of America by Europeans in 1492 meant that a number of unfamiliar vegetables were introduced: kidney beans, maize and nasturtiums (the flowers, leaves and seeds were used). However, potatoes, turkeys and chocolate made the most impact on people's diet. Potatoes were introduced into Britain in 1564, but at first they were regarded with a lot of suspicion and some people even believed they caused leprosy. However, in the eighteenth century, as the price of other foods, especially wheat, rose, they became more important as a food for the poor. In 1744, one cookery book gave 20 recipes for cooking potatoes (but there were as yet no chips!).

Throughout the period fruit tarts were popular, as were cheeses, cakes and biscuits, at least for those who could afford them. Fresh fruit was thought by some people to cause fevers, but great quantities were grown. From the seventeenth century oranges were imported or grown in private orangeries, but were a great luxury at as much as 1 shilling each. Salads contained some interesting ingredients such as violets, cowslips, rosemary and borage. They were often decorated with curious figures cut out of red beetroot. In the 1660s the diarist John Evelyn warned that garlic was 'not for ladies' palates, nor those who court them'.

There was little improvement in the diet of the poorest during the period covered by this book. Rural (country) workers in the south had little room to grow their own vegetables and lived mostly on bread with salt bacon or cheese. The more fortunate might have meat once a week, but they were always short of fuel for cooking. It was important to keep the fire burning, but the poor could not get hold of enough wood; at night the flames were covered with turf so that it would smoulder slowly until the morning. People in the north fared a little better because they had oatmeal and potatoes and were less dependent on increasingly expensive wheat. Traditionally they had been able to supplement their diet with the game – fish, rabbit and hare – that they might catch in the fields, woods and streams around the village. However, the Game Act of 1671 outlawed this. The labourer who wanted a rabbit for his pot now had to risk the penalties for poaching, usually death by hanging.

Food storage

Throughout the period fresh meat was scarce in winter because it was difficult to supply good feed for the cattle. Animals were slaughtered in the autumn and meat was preserved by pickling, salting or smoking. Hams were rubbed with salt, pickled in ale and brown sugar, and then hung over smoke from a wood-fire. Vegetables were also pickled; fruit and flowers were made into wine. These items were supplemented by fresh game, poultry and pigeons, and fish.

It was also difficult to keep food fresh in the summer. Without refrigerators, housewives would wrap salted beef in dry cloths and keep it in a tightly closed cupboard. Fish was sometimes fried in oil and then steeped in white wine vinegar. Despite these precautions, incidences of food poisoning were very common. Many children died from the diarrhoea caused by eating rotten food.

Drinks

Home brewed ale or beer was the normal drink, available from public breweries in the towns. Children drank a lighter variety called 'small beer'. A favourite was buttered ale – warmed beer flavoured with cinnamon, sugar and butter. In fruit-growing districts housewives made cider and perry. Wealthier people could afford to drink French wine and brandy. Stuart governments began to tax wine and beer in the late seventeenth century so many of the poor turned to gin. Originally this came from Holland but by the eighteenth century it was being made in London in huge quantities. There was a good deal of drunkenness among all classes. Nevertheless, it was perhaps safer than drinking the water which was often contaminated.

Managing the home

In the seventeenth century, prosperous families who had made fortunes from overseas trade were building fine houses and gardens. Then, as now, there were books available to encourage them in their new lifestyles. Manuals about gardening, farming and cooking abounded. The lady of the house was expected to know how to manage the gardens, the dairy, the stillroom (pantry) and the kitchen. She was also expected to know how to prepare herbal medicines and treat the sick.

Until the seventeenth century these remedies would have been handed down by word of mouth but now they began to be collected and printed. One remedy recommended fried mice to cure bedwetting, while another, a cure for consumption, included the ingredients 'a peck of small garden snails and a quart of earthworms' (a peck and a quart were measures). Even so, cookery books greatly encouraged an interest in food.

Tea and coffee

It was not until the seventeenth century that hot drinks such as tea, coffee and chocolate became popular in Europe. The reason was the growing trade with Asia and America. Tea was very expensive, so it was drunk in the Chinese style – very weak, with sugar but no milk and served in shallow handleless porcelain dishes. In wealthy houses, the tea was stored in a small locked chest called a caddy. Only the lady of the house had a key to this so that the servants could not steal any tea. As more was imported from India the price fell and, in the eighteenth century, poorer people began to enjoy it. They drank the cheapest kind of tea, which was often mixed with other leaves. They only used a few leaves at a time and often these were dried after use so that they could be used again. Tea became the usual breakfast drink with bread and butter or toast and was enjoyed again in the afternoon and after dinner. By the middle of the eighteenth century, drinkers were adding either milk or cream to taste.

The first coffee shop opened in Oxford in 1650 quickly followed by others in London. Samuel Pepys, the seventeenth-century diarist (see pages 120–2) frequently visited coffee houses. They became fashionable places for men to spend part of the day, with people from different backgrounds often mixing together, gambling and discussing business and politics. In the eighteenth century, however, they became more exclusive, with only the rich and fashionable allowed in. Chocolate as a drink has been popular since the seventeenth century and by 1700 it was also taken as a breakfast drink.

Tea, coffee and chocolate are naturally rather bitter and, as the consumption of these drinks increased, so the demand for sugar rose. Sugar plantations run by slave labour in Brazil and the Caribbean had been supplying England since Queen Elizabeth's reign. A German traveller who met Queen Elizabeth l commented on her black teeth, 'a defect the English seem subject to, from their too great use of sugar'.

A contemporary illustration of a London coffee house in the seventeenth century.

Activity time

1 There were many changes taking place in the food and drink that people were consuming during this period. Make a list of the changes. In a separate column write down for each change which sort of people would have been affected by it: nobles and gentry, yeomen, merchants, labourers and cottagers.

Change	People affected

Can you draw any conclusions from this evidence about whether life was getting better or worse for English people?

Towns

In the sixteenth century, towns were growing quickly. London was already by far the largest city in England, with a population of 100,000 by the end of Elizabeth's reign. One-twentieth of all the people in England lived there in 1600, but by 1700 it had grown so much that it was nearer one-tenth. London was actually still two cities rather than one when James I became king in 1605. The old city, surrounded by its medieval walls, was separated from Westminster, where the Palace of Whitehall was, by a row of noblemen's palaces whose gardens lined the River Thames. As the city grew it became more overcrowded. London's population was bursting through its walls, and one by one the great palaces were pulled down as the nobles moved on – not before making a fortune by building houses on their palace gardens!

SOURCE A

London in the seventeenth century from the River Thames, showing London Bridge. Print dated 1647.

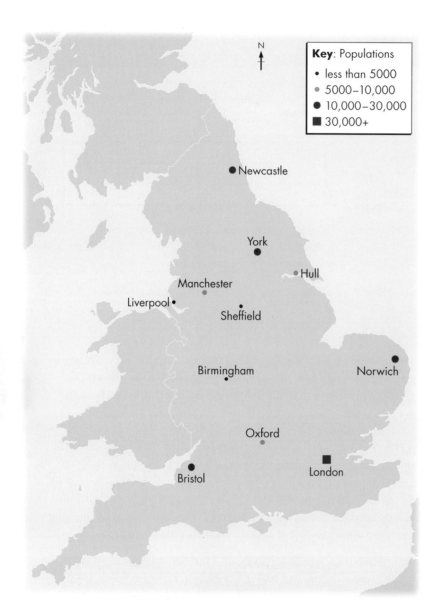

Outside London towns were much smaller. The big cities of today hardly existed; Birmingham, Manchester and Leeds were still quite small in the seventeenth century. The largest towns were Bristol, York and Norwich, but even these were small compared to London. Bristol had only a population of about 12,000 in 1600. After the Restoration period (beginning 1660) many towns began to grow rapidly (see the table below).

England in 1670.

Size of population		
	1670	**1750**
London	300,000	670,000
Norwich	21,000	36,000
Bristol	18,000	50,000
Newcastle	11,800	29,000
York	10,500	11,400
Oxford	7500	8200
Hull	6300	11,500
Manchester	5500	18,000
Birmingham	4000	23,700
Sheffield	2000	12,000
Liverpool	1200	22,000

Population growth of towns 1670–1750.

Activity time

1. Using a computer, enter the figures in the table above on to a spreadsheet. Use it to draw graphs showing the growth of towns. You should make a separate graph for London. Choose carefully which type of graph shows the information most clearly. Label your graphs, then print them.

2. Now answer the following questions:
   a. Which towns listed in the table have grown the most quickly? How can you tell this from your graph?
   b. Which have grown least quickly?
   c. Try to find reasons for their growth, or why they didn't grow, using this chapter and the next, and your own knowledge.
   d. Use an encyclopaedia or the Internet to find the population of two of these towns today. By how much have they grown since 1750?

Life in the towns

People in towns lived much closer to their food supplies than we do today. Throughout the period pigs scavenged in city roads; sheep and cows were driven through the streets to the butcher's shop. Offal and stale fish littered the streets; in London, the smell from the River Fleet where butchers washed freshly killed carcasses forced residents to send a petition to Charles II in 1660. Small market gardens grew up to the north and west of London to provide the markets with fresh food. The vegetable growers would obtain their manure direct from carts carrying the Londoners' waste out of the city (see page 209).

As well as the markets where people could buy what they needed, street vendors (sellers) offered a wide range of goods and called out their wares as they walked through the streets. Milkmaids brought milk direct to the door. Where transport was available, traders from the countryside preferred to send their produce to town markets because they could get higher prices. However, the housewife had to beware of dishonest traders. Stale fish was sometimes washed to make it appear fresher; meagre meat joints were padded out with cloth; bakers sold underweight loaves; and wine sellers mixed the wine with starch or gum, or sold fake wine which was not made from grapes.

Clothing and fashion

Just as people's changed in style and appearance, so too did the clothes that they wore.

Only the rich regularly wore new clothing. They set the style and, increasingly, everyone else did their best to copy it.

Tudor times

In the sixteenth century, the monarch and the aristocracy did not like the idea that people of lower birth might dress in the same way as they did. There was obviously a lot of snobbery, especially shown by nobles towards merchants. The sumptuary laws of the reigns of Henry VIII and Elizabeth I were designed to preserve the differences between the social classes. Among other things, they laid down the quality of dress permitted to men in each level or rank of society, from royalty to servants and labourers. Women's dress was not thought to be socially important so it was not covered by the laws.

A Tudor gentleman wearing doublet and hose. The codpiece was popular for men during Henry VIII's reign. It was a piece of cloth designed to conceal a gentleman's genitals and it became necessary, because the doublet, or coat, was worn so short that it was very revealing! A range of showy and sometimes large codpieces was fashionable at Henry's court. The aim was obviously to impress the court with the size of what was hidden. This painting shows Sir William Drury and was painted in 1587.

According to the sumptuary laws, among the higher Tudor nobility, dukes could clothe themselves and their horses in woven cloth of gold. Earls could wear sable fur, and barons could use cloth embroidered with gold and silver. Those of the rank of Knight of the Garter and above could wear crimson or blue velvet, while ordinary knights were restricted to velvets in other colours. Further down the social scale, annual income rather than social rank determined how much you could spend on your clothes. Gentlemen worth £100 a year could wear velvet doublets, but only satin or damask in their gowns and coats. An income of £20 a year would allow satin and damask doublets, and silk or camlet gowns and coats. Only gentlemen and above could wear imported furs and those below the rank of knight were restricted in the amount of material which could be used to make their gowns.

Servants and agricultural workers and those worth below £10 a year had to make do with clothes made from cloth costing less than 2 shillings per yard. Those who broke the law were fined, except for servants and labourers whose punishment was to be put in the stocks for three days.

In Elizabethan times women were still wearing the farthingale. Originally this was a petticoat with hoops of whalebone stitched in; later it was a horseshoe-shaped bolster stuffed with hair or rags and tied round the waist to make the skirt stand out. As you can imagine, it took up a great deal of room and must have been very hot and uncomfortable to wear. Men's clothes were similarly oversized, with wide, puffed breeches padded out with hair or bran, and flowing gowns with loose sleeves and ornate ruffs. Hair was worn long, and by 1600 curling on the shoulders or tied back with a bow.

Stuart styles

Parliament had passed the sumptuary laws in an effort to halt change, and to stop the lower classes from copying their 'betters'. Even in Tudor times it was very difficult to enforce these laws. For all sorts of reasons, society was changing, and laws and fines could not prevent this. By the time of Samuel Pepys, in the reign of Charles II, the sumptuary laws were a thing of the past. Pepys spent a large part of his savings on his clothes – far more than he allowed his wife for her wardrobe. In 1663 his account books showed he had spent about £12 on clothes for her and about £55 on his own clothes, including a velvet cloak, two new suits, a gown, a hat and two wigs. In 1665 he paid £24 – about six months' income for a middle-class family – on a silk suit 'the best that I ever wore in my life'. Even though he spent much more on himself, he could still get angry with his wife when he thought she was extravagant (spent too much money).

SOURCE C

And upon my being very angry, she doth protest she will here lay up [put aside] something for herself to buy her a necklace with – which madded [angered] me and doth still trouble me, for I fear she will forget by degrees the way of living cheap.

Samuel Pepys, writing on 29 September 1664 about his wife's extravagance.

Digging deeper

How did the Tudors and Stuarts do their laundry?

We sometimes imagine that before modern times nobody washed either themselves or their clothes very much. This is not really a very accurate view. Clothes washing was regarded as an important part of housework despite the difficulties involved. Though standards may have been different from today's, everyone liked having clean clothes to wear. We hear of people, especially children in families who had very few clothes, having to stay in bed while their garments were washed. Wealthy people who owned more clothes and linen might have a washday once a month or less often. It was a hard and heavy job for the housewife, or the servants in larger houses. To be able to complete the task in a day, many women would have had to start in the early hours of the morning.

The original, and most simple, method of doing the washing was to take it to the nearest source of water and beat it clean. This might be with a wooden implement called a beetle or a battledore, or if the laundry was done at a stream or river, it might be beaten against the stones or rocks. Imagine standing in the cold water of a stream in the winter! In Scotland, women did the laundry by trampling on it in a tub, sometimes in pairs. After the laundry had been beaten or trampled, it was wrung and stretched out on the grass or a nearby hedge to dry. The sunshine would help to keep the clothes white.

On its own, however, cold water could not get dirty, sweaty, soiled clothes clean, so another method involved the use of a cleansing agent. Of course people of this period could not go to the supermarket for a pack of washing powder, so what could they use that was cheap and easily available? Urine was the answer. It contained ammonia which bleaches clothes – but it had to be stale, to allow the ammonia to be concentrated. Ships would bring huge barrels of horse urine to London from ports further north like Hull. Poor people also used urine for washing themselves. Some villages kept a communal barrel, which must have made for an unpleasant smell on washday! Sometimes animal dung was used for cleaning clothes, again because of the ammonia, but some people found it gave them an unpleasant itch! Perhaps they hadn't rinsed their clothes properly.

Another cleanser was lye, made from wood ash or the ashes of plants, such as ferns, thistles, docks and other weeds. Soap was the most efficient cleanser but was expensive and heavily taxed. Its raw ingredients were already in demand for other purposes such as cooking and candle-making, and so extra supplies had to be imported. A further disadvantage was that it required hot water, unlike the other cleansing agents.

There were also remedies for removing stains and spots, some of which are still in use today. Ink stains could be removed with lemon juice; rust marks were cleaned with sorrel juice; fruit stains were rubbed with butter and washed in hot milk. Greasy marks were treated with a mixture of turpentine and ground sheep's trotters, fuller's earth or chalk.

After the laundry was washed and dry, it was pressed with a smoothing iron, either heated over the fire or kept hot by a piece of burning coal or charcoal inside. Women who did not have an iron may have used hot stones, or wooden rollers, or trampled it with their bare feet.

SOURCE D

Restoration costumes of
men and women c.1660.
This is a family portrait by
Cornelius de Vos c. 1630.

When the ruff went out of fashion in early Stuart times it was replaced by a deep lace-trimmed collar which fell over the shoulders. During the Civil War (1642–9) clothes had a political significance with the Roundheads wearing severe, plain clothes and the Cavaliers dressing extravagantly. During Cromwell's rule, fun and frivolity were frowned upon. This was reflected in the drab clothes people wore.

With the restoration of Charles II in 1660 came a new glamour and flamboyant styles reappeared. Men now wore a form of three-piece suit, with long-sleeved, knee-length waistcoats and over the top a long coat with large pocket flaps and wide turned-back cuffs. They had knee-breeches in silk, velvet or cloth, adorned with buttons. The shirt had ruffled cuffs and was worn with a linen or lace cravat. Wide brimmed beaver hats were worn, trimmed with ostrich feathers. As well as a sword, men carried a walking stick. Soft leather gloves completed the outfit, with high-heeled shoes and stockings held up by garters. At home men dressed more informally with a loose gown worn over a shirt and breeches, and slippers. In place of the formal wig they might wear a fur turban.

Wigs became popular during the 1660s and were styled in two peaks either side of a central parting, falling in loose curls over the shoulders. Although wigs were expensive to buy, fashionable men had their heads shaved and wore them instead. Sometimes the wigs were made using their own hair.

Fabrics were still expensive but the cost of making clothes was relatively cheap, so clothes might be altered, restyled, relined and repaired and finally passed on to other people. All but the richest people took advantage of the thriving second-hand market in clothes. In London there were shops and markets specialising in second-hand garments which allowed the lower classes to wear clothes that they could not have afforded new. Some new clothes could be bought 'off the peg'. Typical prices in 1660 might be 7–18 shillings for a waistcoat; 6–20 shillings for a silk petticoat; and 34 shillings for a beaver hat. For poor villagers there was little chance of taking advantage of the second-hand market in the towns. Such people couldn't afford the extravagant clothes worn by the wealthy. A typical labourer's wage was only about 4 shillings a week. Instead they wore plainer clothes that were more practical for work, though quite dull. Men wore a loose-fitting shirt and coarse woollen breeches. Women wore a kurtle (dress) and apron. Boots and hats were made of leather.

SOURCE E

Costumes of men and women c.1700–50. This painting shows the Andrews family, painted by James Willis in 1749.

Fashion in the eighteenth century

During the eighteenth century men began to dress in the rather plainer styles which are familiar today. From the late seventeenth century during the day time a fashionable lady might wear a mantua gown which, although worn over a corset (a close fitting garment that gave shape and support to

Reformation and Rebellion 1485–1750

the figure and was tightened with lacing), was fairly loose. It was open at the front to show an embroidered stomacher (an ornamental covering for the chest worn under the lacing of the bodice). The back of the skirt was gathered up uncovering a petticoat in a different material and colour. The sleeves ended in deep frills. With this might be worn the commode, a headdress consisting of a wire frame covered with lace or linen frills.

Also in her wardrobe the fashionable lady would have lace-edged nightdresses, smocks, velvet slippers, painted and perfumed fans, scented gloves, fur muffs (covers to tuck her hands in to keep them warm), silk stockings and shoes with diamond buckles. Jewellery of pearls, amber and diamonds would add to her fashionable appearance. Her hair might have curls or ringlets over the ears, forehead or neck; she would wear tiny black patches, cut into fantastic shapes, on her face – perhaps to help cover up scars from smallpox. She might pad out her cheeks with plumpers (small balls or discs) to fill out spaces left by decayed teeth.

Activity time

1 Work in groups to prepare a scrapbook or computer presentation of changing fashions and styles in housing and clothing from 1485–1750. Use the information in this chapter to guide you.

- Begin by collecting pictures of houses, rooms and furniture, also clothing and hairstyles from 1485 to 1750.

- You can copy or trace pictures from books and museum guidebooks, or use a scanner or photocopier; you can also obtain pictures from history websites on the Internet, or from reference software like Encarta; if you are using a scanner be sure to set it at low resolution.

- Sort all the pictures first by centuries. You may then be able to sort them within the centuries, e.g. 1600–50.

- Arrange your pictures carefully in your scrapbook, or, if you are using computer software, prepare slides for the different periods, inserting the pictures.

- Add your own labels and titles. Be sure to label important changes.

2 When you have finished, compare each group's work.

- Test other groups' knowledge by showing them your scrapbook or presentation but cover, or remove, the labels.

- Can they guess the correct period e.g. 'late sixteenth century'; or 'around 1660'?

- Can you guess the correct period when looking at other groups' scrapbooks or presentations?

Historical note: It is important that you are able to tell which sort of people would have worn the clothes, and lived in the homes you have collected pictures of. Were they rich or poor? Nobles, merchants, yeomen or labourers?

Digging deeper

Going to the toilet in the seventeenth century

In the seventeenth century, attitudes to personal hygiene were often very different from ours today. Elizabeth I was thought exceptional because she had a bath four times a year 'whether she needed it or not'. Louis XIV of France never had a bath in his life! Most people rarely washed their bodies, thinking it enough to wash hands, faces, necks and, on occasion, their feet. Part of the reason was the fact that soap was very expensive. Clothes smelled of stale sweat; men's wigs were often full of lice; bad breath was common. There were toothbrushes from the middle of the seventeenth century but they were not in common usage until much later. At this time tooth-cleaning was done by rubbing the teeth with a piece of cloth or handkerchief, and picking between them carefully with a wooden or ivory toothpick. There were recipes for home-made mouthwashes, but some women used a substance called *acqua fortis* which, if over-used, caused the teeth to fall out. Public bath-houses were opened towards the end of the seventeenth century, but later became regarded as places with bad reputations.

Most people considered a bathroom an unnecessary luxury. Pepys entered in his diary that he had visited a man called Thomas Povy who had a bathroom at his home in Lincoln's Inn Fields in London. Celia Fiennes, who journeyed all over England, described the magnificent bathroom at Chatsworth House in Derbyshire.

However, most people, if they bathed at all, made do with a wooden or copper tub in front of the fire in a bedroom, with the water heated over the kitchen fire and brought upstairs in cans by servants.

In some ways, the seventeenth century took a step backwards in matters of sanitation. In the Middle Ages, larger houses had their *garde-robe* or privy (toilet) where people could relieve themselves, usually away from the main rooms and in a position where the human waste could be disposed of easily. By Stuart times, only the richer houses had a 'house of office', usually tucked away in a corner of the cellar or roof space. In the absence of a privy, at best chamber pots were used; failing that, fireplaces, cellars, or coal houses.

SOURCE G

I waked in the morning about six a-clock. I lacked a pot but there was none, and bitter cold, so was forced to rise and piss in the chimney, and to bed again.

On cold winter nights, even rich people like Samuel Pepys might find themselves caught short.

In fact, the water-closet (the WC) had been invented by 1594, and some had been installed in Richmond Palace and Windsor Castle, but it would be many years before they were fitted in ordinary homes.

Chamber pots, and later commodes or close-stools, which were stools with chamber pots beneath them, were kept in bedrooms and often in rooms downstairs too. The word 'stool' came to mean the solid contents of the chamber pot – one of the few polite words in English to describe this! Men were quite happy to use the chamber pot in public, and it was quite common to keep one in a sideboard in the dining room to be used after the ladies had left the room. Samuel Pepys recorded in his diary that he

A chamber pot might be hidden behind the panelling of the dining rooms, as is this one at Penrhyn Castle.

carried on a conversation with Lady Sandwich as she used a chamber pot in his dining room, but this was an accident because he had come in unannounced. There was blushing on both sides as she told him the news from Parliament!

Some coaches had chamber pots under the cushions for the benefit of travellers. Close-stools were a little more comfortable – William III had one with a seat covered in red velvet. Another luxury for him was the presence of the Groom of the Stool, who would wait with a linen cloth and a jug of water ready to wipe the royal bottom! Bess of Hardwick (see page 189) had a close-stool covered with 'blewe cloth sticht with white, with red and black silk fringe'.

The use of toilet paper was almost unknown until 1676; instead people made do with shells, or bunches of feathers or herbs. Paper was too expensive to be wasted. However, a Tudor writer says that some people bought the books from dissolved monastery libraries 'to serve their jakes'. (Jakes is an old word for toilet, and from this comes 'jacksie' meaning bottom.) The close-stool room was known in France as *le lieu d'aisance* (the place of ease) or *le lieu* which became the English word 'loo'.

Pots and commodes had to be emptied, either into a vault in the cellars or into the cesspit outside. Unfortunately, it was the more usual practice to empty the contents straight into the street where pedestrians had to pick their way carefully. In fast-growing London, the problem of sewage disposal was already serious by the 1600s and was contributing to many deaths from disease. Some town authorities employed scavengers or rakers to clear away the worst of the filth but the smells and flies must have been appalling. Emptying the vaults and cesspits was the work of the night-soil men, but often the sewage overflowed between visits and leaked into cellars or contaminated water supplies. This was a problem familiar to Pepys, who was much troubled by his neighbour's dung heap which was leaking into his cellar where he stored his wine. As we have seen the night-soil (human waste) would be taken out of the city and used by the farmers as manure.

Public toilets were not to come into existence until much later, in the middle of the nineteenth century, but in the seventeenth century people seemed to be quite happy to relieve themselves whenever and wherever the need arose.

SOURCE I

My wife was ill, and so I was forced to go out of the theatre with her to Lincoln's Inn walks, and there in a corner she did her business, and was by and by well, and so into the house again.

Samuel Pepys writing in his diary after a visit to the theatre.

On a visit to London, Count Casanova went to St James's Park and complained to his friend, the Earl of Pembroke, that he had seen 'six or seven people [relieving themselves] in the bushes with their hinder parts [bottoms] turned towards the Publick'. He thought it disgusting, but to Pembroke it was a normal occurence. However, for a small fee, it was possible to use the services of a human lavatory or flyter – a man with a bucket and a large cloak who would shield his customers from view while they went about their business.

Life in the village

In 1500 most people in England lived in small villages in the countryside. Little had happened to change this by 1750. Although the population in the cities had risen (see page 200), over 80 per cent of people still worked in farming and England remained a largely rural country. Farming was still a group activity, with families working together in the fields. In any village there was a regular calendar of events which were organised around the farming year and the activities of the Church:

- Most saints' days had been abolished after the Reformation but many continued to be marked in other ways, especially with feasts.

- Beating the bounds continued once a year when villagers walked all round the boundaries of their parish. This helped to prevent disputes between farmers from neighbouring villages.

- Feasts were held to mark the end of harvest, or sheep shearing, or hop gathering, and farmers would provide food and drink to thank their labourers for their hard work.

- Plough Monday in early January at the start of the ploughing season would see the plough decorated with flowers and blessed by the parson.

- Some feast activities were quite boisterous, such as Lent Crocking (the season of fasting before Easter) when crockery would be smashed if money was not given to the poor labourers.

- The Lord of Misrule ritual at Christmas time had survived from the Middle Ages. It usually involved someone from the lower classes becoming master for the day, and leading the young men of the village on a series of pranks.

- On Shrove Tuesday (the day before the start of Lent) in Leicester, gangs armed with whips would attack the wealthy and whip them below the knee. These activities lasted only a day and so were usually accepted by the gentry as high spirits. They may have helped the poor to let off steam particularly as life was hard with little opportunity to have fun.

Changes in rural life

There were some changes in the countryside that made life difficult for the poorer villagers:

- The landlord, or squire as he was called in the eighteenth century, was keen to make more money from his estates. Sometimes this meant that traditional country activities, like wood gathering or gleaning (gathering what is left in the fields after harvesting), now became crimes, as the farmers sold off the woods to merchants, or enclosed the fields for sheep.

- Enclosure meant the end of the common pasture where poor villagers had been able to keep an animal or two.

- Poaching in the woods also became a crime, punishable by hanging.

- Sometimes a gentleman wanted to improve the view from his house and so would simply demolish a village that was on his estate.

This is why the population in towns was increasing – countrymen and women went there in search of work. But it also explains why there was a growing problem of poverty, resulting in an increased number of beggars, thieves and highwaymen.

So life for the poor in 'merry olde England' could be grim. By 1700 there was growing impatience among the upper classes with the feasts and ceremonies enjoyed by the poor. Gentlemen farmers wanted to get more work out of their labourers and hated seeing them idle. During Cromwell's time leisure was seen as idleness; this view was revived in the eighteenth-century. For example, the Whit Ales was an annual celebration held in Oxfordshire, and traditionally had been a week-long carnival of food and drink. Gradually it had stretched to thirteen days and was a time of riotous and unruly behaviour. Because this upset the gentry, as well as disrupting the farming year, the festivities were greatly toned down. Similarly, the Birmingham Wakes was a parish feast originally held to mark the local saint's day but it had become an annual social event. Activities included nude racing, goose-riding and bull-baiting. The middle classes came to see it as immoral and their efforts to stop it led eventually to the decline of the feast.

A man in the stocks c. 1800. This was a form of punishment as well as a way of providing entertainment.

Entertainment

Perhaps life in some villages was becoming quieter, but not too far away there was always a town, where there would be a market. Market day was always a lively affair with crowds gathering to buy and sell, but also to enjoy the free entertainment. During the Tudor and Stuart period people enjoyed sports and entertainment which we would probably find cruel today. For example, people enjoyed public executions, rushing to obtain a good view. A day out might be a visit to an asylum to watch the lunatics, or to throw all sorts of things at villains in the stocks.

Fairs were a great source of enjoyment, particularly for the curiosities which were exhibited. It was thought fun to ogle at freaks in sideshows: notices from the time advertise 'a cannibal giant', 'a living skeleton', 'a fairy child' – plus the more usual spectacles of tightrope walkers, tumblers, puppet shows, musicians and dancers.

Brawling and fist-fighting soon drew crowds, some of whom lay bets on the likely outcome. The fighting was not confined to men – sometimes women would strip to their shifts (undergarments) and fight. People liked to watch sports where animals were made to fight each other: cockfighting, bull- and bear-baiting were also popular with gamblers. In the bear pit, trained bulldogs would attack a bear that was chained and muzzled, and could only defend itself with its paws. Not everybody enjoyed watching the bear die: the French ambassador who visited Lord Burghley (see page 189) was sickened by what he saw in the bear pit at Southwark.

Most people did not actively participate in sports themselves. Some would play bowls, or a form of football in which there were no goals, resulting in much damage to property. In London the theatres were closed down by the Puritans, but reopened when Charles II came to the throne in 1660. They quickly regained their popularity. Plays were usually performed in the afternoon, from about 3pm, with music and dancing before the performance and again during the interval.

Question time

1 What entertainments were available to you if you lived in:
- a country village
- a small town
- London?

2 In what ways did life become harder for the poor from the beginning of the eighteenth century?

3 How has our view of what is fun changed from the early eighteenth century?

Digging deeper

A day out in the country

By the 1660s London had grown so large that it became a pleasure to escape from the city for a day in the country, complete with a picnic. Nowadays this is a pleasure enjoyed by most of us who live in large towns, but then only the rich could afford to do it. One Sunday in July 1667, Samuel Pepys woke his wife early, in order to go by hired coach for a day out at Epsom, in the Surrey hills. They were accompanied by a friend, Mrs Turner. They climbed into the coach pulled by four horses, taking with them 'some bottles of wine and beer and some cold fowl'. It was a lovely summer's day, and they enjoyed the views of the countryside, although the road was very dusty. They reached Epsom by eight o'clock, where there was already a crowd gathered at its famous well. The salty water was believed to be excellent for the health. 'I did drink four pints and had some very good stools by it' wrote Pepys. Mrs Turner and Mrs Pepys did not fancy the water but preferred to walk about with the fashionable women.

SOURCE A *In the late seventeenth and early eighteenth centuries, it was fashionable to visit the country for a day, to take the waters and be seen by the right people. This view of the Old Horse Guards Parade from St James's Park was painted by Thomas van Wyck (1616–70).*

After talking a while with other Londoners who were also here for the day, it was getting hot. It was time for dinner, the midday meal, so they went into the little town of Epsom to the King's Head inn. 'The day being wonderful hot,' after dinner they all lay down for 'a good nap'. Pepys wanted to go back to the well to fill some bottles of water to take back to London, but after this they went for a walk in the countryside. They walked in the woods belonging to his cousin, and Pepys managed to get the three of them lost: 'I could not find the way into any of the walks in the wood, which indeed are very pleasant if I could have found them.'

As he tried to leap over a ditch, he sprained his ankle, but at last they found their way, and now, joined by Mr Hewer, they walked on the Downs among a flock of sheep. They found the shepherd and his little boy, who was reading the Bible to him. Pepys then made the boy read a little to them, 'which he did in the forced tone that children do usually read, which was mighty pretty'. They marvelled at the old shepherd's woollen knitted stockings and his shoes which were shod with iron, and had great nails sticking out of them. They learned that the shepherd earned 4 shillings a week for looking after 360 sheep.

After giving the man and the boy some money, they wandered on with Mrs Turner picking wild flowers. They returned by coach to the inn, stopping a milkmaid on the way, 'and in my gilt tumblers did drink our bellyfuls of milk better than any cream'. It was now seven in the evening so they paid the bill at the King's Head, and began the journey home. It was still a lovely day, as they watched families walking alone 'to take the air'. As the sun went down they had great pleasure chatting about the day they had had. Pepys had made up his mind that he would not buy a country house, but would instead get a coach, so that he and his wife could 'go sometimes for a day to this place and then quite to another place'. As it grew dark they were delighted to see several glow-worms, 'which was mighty pretty'.

 Activity time

From reading this diary of Pepys you have learned of a new development in England's history – the start of what now is called tourism.

How does Pepys' description of his day out compare with that of a town dweller's today? Think of a day out you may have had recently. What parts are similar? What is different? You might call your work 'Tourism: Then and Now'.

Assessment section

1 This chapter has concentrated on explaining how the different people of England lived during the period from 1485 to 1750. There were many changes. Using the information in this chapter, describe and explain how the home life of *two* of the following had changed between 1485 and 1750. Be sure to describe how the changes might have affected the whole family.

- Noble or gentleman

- Town dweller

- Peasant farmer

- Cottager or labourer

In your answer you will need to explain how life had been at the beginning of the period, and how it was different at the end. Refer to some of the following:

- houses

- food

- clothing

- hygiene

- entertainment

Think carefully about the sentences you write. Here are some examples:

In 1485 a noble would probably have lived in a castle, but by 1750 his descendant's home looked very different.

At the beginning of the Tudor period a peasant farmer would have lived in a one-roomed cottage with no windows and a fire in the middle of the floor.

By the middle of the eighteenth century many of the better off farmers had houses with windows and fireplaces.

It is important that you include accurate detail in your descriptions.

2 Did you find it easier to find more about the nobles and gentry? There is certainly more about them in this chapter than about craftsmen and labourers. This is quite common in history books for this period. Why do you think this is so?

3 There are many references in this chapter to what some people wrote in their diaries. Try to obtain a copy of a seventeenth-century diary. Samuel Pepys' diary is available in most libraries, and you may also be able to find the diaries of Celia Fiennes, or John Evelyn. Lady Anne Clifford's diary is also useful for the middle of the century. Be careful! Sometimes diaries can be difficult to understand.

a What use are diaries to historians?

b Why do you think people kept diaries?

c Do you think diaries will give us a reliable picture of life in the seventeenth century?

d Try to suggest some drawbacks of using diaries as historical evidence.

4 The Tudor and Stuart period has sometimes been presented in history books as a 'Golden Age' of British history. This means not only a time when great and exciting deeds were done by heroes, but also a period in which it was good to live because the problems which people faced were small when compared with now.

What are your views on this issue? Having read this chapter you should begin to form your own opinion about whether this period was a Golden Age in which to live. If you think it was, then ask yourself whether everyone shared in 'the good times'.

Summarise your views in your notebook. After reading the next chapter you may need to alter your views.

The 'World We Have Lost'

In Chapter 7 we looked at life in Britain before 1750 and saw that it was very different from now. There were differences in the way people worked, how they got married and raised their children, and what happened when they died. This chapter looks at aspects of the way of life that have disappeared in the last 300 years. This way of life was described as a 'world we have lost' by historian Peter Laslett (1971).

Changes in the world of work

Today we are used to most people working in large towns, either in shops, offices or factories. There were very few large towns in Tudor and Stuart times (see page 200). There were no factories, and even the workshops usually employed fewer than ten people. Most work was done by hand, and the few machines that existed usually had to be worked by hand or foot. There were some important new inventions and processes, especially the printing press (see page 161), but in most trades, the craftsmen of 1500 would still have recognised most of the methods used by their descendants in 1750.

Nevertheless there were changes in this period and, between 1500 and 1750, industry expanded enormously, which meant:

- more workshops
- more looms, windmills, watermills, brickworks and tileries
- more spinners and weavers
- more miners, smiths, brewers, potters, leatherworkers, glassblowers and charcoal burners
- more coal and iron
- more pollution
- more printed books
- more trade, more rich merchants
- more money being made!

Some things that had become common by 1750, had hardly existed in 1500:

- newspapers
- tea, coffee, chocolate
- tobacco, potatoes
- forks, microscopes, telescopes, watches
- stocks and shares
- insurance.

In this chapter we shall look at these changes, but first we must look at the countryside where most people lived and worked. Even here change was taking place.

Farming changes: from serf to farmer

The feudal system of farming based on the manor had broken down by 1500, following the problems caused by the Black Death. No longer were there serfs, who had to work on the lord's land in return for their own strips in the open fields. By now tenant farmers, or husbandmen, all paid a rent in money to their landlord. There was a great variation in rents across the country. In some areas there were large numbers of farmers called freeholders who paid very little. These yeoman farmers were doing well for themselves and were building better houses for their families like those we saw in the last chapter (see page 192). Other farmers were less fortunate. The landlord could easily raise their rents, or they could be evicted, that is thrown off their farms altogether.

Enclosure of the common land

We have heard already about enclosure, where the landlord fenced off the common land to use it for grazing sheep (see page 210). This was because the price of wool had become very high and the lord knew that he could make more money from the sheep than from allowing poor farmers to graze their animals.

Sometimes farmers were evicted from their homes to make way for sheep pastures; elsewhere they just lost the right to graze their few animals on the common. Sheep need only one shepherd with a dog to look after them, so the landlord had no need for labourers who had to look elsewhere for work. Sir Thomas More, beheaded by Henry VIII, said that 'sheep were eating men'.

Digging deeper

Kett's Revolt, 1549

Enclosure for sheep happened quite often in the sixteenth century. It sometimes led to riots, and even a rebellion in Norfolk in the summer of 1549. This began with a dispute between two landowners, Sir John Flowerdew and Robert Kett, over the ruins of an abbey at Wymondham, outside Norwich. Both men had enclosed common land to graze sheep. Flowerdew, however, was a wealthy London lawyer who was disliked because he was an outsider. He had bought the property of the dissolved abbey, but the buildings had been bought by the villagers who wanted to use the abbey church for their services. When Flowerdew stripped the lead off the church roof, the villagers were furious. Kett, a local man, was on the villagers' side against the Londoner, but Flowerdew tried to turn Kett against the villagers, by persuading them to tear down the hedges that Kett had put up on the common.

To Flowerdew's surprise Robert Kett now agreed with the villagers that he had been wrong to put up hedges on the common. He listened to the peasants' complaints, and promised to lead them on a march to

Norwich, to protest about enclosures and high rents charged by the gentry. The rebels tore down some of the new fences, and Kett's force quickly grew to 16,000 men. Many of the peasants in Norfolk were discontented because they were suffering so much hardship. Harvests had been bad, so they were making little money from farming. Even so, the landlords were still demanding high rents. For this reason many of the peasants were eager to join Robert Kett.

After three days of fighting, the rebels captured Norwich on 23 July 1549. Norwich was England's second largest city, and Kett hoped that this would show the government that it must take action to halt the greed of landowners. He sent a petition to Edward VI asking for an end to high rents and enclosure.

However, the ambitious John Dudley, soon to become the Duke of Northumberland (see Chapter 3), had no time for rebels. Like all the aristocracy he believed that the peasants' only duty was to obey their betters. Dudley's royal army met the rebels just outside Norwich. For the rebels the situation was hopeless: they only had farm tools and ropes, which they hoped to use to strangle their attackers. They were cut down brutally by the royal soldiers, using cannon and muskets against them. Then the royal cavalry rode into the rebels, swinging their swords from their horses. The rebels stood no chance and over three thousand were slaughtered as they fled into the fields and narrow lanes outside the city. Kett was soon captured and, after a short trial, was found guilty of treason. He was hanged, drawn, and quartered at Norwich Castle.

In some villages the open fields where the villagers grew their crops were enclosed. The idea was that, instead of having his land in strips scattered all over the fields, a farmer would have all his land together in one place. This would make farming easier, but it was really only the richer farmers who were in favour of enclosure. Most poor farmers could see little to benefit them from change. Luckily for them it was quite difficult for landowners to enclose the open fields because they had to get a law passed by Parliament before they could do it. This was expensive, and many landowners still had little interest in farming. They were happy for their stewards to collect their rents so that they could live in comfort in their country houses, or even in London.

Changes in farming methods

During the seventeenth century some better-off farmers, landlords and yeomen experimented with growing new crops. Turnips had been introduced from Holland. They could be used to feed animals during the winter. Peasants had had to kill most of their animals in the autumn when the grass stopped growing and preserve the meat for the winter by pickling, salting or smoking (see page 197). With turnips, however, there could be a supply of fresh meat during the winter. There was another advantage – the animals eating the turnips produced more manure, which was used to improve the soil.

Another fodder crop sometimes grown was clover. Even so, throughout the period, most peasant farmers were too poor to be able to afford to try new crops. They had no spare land on which to experiment so stuck to tried and tested familiar crops, especially wheat, barley and oats.

Some farmers found other ways to make more money. If they could improve their soil with fertiliser they could grow better crops. The most usual fertiliser was either animal or human manure. For the farmers near to London there was a plentiful supply of this. We saw on page 209 how night-soil men sold the contents of London's privies to the nearby farmers. By the early eighteenth century the River Lea in Hertfordshire was always busy with barges, going in one direction to London with barley malt for the London brewers, and returning full of the contents of Londoners' privies to become manure for the farmers. The large number of horses in the city was another useful source of manure.

The need for more food

The population of England rose steadily between 1500 and 1700 (see below), and then began to rise more rapidly. More people needed more food, but historians still find it difficult to answer these questions:

- Did the rising population encourage some farmers to try to grow more food and so make more money?

- Or did the farmers produce more food which made people healthier so they had more children who lived longer?

It is difficult to decide which came first because there is not enough evidence either about the population or about what farmers were doing.

Population of England	
1500	4 million
1600	5.4 million
1750	7 million

Another way to grow more food to feed the rising number of people was to start ploughing land that had never been farmed before. In Tudor and Stuart times, there were large parts of the country that were still quite wild, but this was usually because they were too difficult to farm. Either the soil was poor, or too wet, or the ground was too steep. It would have cost far too much to make this land suitable for the plough. Even so around most villages some of the countryside that had just been rough land was now ploughed up for farmland. This did not help the poor who had used the wasteland to keep their cow or goats.

Digging deeper

Draining the Fens

It was in Lincolnshire and Cambridgeshire that there was the greatest effort to increase the amount of farmland by draining the fens in the seventeenth century. These were huge marshes where the cottagers spent their lives travelling by boat, fishing and hunting birds among the reeds, or walking on stilts as they drove their cattle along the watery channels to drier pastures. Some of their houses were also built on stilts over the water. The fenlanders were poor people who suffered from the ague (malaria), caused by the large numbers of mosquitoes in summer. However, they were fiercely independent and had no wish to change their way of life.

In the 1620s and 1630s, James I and Charles I employed a Dutch engineer, Cornelius Vermuyden, to drain the fens. Coming from Holland he was familiar with the problem of how to keep water off the land. He built miles of drainage dykes, and pumps operated by windmills. It was enormously expensive, but it made a fortune for the great landowners like the Earl of Bedford and also for the king.

The fenlanders fought back fiercely. Their world was being destroyed. Charles I, always on the lookout for new ways of making money, placed a heavy tax on all land 'hurtfully surrounded' by water.

When the fenlanders didn't pay, the land was confiscated by the king. The fenlanders said the king had no right to the land which belonged to them. They broke down the dykes and burned the windmills, but they could not stop the drainage of the fenlands; their way of life had disappeared by the eighteenth century. Today the fens are not marshes at all. They are amongst England's richest farming areas, with excellent black peaty soil.

Areas of fenland in England c. 1600.

Question time

1. Kett's rebels and the fenlanders were two groups of people who were the victims of change in the countryside in the sixteenth and seventeenth centuries. Make a table showing all the groups of people who were suffering from change, and the reasons why.

2. Kett's Revolt lasted only a couple of months, but the fenlanders fought a bitter war for many years. If a fenman had been brought before a court what might he have said to justify his actions?

3. What arguments might the Duke of Bedford's agents have used against the fenlanders?

The importance of the textile industry

Apart from farming to produce food, England's main industry in 1500 was textiles (cloth making). The sheep that grazed all over England, Wales and Scotland, produced excellent wool. The wool was highly valued in Europe because it produced fine cloth. In Tudor times the best cloth was made in Holland by skilled weavers and then brought back to England to be worn by the fashionable rich. However, in some parts of England the villagers were beginning to specialise in weaving. Villages and towns in the Cotswolds, East Anglia and West Yorkshire were already wealthy through the wool trade by 1500. Over the next 200 years there were a growing number of spinners and weavers in places like Chipping Campden in Gloucestershire, Lavenham in Suffolk, and Halifax in Yorkshire.

SOURCE A

The Piece Hall in Halifax, Yorkshire, was built in Georgian times as a market place for the woollen and worsted cloth made by the handloom weavers in the area. Each Saturday, the weavers would bring 'pieces' of cloth into the Piece Hall to sell them to merchants between 10am and noon. A bell would be rung to signal the end of trading. Anyone buying or selling cloth at other times would be fined 5 shillings.

Today you can still see many fine old houses that belonged to the merchant clothiers who organised the trade in these places. The cottages of the spinners and weavers have also often survived which means they were probably better built than ordinary farm labourers' homes elsewhere. Cloth was still made in the way it had been in the Middle Ages. Spinning wheels and looms did not change much during the sixteenth and seventeenth centuries. The work was done in the homes of farm labourers, where the women of the family usually did the spinning on a wheel by the hearth. Weaving was done by the men of the house using a loom, often in an upstairs room. Extra windows would be added to give more light. The merchant clothier had to take wool to the spinners, and yarn to the weavers, and then see that it was collected from them. He would pay the weavers a piece rate – a wage according to the number of pieces of cloth they had woven. By 1750 it was usual for the clothier to own the looms, so he would deduct a sum from the weavers' wage for the rent of the machine.

Differing rates of wage increases.

Wage increases 1700–50	
London	5%
Oxford	0%
Lancashire	50%

Wages for weaving were good compared with other work. The wages of ordinary labourers who had no special skill depended on how many other labourers were available locally. If there was a shortage of workers, as occurred in rural Lancashire in the eighteenth century, wages could rise rapidly (see table).

Combining different types of work

It was common for labouring families to do more than one type of work. If a family could combine some farm work with spinning and weaving, and maybe keep a cow and a pig, its members could be reasonably comfortable, although still very poor by today's standards. The growth in population meant that there was always a demand for clothing so this usually kept families in work. In parts of Yorkshire, the farm labourers would also knit woollen stockings as an extra job. In the 1720s Daniel Defoe, the author of *Robinson Crusoe*, described seeing Yorkshiremen walking to market, knitting as they went. In other places, cottagers and labourers might also be part-time miners, for coal or iron.

Cotton cloth

As well as woollen cloth, linen was made from flax grown in England. From 1660 there was a growing demand for cotton cloth. Cotton grew in India, where European merchants saw the people dressed in beautiful light cotton fabrics dyed in bright colours. Cotton garments became fashionable among the rich and were imported directly from India by British merchants. The advantages of cotton cloth over wool seemed so great – it was finer, lighter and could be washed more easily. Some clothiers wanted to produce the cloth in England but it was more difficult to spin than wool, and the yarn often snapped on the loom. These difficulties were gradually overcome, especially when wool and cotton were mixed to make worsted.

By the 1750s, the cotton industry was still small but well established in Britain, especially in Lancashire, as the merchants of the port of Liverpool imported cotton from India. In the next 100 years the textile industry would lead a revolution that was to transform Britain and the world, and end forever the rural way of life we have been studying.

Question time

1   Look at the table on page 221. Can you explain why wages in Lancashire rose so rapidly after 1700 in comparison with other areas?

Other industries

There were, of course, many other industries in England between 1500 and 1750, but they were all much smaller than the textile industry. Remember there were no factories or large machines. Goods were produced slowly by hand in small quantities in workshops that were as often in the country as in a town. There were leather works and potteries, breweries and workshops where cloth was bleached. It was a world without plastic or oil. Metals could be produced only in small quantities and were expensive so wood was still used for many items. Even the cogs and gears in a windmill or a water mill would be wooden.

Iron and steel

Iron ore was smelted in furnaces: the rock mined from the ground was heated until the iron contained in it melted. Furnaces were usually in the woods because they needed large amounts of charcoal as fuel. This was produced by charcoal-burners, men who lived in the forests tending slow-burning fires where wood was transformed into charcoal. In forges the iron would then be shaped into tools by blacksmiths working with anvils and hammers, and in foundries molten iron was poured into casts of special shapes. Most iron was either soft or brittle; steel, which is strong but flexible, was difficult to produce and was still used mainly for swords or knives.

In the villages around Birmingham, there were large numbers of workshops where nails were made, while around Sheffield workshops were making steel cutlery. These are areas that are still well known for producing metal goods today. Some of these industries were already dreadful polluters.

SOURCE B

Very populous and large, the streets narrow and the houses dark and black, occasioned by the continuous smoke of the forges, which are always at work.

Daniel Defoe's impression of Sheffield after a visit there in 1727.

Mining

Tin, iron and coal had been mined in some places for centuries, but this was still on a small scale. Usually the mines were shallow and were not designed to reach deep mineral seams. Landowners who discovered iron or coal near the surface of their land were keen to profit from it, so they would employ labourers to dig using simple tools, and candles for light. In the north-east of England, around Newcastle, the coal seams came to the surface, so here coal was mined more extensively. It could then be shipped directly to London, where 'seacole' had become an important fuel for heating homes from Tudor times. The brewers also used large quantities of seacole. Newcastle grew rich on the trade. The expression 'taking coals to Newcastle' is still used to mean giving someone something of which they already have lots.

Trade and merchants

Apart from the nobles and gentry who owned the land, the really rich people in Tudor and Stuart times were not the manufacturers who made things, but the merchants who bought and sold them. Today we would use the words business men and women to describe merchants.

In earlier times there was little difference between merchants and craftsmen. The same people who made goods also sold them. They belonged to a guild. This was an association that looked after the interests of a particular trade, that controlled prices and wages, as well as the quality of the goods made. The guild set rules for the training of apprentices. The idea of the guild was to protect the business and all who worked in it. Guilds were still powerful in Elizabeth's reign and continued to regulate trade, but as merchants became richer and more independent the power of the guilds began to decline. We have already seen how cloth was being made in country cottages (see page 221), where the spinners and weavers did not belong to a guild. They found that the merchants who supplied the looms, the wool and the yarn, and fixed the wages, closely controlled their lives.

Overseas trade

The wealthiest merchants were those who engaged in overseas trade. They included cloth merchants and cotton importers, wine merchants and traders in naval supplies – timber, tar and rope – from northern Europe. There were also merchants trading in some of the most eagerly desired goods after 1660: tobacco, tea, coffee, chocolate and, the most valuable of all, sugar. All these were coming from England's growing number of colonies in India, Africa, the West Indies and North America (see page 186).

England was becoming rich through trade, but there was a dark side to this wealth. Many merchants' fortunes were made from the highly profitable trade in slaves. In the eighteenth century a very large number of West African men and women were taken forcibly across the Atlantic Ocean to America and the Caribbean to work on the plantations where sugar, cotton and tobacco were grown. One in every five Africans died on the voyage, chained below decks in terrible conditions. The sea captains refused to let them up on deck because the slaves would often throw themselves overboard, preferring to perish in the sea rather than suffer any more. London, Liverpool, Glasgow and Bristol grew rapidly through this trade.

Population growth of Bristol and Liverpool 1670–1750.

Population Growth		
	1670	**1750**
Bristol	18,000	50,000
Liverpool	1200	22,000

The Duchess of Portsmouth
(1649–1734), one of Charles II's
mistresses, with a black
slave girl. Contemporary
portrait by
Pierre Miguard.

Many noble families owned plantations where the slaves worked. There were even slaves in England, although here they worked as indoor servants. By 1700 it had become quite fashionable for a wealthy lady to have a little 'black boy' with her (see Source A). The child would be dressed in fashionable clothes and well looked after, like a pet, but then discarded when he became too old. Rarely do we know what happened to them later. You can read more about the slave trade in Book 3.

This trade seemed to bother very few people in England. Perhaps this was because little was known of the cruelty on slave ships, or on the plantations, but it was also because racism was widespread and considered normal. One writer in the 1690s criticised Shakespeare because he had shown too little colour prejudice towards the character of Othello!

The social status of merchants

As merchants became richer their importance in society grew. They built themselves fine townhouses, with workshops behind so that they could keep a close eye on the craftsmen they employed. Where there was a river, the workshops would be linked to a jetty or staithe, where boats would tie up to load and unload cargoes. By 1700, 400 miles of river in England were being used by cargo-carrying boats. Many inland towns could trade directly overseas using their local river.

Merchants' houses were large and elegant. They would employ builders to construct elaborate pediments over the front doors. Inside they would have decorative plaster ceilings and fine furniture. As well as living in grand houses, they tried to imitate the lifestyle of the aristocracy. A merchant might hope that his sons and daughters would marry into the gentry to give his family more status. Some of the aristocracy looked down their noses at merchants as vulgar tradesmen, but they were often happy for their sons to marry a wealthy merchant's daughter if she brought a large fortune into the family. It was also common for the younger sons of the gentry to go into the City of London to work in trade. Their older brothers would inherit their father's estates, so they needed to make a living – trade was becoming more respectable. At the same time, merchants who did well could buy themselves country estates, so becoming gentlemen! In the early eighteenth century James Bateman, for example, started his career as a merchant in the East India Company, but ended up the Governor of the Bank of England. He was knighted and his son married the daughter of an earl. Daniel Defoe was sure this was good for Britain.

SOURCE B

Our tradesmen are not, as in other countries, the meanest of our people. Some of the greatest and best and most flourishing families, not only among the gentry but even the nobility have been raised from trade.

The eighteenth-century writer, Daniel Defoe, speaking out in support of people in trade.

In 1485 the difference between a merchant and a knight or noble had been very great in terms of wealth and social class. By 1750 it was sometimes difficult to tell merchants and gentry apart with many more people now in the middle social band (see below).

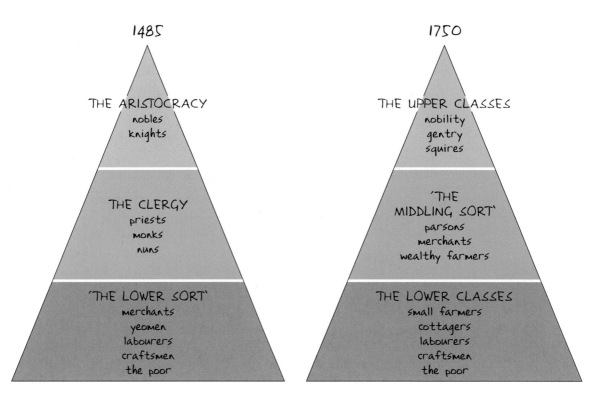

1485

THE ARISTOCRACY
nobles
knights

THE CLERGY
priests
monks
nuns

'THE LOWER SORT'
merchants
yeomen
labourers
craftsmen
the poor

1750

THE UPPER CLASSES
nobility
gentry
squires

'THE MIDDLING SORT'
parsons
merchants
wealthy farmers

THE LOWER CLASSES
small farmers
cottagers
labourers
craftsmen
the poor

Digging deeper

Merchant towns in 1700

By looking at contemporary sources, you can build up a picture of what life was like in a prosperous merchant town in the first half of the eighteenth century.

In 1600 Shrewsbury, in Shropshire, was a small market town where local farmers would come to market to sell their produce and buy tools, candles and cloth. Celia Fiennes was an adventurous traveller who rode round many parts of Britain at the end of the seventeenth century. She was fascinated by what she saw and recorded her journeys in her diary. From her account of her visit to Shrewsbury it is clear that the town had changed dramatically in 100 years.

> **SOURCE C**
>
> … with gravel walks set full of all sorts of orange and lemon trees. There was also firrs, myrtles and hollys of all sorts and a greenhouse full of curiosityes of flowers. Out of this went another Garden much larger with several fine grass walks kept exactly cut and rolled for Company people to walk in. Every Wednesday most of the Ladyes and Gentlemen of the town walk there as in St James' Park [in London] and there are an abundance of people of quality living in Shrewsbury, more than in any town except Nottingham.
>
> *Celia Fiennes gives her impressions of the Abbey Gardens in Shrewsbury in 1699.*

There was another even more impressive area of parkland called the Quarry, where graceful tree-lined walks stretched down to the River Severn.

A census is an official record of the population of a place. Source D tells us the type of jobs people did who lived in Shrewsbury in 1695. Look up any words you don't know.

SOURCE D

■ Butchers, bakers, smiths	Large numbers
■ Watchmakers	6
■ Bookbinder	1
■ Gunsmith	1
■ Dancing masters	2
■ Gardeners	12
■ Grocers	13
■ Vintner	1
■ Distillers	2
■ Tobacconists	9
■ Barbers	12
■ Surgeons	3
■ Apothecaries	10
■ Milliners	2
■ Furrier	1
■ Perfumer	1
■ Tailors	52
■ Goldsmiths	3
■ Stationer	1
■ Booksellers	2
■ Musicians	Several
■ Schools	Several, including Mrs Saxfield's for the 'daughters of gentlemen'

From a census of Shrewsbury, 1695.

William Harper had worked all his life as a cobbler in Birmingham. As a trained craftsman, he was better off than journeymen – labourers who were paid by the day (from the French *journée* meaning 'day'). An inventory is a list of a person's property made, in this case, when a person dies.

SOURCE E

One table	
One trestle	
One stool	
Two bedsteads	
Some linen	
One knife	
Pots and pans	
TOTAL VALUE	£3.17s.9d

Inventory of William Harper, cobbler of Birmingham, died 1693.

SOURCE F

Engraving of High Street, Shrewsbury, c. 1750.

1 How can Sources C, D and F help us to understand what Shrewsbury was like around 1700–50? What conclusions can you make about Shrewsbury from the list of occupations of the inhabitants?

2 Source E shows you the total wealth accumulated by a cobbler in Birmingham after a lifetime of hard work. Find examples of extravagant wealth elsewhere in this chapter, or in Chapter 7, to compare this source with. For example, find out what Sir Robert Walpole spent on candles (see page 191).

3 A cobbler or tailor in Shrewsbury would have earned a similar amount to William Harper. Now read Source G.

SOURCE G

In English towns in the seventeenth and eighteenth centuries wealth was shared out very unevenly. Those who worked hardest had the least.

A modern historian's view of work in the seventeenth and eighteenth centuries.

Use the evidence in this section, and elsewhere in the chapter, to judge whether this opinion is correct. You must back up your reasons with evidence.

Marriage and childbirth

Registered births, deaths and marriages

One of the many new laws Thomas Cromwell made in the 1530s required the parish priest to keep a register of all baptisms, burials and marriages. His intention was to make sure that priests were performing their duties, but this law has made it possible for historians to learn about the more private side of people's lives. Unfortunately, not all the parish registers have survived over 500 years, so the picture of the past they give is sometimes a patchy one.

It is a mistake to believe that until recent times all marriages took place in church. This was not the case in the Middle Ages; it was really only during the period 1450–1750 that the church was becoming the usual place to be married. It was a common belief among poor people that all that was necessary for a marriage was the exchange of vows and tokens, usually a ring, in front of witnesses, and the Church continued to accept this as legal until the eighteenth century.

In 1698 there was an interesting case of a broken-hearted husband called Stephen Wilson. His beloved wife, Mary Russell, had left him and had now married again. So unhappy was he that he went to court to prove that she was still married to him. The court heard that he had told Mary that she was 'the first woman he had ever courted and that he had settled his affections upon her'. He had hoped she would not deceive him. She had told him that she would not deceive him. Stephen had then put a ring on Mary's finger and had said, 'I give you this ring as a contract of marriage between ye and me, and that you'll have no other man.' Mary had replied, 'I promise to marry you Mr Wilson and no other man.' To Stephen the case looked clear cut: Mary could not marry another man. But he lost – the court heard that there had been no witnesses and it therefore ruled that the marriage was illegal.

Marriage laws

By 1700, a parson (a vicar) was usually present to perform weddings according to the law, using the service in the Church of England Prayer Book. The law required the reading of banns in church. This is a notice of an intended wedding which is read in church on three successive Sundays before a wedding. It allows an opportunity for anybody to object to the marriage. A license had to be purchased by Non-conformists and Jews. A law of 1696 imposed a tax on both church certificates and licences, which made marriage expensive so some couples found ways around the law.

In London there were many poor parsons who were prepared to forge entries in marriage registers or issue false certificates for only one-third of the price of the licence. Marriage houses existed in the poorer parts of the city, with a sign outside of a man holding a woman's hand. The service conducted there would lack style – parsons were sometimes drunk, wearing dirty vestments, and they cut out much of the service. It was even possible to go to the Fleet prison to get married, because the law did not require a marriage made there to be licensed.

The Fleet prison must have been a strange place. A woman with debts might go there to find a prisoner who would agree to marry her for the payment of £3 because, as a married woman, she could not be prosecuted for debt. She would leave the prison with her certificate, and never see her 'husband' again. When the people she owed money to appeared at her door she would wave her marriage certificate in front of them. As her husband was already in prison they could not get their money back!

The courts and the bishops tried to control marriage, but laws were sometimes difficult to enforce. Despite rules against certain members of a family marrying one another, uncles found ways of marrying their pretty nieces, or a woman who fell for the charms of her brother-in-law could usually marry him if she was determined. Bigamy (being married to more than one person at the same time) was common. Mary Stokes of London first married Thomas Adams, but only stayed with him eight days. Four years later she married Sebastian Judges, but left him after just one night. Despite being convicted of bigamy, she then married William Carter and, later, William Brown. Sadly for Mary, eventually the law caught up with her and she was hanged in 1693 (probably for a felony involving deception or theft).

Marriage customs

Throughout this period brides did not wear white. Those who could afford to wore brightly coloured silks, with red, white or blue garters. In public, there was sometimes very little ceremony, the whole wedding being carried out almost in secret. This was to stop the newlyweds attracting attention from vulgar people who might gather outside their bedroom window on the wedding night and make rude suggestions, and would not go away until they had been given money!

In private, among the better-off there was plenty of ceremony. After a feast (Source A), the bride and groom would each be undressed by their attendants who would then carry them to their marriage bed in nothing but their undergarments. The bridesmaids and the groom's men would stand at the bottom of the bed with their backs to the couple and throw the garters they had removed over their shoulders on to the couple. A direct hit by a bridesmaid on the face of the groom meant she would soon be married. Glasses of punch were then drunk before the newlyweds were left in private.

During the period the age at which men and women married varied according to how rich they were. Only among the aristocracy did marriages take place when the bride and groom were really young. At the age of 13, Henry VIII's sister, Mary, was married to the decrepit King Louis of France, who was 51. Many marriages among the aristocracy had little to do with love and everything to do with property. Parents arranged the marriage for their children who would often not have met until the wedding.

I never saw my lady till an hour before our marriage. I made my addresses [spoke] to her father, her father to his lawyer, the lawyer to my lawyer, and the bargain was struck.

A character in Henry Fielding's Love in Several Masques *(a play written in 1728), saying how he had no time for romance and courtship.*

The bargain referred to in Source B usually depended on how much money the father of the bride was prepared to give as the 'marriage portion'. It was not common for young men and women to defy their parents or even their older brothers after the death of their parents. But it did happen occasionally. Indeed, as soon as her loathsome husband had died, Henry VIII's sister, Mary, married Charles, the Duke of Suffolk, a man with whom she was deeply in love, without her brother's approval.

Among the families of merchants, farmers and craftsmen it was usual for a young man to wait until he was about 30 before marrying. By then he would have made enough money and could afford to take a wife who would usually be up to ten years younger. Among the very poor, women might marry before their twenties, presumably because they had little to gain by waiting.

By 1700 it was not unusual for a couple who intended to marry to start sleeping together. When the girl became pregnant the marriage would take place. This was one way for a husband to ensure that his future wife was fertile and would give him children! Sometimes a man would try to escape his responsibility, and so the parish authorities would chase him into the courts to make him pay for the upkeep of the child (maintenance). It is interesting to note that by 1700 it was increasingly common for a married couple to greet each other by a kiss on the mouth, but it was still rare for them to use each other's first names!

The wife as the property of her husband

Once married a woman became the property of her husband. She promised to love, honour and obey him. It was not at all unusual for a man to beat his wife. A wife might even be sold, or swapped. A woman was expected to behave as a servant to her husband. If she was unfaithful, her lover was regarded as a thief – he had stolen the husband's property. However, there was no law to protect women against husbands who committed adultery. At this time the law was against women – it did not treat them as equal to men. For example, a man who murdered his wife would be hanged as a criminal, but if a woman killed her husband she had committed treason and would be burned alive. In reality this punishment was rare, but it could be used.

Violence against women was very common. When London merchant John Chambers married his wife Elizabeth in 1697, he forbade her children from her first marriage to visit the house. One day he came home to find she had secretly allowed her daughter, Ann, to call. Elizabeth was pregnant but it didn't stop Chambers from throwing her against the bedstead and kicking her. He then chased after Ann but she escaped.

However, by 1750 attitudes were slowly changing. The reason we know about John Chambers' cruelty is because, increasingly, violence towards women was not tolerated and behaviour like his was exposed. A woman's neighbours might come to help her, and some women certainly gave as good as they got!

Childbirth

Having children was very dangerous for a woman right up until the twentieth century when hygiene standards improved and there were medicines to treat infection. Jane Seymour was not the only queen to die as a result of giving birth; in fact Henry VIII's sixth wife, Catherine Parr, died this way after she had remarried following Henry's death. In 1700, 7 per cent of all deaths of women occurred in childbirth. Tragedy was never far away. Because of their inadequate diet, the children of the poor often suffered from rickets which prevented their bones from growing properly. When girls grew up their pelvis was too small for childbirth, and many died in agony delivering their first baby. Only about one-third of all babies would live to their first birthday. In fact the life expectancy for the population as a whole in 1750 was much lower than today.

Average life expectancy.

	1750	2002
Men	31	78
Women	33	81

A woman who married in her twenties might expect to be pregnant up to 20 times over the next 20 years, although many pregnancies would end in miscarriage. Only one or two children would survive infancy. Queen Anne (1702–14) had seventeen pregnancies but all of her children died before her. John Wesley (1703–91), who founded the Methodist Church, and his brother, Charles, were the only survivors of their parents' eighteen children. Mrs Hodgson of York was 38 when she died delivering her twenty-fourth baby.

Midwives and gossips

There were no anaesthetics to numb the pain, and no understanding of the importance of hygiene. A mother was attended by a midwife and by 'gossips'. By 1700 midwives who helped deliver babies were licensed and trained, but their medical knowledge was limited. The gossips were married women who acted as witnesses if the baby died at birth. This protected the mother against being charged with the murder of her baby. The gossips were also there to ensure that the midwife was not a witch! If the baby did not look likely to survive, the midwife could christen it. Otherwise a priest or minister would perform the baptism within the first week, in the belief that if the baby died its soul would go to heaven.

Digging deeper

Death in the family

Was death so familiar in the sixteenth and seventeenth centuries that people took it for granted? We might think that because so many babies and children died, as well as their mothers, that perhaps people accepted death more and were not saddened by it. Perhaps this was sometimes the case with infant deaths, which happened so frequently. Parents would sometimes give two of their children the same name because they did not expect them both to live. We can learn about people's feelings for their children from what they wrote in their private diaries.

An Essex vicar called Ralph Josselin seemed to take the death of his baby fairly well. In 1650 he wrote in his diary, 'it was our youngest and our affections not so wonted onto it', (i.e. we were not so strongly attached to it). This seems harsh, but when his five-year-old son died he wrote how they felt 'inexpressible grief and affliction'. Another diarist, John Evelyn, was woken one morning by his baby's nurse. She had rolled on to the baby in her sleep and had smothered him, something that was all too common. Evelyn wrote of 'our extreme sorrow, being now again reduced to one; but God's will be done'. Another of Evelyn's children, his four-year-old daughter, died because her corsets were too tight. They broke her ribs, which punctured her lungs.

Activity time

1. Look at the figures for life expectancy in 1750 on page 232. Do they mean that most men died at the age of 31 in 1750? Discuss this with your class.

2. Why might a diary be a good source for historians wanting to know about people's feelings and emotions?

3. Read Source A. What does Ralph's tribute to Mary tell us about the emotions of a parent 300 years ago?

4. This chapter is mostly about things that were different in the sixteenth, seventeenth and eighteenth centuries. Not everything changes, however. Discuss what this section on childbirth suggests to you about 'what people were like' then. In what ways were they like us? In what ways were they different?

Remember that what people in the past felt is just as much a part of history as what they did, or what they believed.

SOURCE A

This day a quarter past two in the afternoone my Mary fell asleep in the Lord, her soule past into that rest where the body of Jesus and the soules of the saints are. She was 8 yeares and 45 dayes old when shee dyed, my soule had abundant cause to bless God for her, who was our first fruites. It was a precious child, a bundle of mirth, a bundle of sweetnes; shee was a child of ten thousand, full of wisdom, woman-like gravity, knowledge, sweet expressions of God, apt in her learning, tender hearted and loving, an obedient child to us she was free from the rudenesse of little children. It was to us a boxe of sweet ointment, which now it's broken smells more deliciously than it did before. Lord I rejoice I had such a present for thee. She lived desired and dyed lamented.

The unfortunate Ralph Josselin writing about the death of his daughter Mary, aged eight. Ralph finished by writing directly to Mary: 'Thy memory is and will be sweete unto me.' We can only guess at which of the many possible causes was responsible for Mary's death.

Superstition surrounding childbirth

There was considerable superstition surrounding childbirth. During labour a woman would wear some of her husband's clothes. This was believed to transfer some of the pain to him. She might also hold a lucky charm. If the child was born with a defect it was blamed on an event in pregnancy. A harelip was believed to have been caused by a hare crossing the mother's path. The belief in witchcraft meant that some defects were thought to have been caused by spells. It was believed that Anne Boleyn had courted the devil when she miscarried a deformed baby.

Unmarried mothers

Unmarried mothers suffered terribly. Having a baby with no husband was a great shame for which they might be whipped. Pregnant girls would sometimes arrange a speedy marriage to a stranger, or even a prisoner. If they did not do this and remained unmarried, in their desperation they sometimes concealed the birth, either killing the baby or leaving it at the door of a hospital or church. If they were caught they received no sympathy from the law – they were hanged. Many pregnant girls who had no husbands preferred to kill themselves rather than face the shame. Of course, the men who had made them pregnant suffered nothing.

Childcare

Once born, the baby of better-off parents would be given to a wet nurse. This was a poor woman who had recently had a child, so could breastfeed an extra baby. It was very risky – the baby was at risk of disease from staying in dirty, overcrowded housing, while the wet nurse herself was often underfed and unhealthy. There were stories of babies dying, and being replaced by the wet nurse's own baby, or of the wet nurse simply confusing the two. This allowed eighteenth-century novelists to tell tales of poor orphans who suffered terribly until, in the last chapter, it turns out that they were actually the son or daughter of a duke!

The wealthy often left very young babies in the care of servants while they were away. For example, the late-seventeenth-century diary of wealthy Elizabeth Freke tells how she went to Ireland and left her ten-week-old son with a nursemaid. Somehow, the baby was dropped and broke his hip, but the servant kept this a secret, fearing that she would be blamed for her carelessness. She kept the baby in its cradle for three months and told everybody it was teething. Eventually the injury was discovered, and the baby's bone had reset. He survived, but the servant was dismissed.

In some ways, attitudes to children were quite different from today. Children were expected to be in awe of their fathers who could be very strict, sometimes even cruel. Queen Anne's son was born with a brain defect so he found walking difficult. Nevertheless, as he was a prince he had to learn to walk properly: his father beat him until he could walk upstairs without help. He died at the age of eleven.

Activity time

1   Who do you think was to blame for the injury to Elizabeth Freke's baby: the poorly paid nursemaid for her carelessness, or the mother, for neglecting her baby for over three months? We don't know the age of the nurse, but she may not have been much older than you.

2   If this incident happened today, a social worker might have to write a report. What conclusions would the report come to,

and what action would the social worker recommend?

3   Is it right for us to judge historical people like Elizabeth Freke and the nursemaid by our standards today? There are other examples in this chapter of people behaving in a way we think wrong. In a short speech to the rest of the class, explain when you think we can judge them, or when we can't.

Death and burials

SOURCE A

Illustrations from 1665 showing the effect of the Great Plague in London. Searchers can be seen visiting the houses of the sick, red crosses have been painted on doors, while people are fleeing from the city. The dead are being buried in pits.

Death was so familiar that in any town the church bell could be heard regularly tolling for those who were dying. It would strike nine times for a man, six for a woman, and three for a child. This would then be followed by a strike of the bell for each year of the person's life.

Fear of the fatal infectious disease known as the Plague led to the appointment of searchers. These were usually old women, whose job was to inspect a corpse to find out the cause of death. They would report what they found to the parish clerk. If foul play was suspected, a magistrate would be called, but, if the victim had died of the plague, the whole house would be boarded up with the family inside. A red cross would be painted on the door, sometimes with the words 'Lord have mercy upon us.'

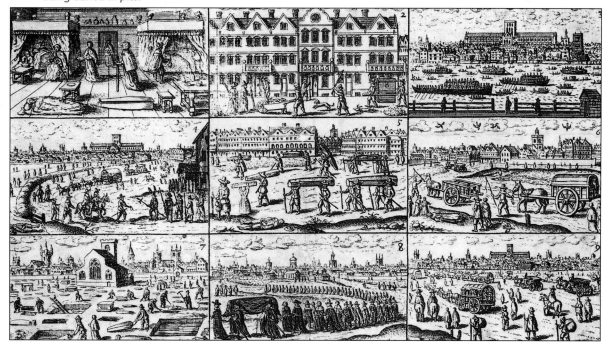

Activity time

1 The worst outbreak of the Plague in Tudor and Stuart times was in 1665. You may already have studied this. We know a lot about the Plague in London because Pepys and other diarists were writing at the time (see page 124), but it affected much of the country. Find out what you can about the Plague outbreak in 1665. Visit the Channel 4 History website, read Pepys' diary for August and September 1665, and present a written report called London during the Great Plague. Your report should cover:

- *Londoners' explanations for the Plague*
- *what people did to protect themselves*
- *what the authorities did*
- *what remedies doctors prescribed.*

Funeral customs

Before the Reformation, the Catholic Church encouraged the family of the dead to say prayers and perform rituals to shorten the time their loved one would spend in purgatory (see page 39). Protestantism came out against the belief in purgatory, and also stopped the practice of buying indulgences, or saying prayers to a saint on behalf of a loved one who had died in order to shorten the time before they were allowed into heaven. Perhaps to make up for this loss of Catholic rituals, funerals now became more elaborate, with processions and mourners.

SOURCE B

An elaborate funeral procession. Engraving dated 1731.

The very rich could afford to have their bodies embalmed – that is, covered with oils and spices to prevent decay. This allowed more time to arrange the ceremony between death and burial. For everyone else it was necessary to bury bodies quickly. Even so the body always lay in state at home for three or four days so that the mourners could view the corpse and offer their sympathy to the family. The government passed a law insisting that bodies must be buried in a woollen shroud (a sheet used to wrap a corpse for burial). This was to encourage the cloth trade, but, as the fine for breaking the law was only £5, the wealthy could afford to ignore it. They preferred to bury their relatives in linen embroidered with fine silk thread.

Funerals were an opportunity for the rich to show off their wealth. Rooms would be draped in black and mirrors would be covered or turned to the wall; anything shiny might threaten the passage of the soul to the afterlife. Widows would wear black mourning clothes with a peaked headdress. It became fashionable for funerals to take place at night. This allowed the use of many large and expensive candles – sometimes mourners were actually mugged and their candles stolen. The funeral procession would often take a roundabout route to the church in order to impress the neighbours.

At the church, the corpse was buried in the churchyard or inside the church itself. In London churches, this caused serious problems as the population rose in the eighteenth century. Churchyards became so overcrowded that grave-diggers often had to move decomposing remains to make way for a new corpse. No wonder mourners carried nosegays or pomanders of herbs and flowers. When bodies were buried in the church itself, it meant that the stones of the floor were frequently disturbed. The congregation sometimes had to put up with the stench of rotting flesh for several weeks! Graveyards could also be dangerous places: sometimes relatives would set traps of spring-guns which would fire and kill the unwary. This was to protect their loved one from body snatchers, who were paid to steal corpses for the hospitals to use for teaching anatomy.

One group of people could not be buried in graveyards: those people who had committed suicide. It was believed that to take your own life was a wicked sin, which showed that the devil had possessed you. Suicides were therefore usually buried at country crossroads with a stake through the bodies to prevent the evil spirit from rising and disturbing the living.

Monuments

In the reigns of Elizabeth I and James I, many people had elaborate funeral monuments placed in their church. These were brightly painted sculptures of themselves with their whole family, even showing children who had been born dead. The sculptures tell us a lot about the merchants and gentry who had them made. Details of their clothing and shoes are clear, and the inscriptions are usually written in English rather than Latin, and tell us about the family and their beliefs.

Hark! Hark! The dogs do
bark! The beggars are
coming to town!

Some in rags and some
in jags [jackets], and
some in velvet gowns.

*From a children's nursery
rhyme.*

Crime

In most parts of Britain in 1500 there was little serious crime. Thefts did happen in villages, and there were fights which sometimes resulted in injury and death. But there was little crime carried out by strangers who were full-time criminals. However, during the next 200 years there was a growing number of 'masterless men' – people who had no land to farm and no work, and therefore no master to supervise them and to make sure they behaved. In Elizabeth I's reign (1558–1603) this led to fear of the bands of beggars who roamed the countryside attacking travellers.

Crime in the eighteenth century

By the eighteenth century merchants and travellers were at risk from highwaymen and footpads (see page 239). These criminals would often attack and rob at the point of a pistol thrust into the unfortunate victim's face. As the population of London and the larger towns grew, there was a rise in the amount of crime. London could be a dangerous place at night.

Why was there so much crime in towns in the eighteenth century?

- There was no police force.

- Cruelty to apprentices meant up to 50 per cent ran away.

- Towns were much larger than in 1500 (see page 200).

- There were low wages for labourers; not enough work was available.

- The closure of the monasteries (see page 56) put an end to the charity given to the poor and needy.

- The very rich lived near the very poor.

- The enclosure of land (see page 216) meant that landless labourers came to towns from country.

- Thieves were branded with the letter 'T' on their forehead or cheek – who would then give them a job?

- Some criminals were mutilated as a punishment – a hand or a foot was cut off. This meant that they could only live by begging or crime.

- There was little security – the wealthy had nowhere to leave their money and valuables safely.

The diarist Samuel Pepys describes lying in bed at night in terror after hearing a noise outside, knowing that all his money was stored downstairs. During the Great Fire of London in 1666, Pepys buried a large parmesan cheese (a very expensive cheese) in his garden, to guard against looters if his house burned down.

What did criminals do?

- **Footpads** – lurked in the streets of towns at night, robbing passers-by.

- **Highwaymen** – attacked and robbed stagecoaches.

- **Clouters**, **cutpurses, pickpockets** – were very quick and could remove purses, watches, snuff-boxes and handkerchiefs, even the sword from a gentleman's side.

- **Anglers and hookers** – visited houses during the day pretending to be salesmen, but carefully noted what valuable objects were near the window. They would then return at night with a long rod and a hook to 'fish' them from the window.

- **Buttock and twang** – a woman would lure a man from an alehouse but would then pick his pockets.

One early-eighteenth-century criminal, Moll Hawkins, could make herself appear respectable by disguising herself as a milliner's apprentice. She would arrive at a wealthy person's house with hats to show the lady of the house. While the maid went to fetch her mistress, Moll would quickly seize what she could and escape. When she visited Lady Arabella Howard's house with gloves and fans, she stole silver worth £50 from the parlour. Some women made a living out of being dishonest servants, robbing one household after another.

Shoplifting in London had become a serious problem by the end of the seventeenth century, even though the punishment for stealing more than 5 shillings was hanging.

Begging

There were also a lot of beggars who found clever ways of persuading people to give them money:

- **The ruffler** – would appear in lonely places, and frighten his victim who would give him money to avoid a beating.

- **The freshwater mariner** – pretended to have been wounded at sea serving with a great naval hero like Drake or Hawkins.

- **Counterfeit crank** – pretended to be ill by smearing himself with blood.

- **The courtesy man** – wore smart clothes and spoke well. He persuaded his listener to lend him money, but of course never paid it back.

- **The Abraham man** – pretended to be mad to gain sympathy and money.

Begging was a serious
problem in the
seventeenth and
eighteenth centuries. This
seventeenth-century
woodcut shows Nicholas
Jennings in the guise of
both a sham cripple and a
gang leader.

Parliament was very hostile to these beggars and passed harsh laws against
them. They were tied to the back of a cart, led through the streets, and
whipped until they were bloody. They were also branded with the letter 'V',
for vagrant, on their forehead. Beggars who repeated their crime could be
imprisoned or hanged. Some were transported to the colonies to work as
slaves on the plantations in the West Indies. It was hoped that harsh
punishment would frighten people into obeying the law, but, since there
was so little chance of getting caught, crime continued to flourish. It was
usually left to the victim to try to catch the criminal.

SOURCE C

*Adverts like this were
quite common in the
eighteenth century.*

WHEREAS, on yesterday morning between eight and nine
a clock in the morning, **THREE FOOTPADS** between
Islington and Holloway, committed a robbery on the body
of one Thomas Waller, and took from him the sum of three
and twenty shillings in silver; one of the footpads, being a
TALL MAN with straight hair, long faced, and a large red
nose, and full of pimples about the mouth, and a small
blew spot on the bottom of his chin; whoever secures him,
and gives notice to Mr Waller (so as he may be had before
a Justice of the Peace) shall have **2 GUINEAS REWARD**,
and reasonable charges.

Even though crime was worse by 1750 than it had been 200 years earlier, it was mainly a problem that affected the bigger towns. For many people living in small villages, crime usually meant little more than the occasional theft among neighbours, or fights which rarely led to bloodshed. In small villages it would have been much more difficult to escape arrest.

Question time

1 What does the newspaper article tell you about how criminals were caught? Why were adverts like this necessary?

2 Look at the explanations for the rise in crime between 1500 and 1750 on page 238. Now consider these two views:

- Crime became worse because the growth of population meant that there were now more dishonest people.
- Crime became worse because of changes in society.

Examine both views to decide which one fits the facts. Use all the information in this chapter, and your knowledge of the period, to write a detailed answer to the question: 'Why did crime become a more serious problem in the eighteenth century?'

Prison

There were few prisons outside the larger towns. The culprits of minor crimes would usually be dealt with by the stocks, whipping, branding or mutilation. Hanging, rather than prison, was the normal punishment for more serious crimes. The number of capital crimes (crimes punishable by death) rose from about 80 in early Stuart times to over 350 by 1750. It was possible to escape the death sentence by pleading benefit of clergy. This meant that if you could prove you were a clergyman (or capable of being one) you were let off your sentence, because clergy could not be harmed, according to the Bible. The proof came when the prisoner read a passage from the Bible, since it was mostly only clergy who knew how to read. This came to be called the 'neck verse'. Pregnant women could also 'plead the belly', but this only delayed their hanging until the baby was born.

The conditions for the prisoners in London were dreadful. The worst prison was Newgate which housed about 150 inmates, some of whom would be waiting for their death sentence to be carried out. As new prisoners entered Newgate they would be overwhelmed by the smell and the noise. The shouts and cries of prisoners would be mixed with singing and laughter from the better-off inmates who had bribed the jailers to obtain rooms for themselves, and permission to visit the women prisoners. The stench from the prison cesspits spread everywhere.

On arrival, the jailers would search the new inmates. If they could afford it, now was the time to offer the jailers money.

With bribes the prisoners could obtain fresh bedding, a cleaning woman, newspapers and food. A bribe would also be necessary to allow friends to visit. However, new prisoners without money would have all their possessions taken by the guards and thrown into a cesspit.

Prisoners slept on the filthy floor with rags to cover themselves, and only cold or raw food unless they could find the 3d needed to bribe the cook. To feed themselves prisoners tried to catch the many rats and mice that infested their cells. The filth made Newgate prison a very unhealthy place. Typhus was common and spread quickly. When prisoners died, their relatives had to pay a fee to recover the body – sometimes the bodies of prisoners would lie where they had died for months or even years. Of all those condemned to death, only one-quarter lived long enough to be hanged. On the other hand, one prisoner in 1700 had been there 40 years, had married twice and raised a family. He even kept pets!

Public hangings in 1700

Hangings in London took place outside the city walls at Tyburn, where Marble Arch in the West End is today. They were popular public affairs – people were fascinated by the spectacle of watching criminals die. Some of those hanged were no doubt ruthless and cruel murderers, but many were just petty thieves driven into crime by desperate poverty. Others were rogues and villains who were well known, and even liked by Londoners. In the sixteenth and seventeenth centuries the number of people executed was very large, perhaps 2000 a year: in 1598, 74 people were executed in Devon, while in Middlesex there were on average 78 executions each year. By the early eighteenth century, the number of capital crimes had grown enormously (see page 241), but the number of hangings was falling, because juries were increasingly unwilling to find prisoners guilty for minor crimes if the penalty was death.

Public enthusiam for a hanging

The public's enthusiasm for watching a hanging can be explained by remembering that England was a violent country. It was not just criminals who used force. Remember the violence of:

- evictions and enclosure

- beatings of servants and apprentices

- the slave trade

- the burnings of heretics

- whippings, brandings and mutilation of beggars

- husbands and fathers beating their wives and children

- cock fighting, bear-baiting and bare-fist fighting at fairs

- hanging of witches (see page 247).

All of this helped make people used to violence.

Digging deeper

Going out in a blaze of glory

In the eighteenth century, a London hanging was not usually a grim affair. Many prisoners were determined to go to the gallows in a blaze of glory. The prisoner would order new clothes. He could make money to pay for them by selling his memoirs since there was a growing market for pamphlets telling grisly stories about the life and death of a criminal. This might also pay for his coffin and leave something for his family. One chaplain at Newgate prison ran a successful business selling printed versions of last confessions he had heard from condemned men and women.

There were only eight days a year when hangings took place in London. The event would be announced by the ringing of muffled church bells. Crowds gathered along the route from the prison to the gallows, to jeer at unpopular criminals who might be pelted with rotten fruit or the contents of chamber pots. The condemned men and women travelled through the streets in an open cart, although rich criminals could pay for a carriage. It was customary to stop at alehouses on the way where the condemned criminal would be given free drink. One prisoner promised to pay on his way back! Sometimes visits were made to the houses of friends.

Some of the condemned were heroes to the crowd who gave them flowers and cheered them. Sometimes prisoners were determined to be cheerful, but others, little older than children, prayed or wept. Sometimes there would be chaos, as fighting broke out between the dense crowd and the armed constables guarding the condemned men and women. Occasionally rescues were attempted, especially when the crowd was so dense that the prisoners had to leave the cart and carry on to Tyburn on foot.

The gallows

At the gallows, the hangman would inspect the prisoners to see what they were worth. Relatives would have to pay a fee if they wanted to reclaim the body and clothes after the hanging. Otherwise the hangman would sell the prisoner's clothes, while he could get a good fee for the bodies from surgeons wanting to practise dissection.

The gallows at Tyburn could be used to hang up to 24 people at once. It was nicknamed the three-legged mare since it had three large beams, from each of which eight people could be hanged. The hangman was often drunk, and on one occasion nearly hanged a priest who was hearing a condemned man's confession. Nooses were thrown around the condemned men's necks, and the cart pulled away. Death might take ten or fifteen minutes while the crowd stood in awe watching the victims kick out in agony. Sometimes the public cheered or groaned; a relative of the victim might pull hard on the prisoner's legs to put him out of his misery.

A more shameful end came to those who were put on the gibbet, like Robert Aske after the Pilgrimage of Grace (see page 60). Here the punishment was for the condemned person to be hanged in chains until the flesh rotted or was eaten by birds. Crows and birds of prey would sometimes pluck out the eyes of victims before they had died.

Traitors would be hanged, drawn and quartered (see page 55).

Tyburn gallows in London, c. 1750.

Question time

1   This section has shown that hangings were a popular event in the sixteenth and seventeenth centuries. Explain why this was, using the bullet points on page 242 to help you. You can also use the knowledge you have gained from reading this book.

2   We use the word 'ghoulish' to mean showing an interest in cruelty or pain suffered by other people. Today this kind of an interest would be frowned upon or discouraged. With this in mind, answer the following questions:

   a   Does this make us better than people of 300 years ago?

   b   How do the attitudes of people in Tudor and Stuart Britain compare with those of today?

   c   What features of Tudor and Stuart society would we condemn today?

   d   Are there features of our society today that are equally ghoulish?

3   This book has presented you with some unpleasant facts about Tudor and Stuart Britain. Do you think it is right for pupils of your age to learn about such things?

Witchcraft

Spirits and goblins, dwarfs and sprites seemed very real to most people in Tudor and Stuart times. Fear of witches and the power they had grew during the reign of Elizabeth I and for much of the seventeenth century. In daily life so many things could go wrong without explanation. Overnight, healthy cattle could sicken and die; diseases afflicted crops; milk could go sour; and people fell sick. The explanation for these sudden events was believed to lie in the influence of the world of evil spirits. It was believed that witches could use magic spells to bring down evil upon those whom they cursed.

Superstition was widespread even among the educated. James I believed in witches, as did Sir Isaac Newton (see page 176) who founded modern science. The diarist Samuel Pepys always carried a hare's foot to protect him from the colic. Among uneducated, rural villagers strange tales were told and believed. In 1569 a servant girl, Agnes Bowker, was reported to have given birth to a cat in Market Harborough, Leicestershire. The story attracted huge attention and several important people, including the Earl of Huntingdon, the Bishop of Lincoln, and even the Queen's Secretary, William Cecil, were brought in to investigate.

People believed that kings and queens had healing powers if they touched people with skin diseases (see page 176). The Stuart kings made use of this belief to increase the awe which people felt for monarchs.

SOURCE A

The king coming at him Evans kneels down and cries 'God Bless Your Majesty'. The good king gives him his hand to kiss, and he rubbing his ulcerated and scabby nose therewith, which was plentifully stocked with purulent and fetid matter [rotting and filled with pus]: within two days after his reception of his sacred majesty's favour, I saw this Evans cured, and his ulcerated nose dried up and healed.

Large numbers of the sick, like Evans, would queue patiently waiting to be touched by Charles II.

How can you tell a witch?

Witches were said to do the work of the devil, but they could also control evil spirits that lurked in the countryside. People thought they could be identified by the mark of the devil on them. This might be a wart or a mole, or perhaps a deformity. A witch would be accompanied by her familiars – a black cat, or a toad – which it was said she used to speak with the devil. If a woman was suspected of witchcraft she could be tried by the ordeal of ducking in a river or pond. She would be thrown in with her hands and feet tied. If she floated she was a witch and would be hauled out for her punishment. If she sank, she was innocent but it was probably too late! Water was thought to be a good element so would reject something evil.

Who was accused of witchcraft?

Here are some facts about witches:

- Most witches were old women.

- They were usually widows.

- They lived on their own.

- Witches were nearly always poor.

- They had usually fallen out with their neighbours.

- They were unpopular.

- Their behaviour seemed odd to their neighbours.

- They were often aggressive or bad tempered.

It is also interesting to note that witchcraft was found in the country, not in the towns.

SOURCE B

A contemporary print showing the witch Mary Sutton getting a ducking in 1612.

Many witches condemned themselves by their own admissions of guilt. Some seem to have genuinely believed they were witches. In England witches were usually hanged. On one occasion near Ipswich, in 1645, eighteen witches were hanged together.

SOURCE C

Janet MacMurdoch was a widow who lived in the little village of Broughtone in Scotland. She was very poor but tried to make a living by keeping a few animals which she would graze wherever she could. The problem was that the other farmers were mostly better off than Janet and did not want her animals eating grass which they claimed she had no right to. Her trouble really began when she could not pay her rent and the bailiff took away some of her cattle. She cursed him, 'promising him an evil turn'. Shortly afterwards one of his cows and its calf died. He went to her house and accused her of putting a spell on his animals, but she only promised him worse. Soon after, his child died of sweating sickness.

Another farmer John Murray then appears to have kicked her so violently that he knocked her over, although he told the court that it was 'an accidental twitching of his foot'. A few weeks later two of his cows turned mad and died. Then Janet had a quarrel with Robert Brown, who turned her cattle out of the pasture because he said she had no right to graze them there. She was angry and told him that he shouldn't have so many cattle. In the next twelve months fifteen of them died. Another landowner confiscated some of her animals for the same reason. The very next day his child drowned in a peat bog. William Gordon, another wealthy farmer, chased Janet's animals off his land and lost some of his cattle.

Even Janet's daughter could suffer. The woman she worked for accused her of using her mother's devilish tricks. Janet was cross when she heard this, so she called on the woman and asked, 'Why called you me and my daughter witches, for you shall have something better to think on.' The woman's husband then fell ill. Janet called again and this time was given food and drink. The man got better. This was taken as meaning that the witch had lifted the spell.

Finally in 1667 Janet had a quarrel with Jean Sprot. Jean had let her cow steal some of Janet's grass, but the cow then became ill and died. Shortly after, Jean's husband caught Janet working on Sunday and told her off for committing a sin. She 'bade the devil pick out his eye'. Within a week he fell ill with a disease. Jean had asked Janet to come to the house to lift the curse, but she refused and he died.

Jean then reported Janet for witchcraft, for which she was tried. Surprisingly, Janet did not attempt to defend herself, except to accuse Jean of also being a witch. Eventually Janet was burned alive.

The story of Janet MacMurdoch, adapted from The Prospect Before Her *by Olwen Hufton, 1995.*

Activity time

1   Read the following points which may help explain what happened to Janet MacMurdoch:

  ● As men and women grow old, and lose hair and teeth, they can seem ugly to younger people.

  ● In the sixteenth and seventeenth centuries, there was little or no treatment for warts, moles or skin defects; cataracts would form over the eyes of the elderly, making them blind, but also making them appear frightening.

  ● There were no pensions to support old people. The poor would have to work until they died, unless people helped them.

- The Protestant Reformation had ended many traditional religious ways people had had of protecting themselves from evil, for example, with rosary beads, prayers, pilgrimages and indulgences (see Chapters 2 and 3).

- In the sixteenth and seventeenth centuries, cattle plague and other animal diseases were very common. There was no known scientific explanation for them.

- Life expectancy was very short (see page 232); large numbers of children died of disease; there was little understanding of disease and the causes of death.

- Farmers were at the mercy of the weather. Crops could be ruined by drought, rain or hail.

- People living in small villages had little or no education; they had little contact with the outside world.

- People with problems sometimes join together and pick on someone who cannot fight back; that person is made a scapegoat, and is blamed for the problems. They are punished by the community. Today we would call this behaviour bullying.

2   In small groups, discuss the story of Janet MacMurdoch. Use the points above to help you answer the following questions:

   - Why do you think Janet was accused of witchcraft?

   - Was she a victim of bullying? Can you find evidence in the story to support this?

   - Why didn't she defend herself?

   - Would Janet be treated better today? How would her treatment be different?

   - Can you find examples from history of people being treated as scapegoats for a community's problems?

   - Can you think of any examples of behaviour that you have witnessed or heard about that might be similar to the way Janet was treated?

3   After the discussion, write your explanation for the way Janet MacMurdoch was treated in her village. You do not need to tell the whole story; concentrate on giving your explanation. You will need to consider what you know about beliefs and superstitions in the seventeenth and eighteenth centuries, as well as the way people lived. Remember what you learned in this chapter about how changes in farming affected the poor (see page 216).

The decline of superstition

By the eighteenth century, attitudes towards witchcraft had changed. While ordinary people continued to believe in witches, charms and spells, many educated people were scorning the notion that there was such a thing as a witch. The last witch to be hanged died in 1713. Among the educated there was a growing belief that there was a scientific explanation for events which before people had believed to be the work of spirits. The progress which science had made (see Chapter 6) was beginning to lead some people away from religion and the Church.

In 1550 almost everyone would have believed that the devil existed and was the cause of all evil, but 200 years later the Bishop of Durham could complain: 'The influence of religion is more and more wearing out of the minds of men.'

Assessment section

1. Find out about the trade and industry in the area where you live during the period from 1500 to 1750. Produce a written account which can be illustrated with a map and perhaps pictures.

   You will need to go to a library. Your school library may have a good collection of booklets on Local History. You may have a local museum which will be able to help you. Be sure to cover the right period!

   Here are some suggestions for your research. You should be able to find answers to some of these questions:

   a. Were there any weavers? What did they weave? Wool or linen? Where did they sell their cloth?

   b. Were there any mines? What sort? Coal, iron, tin, alum?

   c. Were there any potteries? Where did the clay come from?

   d. What other work was common? E.g. knitting, nail making, brewing, etc.

   e. Which was the nearest market town? Have any old buildings survived? Are there any merchants' houses?

   f. Is there a river that was used for trade? Where were the boatyards? Where were the wharves (where the boats were loaded and unloaded)? What cargoes were transported on the river? Where to?

2. Look again at the figures for life expectancy on page 232. Draw a table with two columns. In the left column write the heading 1750. Using the information in this chapter and the last one give as many reasons as you can for the low life expectancy in 1750. In the right column put the date 2002, and then put as many reasons as you can think of for the much higher life expectancy today.

3. It is over 250 years since the last woman in Britain was hanged for being a witch. What beliefs in our society might a person find odd or even silly in 250 years' time?

4. Was England a more understanding and tolerant society in 1750 than in 1485?

YES	NO
• fewer hangings	• slave trade
• growing sympathy for suicides	• slavery in the Empire
• no more witch trials	• no tolerance towards Scots Highlanders
• no more heresy trials	• no tolerance towards Irish Catholics
• decline of Church influence	• much hardship and poverty
• tolerance for dissenters	• loss of rights for small farmers

Using the points listed above and your knowledge of Tudor and Stuart times gained from reading this book, write an essay explaining how the life of people changed over the period from 1485 to 1750. You should concentrate on what had improved and what had got worse.

5   Much of this book has concentrated on changes during a period of nearly 300 years. Change seems more exciting than things just staying the same, but we must remember that an important part of history is about continuity, not change. Source A shows one thing that did not change for women.

Before, during and after our period, women were expected to fetch water just as they had done for centuries. It was a major task for many women every day of their lives. Do you think the illustration gives a true picture of what this chore must have been like?

SOURCE A

A woman drawing water from a village well c. 1650.

Further reading

Liza Picard, *Restoration London* (Weidenfeld and Nicolson, 1997)

Roy Porter, *London: A Social History* (Hamish Hamilton, 1994)

Maureen Waller, *1700: Scenes from London Life* (Hodder and Stoughton, 2000)

Index

A

Act of Six Articles 63, 66
Act of Union 1536 152–4
Act of Union 1707 144–5
alcohol 197
Anne, Queen 144
Anne Boleyn, Queen 22, 51–2, 53–4
Anne of Cleves, Queen 23
anti-clericals 42, 53
Aske, Robert 59–60, 243
astronomy 173–4

B

Babington Plot 28, 29
balance of power 127
Barebones Parliament 115–6
Battle of Bosworth 12–3
Battle of Culloden 149–50
Battle of Edgehill 105–6
Battle of Marston Moor 106–7
Battle of Naseby 107
Battle of the Boyne 136–7
begging 239–40
Bible 62, 87
bigamy 230
Bill of Rights 126
Bloody Assize 125
Bonnie Prince Charlie 148, 151
Burghley, Lord 189–90
burials 235–7
burning of heretics 80–4

C

Cabot, John and Sebastian 185
Calais 85
Calvin, John 67–70
Calvinists 67–70, 72
Campbell clan 142
Campion, Edmund 91
Catherine Howard. Queen 23
Catherine of Aragon, Queen 22, 51–2, 54
Catherine Parr, Queen 23
Catholic Church
    ceremonies 70–2
    corruption in England 48–50
    discontent in England 45–6
    priests persecuted 90–1
    restored 80–5
    succumbs 87–9
Cavaliers 101, 105, 205
Caxton, William 162–3
Charles I, King 95, 97, 98–103, 113–4, 133, 138
Charles II, King 115, 119, 121–2, 123–5, 140, 205
Charles V, Holy Roman Emperor 44, 51, 52, 62
childbirth 232–4
childcare 234
chimneys 190, 191
China 182
Civil War 96–112, 139, 205
Clitheroe, Margaret 92
clothes 202–7
codpiece 202
coffee 198
coffee houses 198
Columbus, Christopher 185
Commonwealth 115
Copernicus, Nicolaus 173
Corpus Christi procession 71
cotton cloth 221
Court of Star Chamber 14, 15, 100, 101
Cranmer, Archbishop Thomas 53–4, 62, 66, 72, 74, 76, 80, 83
crime 238–41
Cromwell, Oliver 105, 114, 115, 116, 118–9, 122, 134–5, 139
Cromwell, Thomas 53–4, 56–7, 62, 63–4, 229
crop changes 217–8
Cumberland, Duke of 149–50

D

Da Gama, Vasco 185
da Vinci, Leonardo 168, 171–2
Darien, Panama 143
days out 212–3
death 233, 235–7
Defender of the Faith 38
Diet of Worms 44
Diggers 117
dissolution of the monasteries 19, 56–7

divine right of Kings 96, 97, 125
Drake, Sir Francis 186
drinks 197, 198
Drogheda massacre 134
Dürer, Albrecht 168

E

Easter rituals 71–2
Edinburgh 148
education 159–60
Edward VI, King 65–6, 76
Edwardian Reformation 70–2
Elizabeth I, Queen 24–8
enclosures 216–7
entertainment 211–2
executions 55, 113–4
exploration 181–6

F

farming 216–20
farthingale 202
fashion 202–7
Fawkes, Guy 35–6
Fens drainage 219
Field of the Cloth of Gold 8, 21
Fifth Monarchists 118
Fisher, Bishop John 52, 54
food needs 218
food storage 197
Francis I, King of France 8, 21
funerals 236–7

G

Galileo 174
Geneva 67–9
gentry 188–91
Glencoe massacre 142
Glorious Revolution 125–7
Glyndwr Rebellion 152
gossips 232
Grand Remonstrance 101
Great Fire of London 124
Great Plague 124
Greek scientists 173
Grey, Lady Jane 76, 79
Gunpowder Plot 35–6
Gutenberg, Johann 161–2
Gwynn, Nell 123

H

Hampton Court Palace 46–7
hangings 242–4
Hardwick Hall 189–90
Harrison, John 183
Harvey, William 175, 178–9
Henry VII, King (Henry Tudor) 8–16
Henry VIII, King 5, 8, 19–23
Henry VIII's wives 22–3
Highlands 140–1
home management 197–8
Hooke, Robert 177
Hooper, Bishop John 82
House of Lancaster 8–9
House of Stuart 140
House of Tudor 8–13, 77
House of York 8–9
houses
    labourers 192–3
    merchants 225
    nobility 189–91
    yeomen 192
Hudson, Henry 185
humanists 42–3, 66
Hunne, Richard 45–6

I

indulgences 40–1, 169
industry 215
Ireland 15, 130–7
Irish land policies 130, 131–2, 136
Irish Rebellion 101, 133
iron 222
Italy 158, 181

J

Jacobite Rebellions 146–51
James I, King (James VI of Scotland) 33–7,
    133, 138
James II, King 125–7, 135, 140
Jane Seymour, Queen 23, 65–6
Jeffreys, Judge 125
Jonson, Ben 165

K

Kett's Revolt 216–7
King's Great Matter 51–2
kitchens 193–4
knitting 221
Knox, John 87

L

Latimer, Bishop 81–2
Latin 160
Laud, Archbishop William 98–9, 100
laundry 204
Levellers 117
life expectancy 232
London 124, 199
Londonderry 135–6
Long Parliament 100
Lord of Misrule ritual 210
Lord Protector 116, 118
Lowlands 141
Luther, Martin 38, 39–41, 43–4, 48–9, 169

M

MacDonald clan 142
Machiavelli, Niccolò 20, 159
Marlowe, Christopher 165
marriage 229–32
Mary, Queen of Scots 26–9, 33, 89
Mary I, Queen (Mary Tudor) 76, 78–83, 85
meals 195–7
Medici, Cosimo de' 158
medicine 176–7
merchants 223–7
Merry England 72
Michelangelo 168–9, 170
microscope 177
midwives 232
Milton, John 170
mining 222–3
monarch as head of the Church in England 53, 87
Monck, General George 119, 123
Monmouth, Duke of 125
Monteverdi, Claudio 170
monuments 237
More, Sir Thomas 54, 55
Muggletonians 118
music 170

N

newspapers 163–4
Newton, Sir Isaac 176, 245
nobility 188–91
Norfolk, Duke of 59–61, 63, 66, 89
Northern Rebellion 89
Northumberland, Duke of 75–6

P

painting 168–9
Palladio, Andrea 191
Parliament 31–2, 33, 37, 113, 115–6, 119, 126
Pepys, Samuel 120–1, 198, 203, 208, 209, 212–3, 245
personal hygiene 208–9
personal rule 100, 101
perspective 168, 169
Philip II, King of Spain 79
Pilgrimage of Grace 59–61
Plague 124, 235, 236
Plantation of Ulster 132
plays 165–7
poetry 170
Polo, Marco 182
Pope Leo X 44
Pope's authority 40, 43–4
population changes 218
Portsmouth, Duchess of 224
Portugal 185
power balance 127
power under the Tudors 6–7
Poynings Law 15
Prayer Book 72, 76, 80
Prayer Book Rebellion 74–5
Pride's Purge 113
Prince, The 20, 159
Princes in the Tower 8–10
printing 160–4
prison 241–2
privateers 185–6
progress (Queen's) 30–1
Protectorate 115
Protestantism
    Edwardian Reformation 70–2
    Reformation 38–54
    rejected 63
    triumphs 87–9
Prynne, William 98–9
Puritans 70, 87, 98, 116
Pym, John 100, 101, 106, 139, 163

Q

Quakers 117

R

Ranters 118
Raphael 168
Reformation 38–54, 70–2, 76–80, 87–9
register of births, deaths and marriages 229
relics 39, 62
religious differences 34, 38–9, 131
religious settlement 88, 131
Renaissance in general 156–8
Renaissance man 19
Restoration 123
Richard III, King 6–13
Ridley, Bishop 81–2
Ridolfi Plot 28, 89
Rome 169–70
Roundheads 105, 205
Rump Parliament 113, 115–6, 119

S

Sailors' risks 184
St George's Day ceremony 71
St Peter's Basilica 169–70
sanitation 208–9
scientific revolution 175–80
Scotland 138–51
Scottish Presbyterians 99
Scottish Rebellion 106, 138
sculpture 168–9
second–hand clothes 206
Shakespeare, William 165
Ship Money 102
Shrewsbury 226–8
Simnel, Lambert 17
slave trade 223–5
Society of Friends 117
Somerset, Duke of 66, 74–5
Spain 185
Spanish Armada 93
squire 210–1
statues 62
steel 222
Stuart, Charles Edward 148, 151
Stuart, James Edward 147
sumptuary laws 195, 202, 203
superstition 248
Sword Rule 118

T

table customs 196
tea 198
Tetzel, John 40–1, 169
textiles 220–1
toilets 208–9
tourism 213
town growth 199–201
trade 181, 223–7
Treaty of Etaples 15
Tyndale, William 48, 53, 87

U

Union flag 145
United Kingdom unification
    Ireland 130–7
    Scotland 138–51
    Wales 152–4
unmarried mothers 234

V

Vesalius, Andreas 177
village life 210–1

W

Wales 152–4
Walsingham (shrine) 62
Walsingham, Sir Francis 28, 89–91
Warbeck, Perkin 18
Wars of the Roses 8, 14
water fetching 250
Wesley, John 232
wife as property of husband 231–2
William III of Orange, King 126, 135, 140–1, 164
witchcraft 245–8
Wolsey, Cardinal Thomas 45, 46–7, 52, 53
women in the Civil War 112
woollen cloth 220–1
Wren, Sir Christopher 175
Wyatt's Rebellion 79